Landscape Architect's Pocket Book

Siobhan Vernon,
Rachel Tennant and
Nicola Garmory

ELSEVIER

AMSTERDAM • BOSTON • HEIDELBERG • LONDON •
NEW YORK • OXFORD PARIS • SAN DIEGO • SAN FRAN-
CISCO • SINGAPORE • SYDNEY • TOKYO
Architectural Press is an imprint of Elsevier

Architectural
Press

Architectural Press is an imprint of Elsevier
The Boulevard, Langford Lane, Kidlington, Oxford, OX5 1GB
30 Corporate Drive, Suite 400, Burlington, MA 01803, USA

First edition 2009
Reprinted 2010, 2011

Notice
No responsibility is assumed by the publisher for any injury and/or damage to persons or property as a matter or products liability, negligence or otherwise, or from
any use or operation of any methods, products, instructions or ideas contained in
the material herein.

British Library Cataloguing in Publication Data
A catalogue record for this book is available from the British Library

Library of Congress Cataloguing in Publication Data
A catalogue record for this book is available from the Library of Congress

ISBN: 978-0-7506-8348-7

For information on all Architectural Press publications
visit our web site at www.elsevierdirect.com

Printed and bound in China

11 12 13 14   7 6 5 4 3

Contents

Preface   *ix*

Acknowledgements   *xi*

1   Hard Landscape   **1**
    1.1   Natural Stone   1
    1.2   Metals   8
    1.3   Stainless Steel   14
    1.4   Timber   23
    1.5   Exterior Finishes to Timber   33
    1.6   Bricks and Brickwork Construction   37
    1.7   Concrete   51
    1.8   Mortar   54
    1.9   Damp-proof Courses   59
    1.10   Damp-proof Membranes   65
    1.11   Lighting   66
    1.12   Drainage   73
    1.13   Sustainable Urban Drainage Systems (SUDS)   76
    1.14   Sustainability of Materials and Life Span   82
    1.15   Recycled Materials and Products   84
    1.16   Typical Footpaths   86
    1.17   Typical Footpath Edging   88

2   Soft Landscape   **91**
    2.1   Definition and Specification of Tree Sizes   91
    2.2   Definition and Specification of Shrub Sizes   94
    2.3   British Native Trees and Shrubs   97
    2.4   Plants for Encouraging Wild Life   102
    2.5   Common Poisonous Plants   105
    2.6   Grass Seed Mixes   107
    2.7   Wild Flower Mixes   110
    2.8   Topsoil   112
    2.9   Times of Year for Planting   117
    2.10   Tree Planting   118
    2.11   Plant Protection   123
    2.12   Composts, Mulches and Manufactured Soil   127
    2.13   Soft Landscape Maintenance   133
    2.14   Soft Landscape Maintenance
        Programme – Routine Operations   140
    2.15   Green Roofs   142
    2.16   Geotextiles   148

3 Planning and Legislation   **151**
    3.1 Planning and Development Control   151
    3.2 Listed and Protected Areas for Heritage, Amenity,
         Landscape Quality, Cultural and Natural Habitat   155
    3.3 Tree Preservation Orders   161
    3.4 Hedgerow Legislation   163
    3.5 Notifiable Weeds   165
    3.6 Environmental Impact Assessment (EIA)   167
    3.7 Landscape and Visual Assessment   170
    3.8 Landscape Character Assessment   172
    3.9 Planting and Water Bodies Near Airfields   174
    3.10 Guidelines for Construction Around Trees   177
    3.11 Glossary of Contracts   180
    3.12 Construction (Design and Management)
         Regulations 2007   185

4 Design Guidelines   **191**
    4.1 Dimensional Data   191
    4.2 Senses, Communication and Space   203
    4.3 Walkable Neighbourhoods   204
    4.4 Creation of Positive Outdoor Space   206
    4.5 Steps and Ramps   207
    4.6 Guarding and Handrails   211
    4.7 Tactile Surfaces and Warning Paving   213
    4.8 Design of Cycleways   219
    4.9 Playgrounds and Playground Equipment   220
    4.10 Designing for Schools: Rules of Thumb   223
    4.11 Standard Sports Markings   226
    4.12 Construction of Free Standing Walls   233
    4.13 Water Features and Ponds   237
    4.14 Signage   242

5 General Information   **245**
    5.1 Landscape Architectural Work Stages   245
    5.2 Setting a Sundial   247
    5.3 Conversions and Calculations   251
    5.4 Gradients   253
    5.5 Weights of Materials   255
    5.6 Volumes in Relation to Depth and Area   260
    5.7 Rules of Thumb for Planting Plans   263
    5.8 Quantities and Rates of Sowing Grass Seed for
         Sports Use   264

6 Graphics **265**
  6.1 Paper Sizes 266
  6.2 Common Digital File Extensions 267
  6.3 AutoCAD Printing Scales 268
  6.4 Typical Survey Annotations 269
  6.5 Common Graphic Symbols 273

Glossary *275*

Associations, Institutes and Further Sources of Information *279*

Bibliography *287*

Index *289*

Preface

This book is intended to provide a concise reference guide and a first point of call for those seeking more extensive, supplementary sources of information. The content has been collated from a huge range of sources and has been distilled into what we hope are clear explanations, concise and accurate information covering a range of topics. When researching the topics and compiling the chapters we found that there were many sources of conflicting information and that some information quickly went out of date, even within the timeframe of preparing the book. We have endeavoured to be as accurate as possible; however, the user should be aware that legislation and standards will be updated and changed at various stages. Further sources of information and websites have been provided in order that current guidelines and legislation can be obtained and verified.

Acknowledgements

Many people are due thanks for their input, help, advice and support towards the production of this book including the technical representatives and publishers listed throughout the book.

However, we would like to state our special appreciation and thanks to the following:

Isobel Macintosh, Robert Macfarlane, Gillian McVitie, Graham Ross, Bob Ross, Lesley Samuel, Catriona Scott, Wendy Tippett and Austin-Smith:Lord LLP.

Sketches are provided by Gillian McVitie.

Thank you

1 Hard Landscape

1.1 Natural Stone

Natural stone can be grouped into three classes:

1. **Igneous rock** is formed when molten rock (called lava or magma) cools and hardens. Granite is an example of an igneous rock.
2. **Sedimentary rock** is formed from biological deposits that have undergone consolidation and crystallization. Limestone and sandstone fall into this category.
3. **Metamorphic rock** is formed when other kinds of rocks are changed by great heat and pressure inside the earth. Marble, slate and quartzite are examples of metamorphic rocks.

Typical properties and characteristics of common stone which fall within commercial definitions

Stone/group	Thermal movement mm/m per 90°C %	Water absorption %	Hardness Moh's scale*	Porosity	Moisture movement mm/m for dry/wet change	Compressive strength kg/cm²
Igneous						
Granite	0.93	0.2–0.5	5–7	Negligible	None	1000–2200
Sedimentary						
Sandstone	1.0	Less than 1.0	6–7	Low to very low	Approx. 0.7	365–460
Limestone	0.25–0.34	Less than 1.0	3–4	Quite low	0.8 – negligible	1800–2100
Metamorphic						
Slate	0.93	1.0–1.5	2.5–4.0	Low to very low	Negligible	170–240
Marble	0.34	Negligible	2.8–3.5	Negligible	Negligible	900–1250

See page 3 for a description of Moh's Scale of Relative Hardness

Points to note on the table on the previous page:

- The thermal coefficient of expansion of limestone and marble is low in comparison to granite, slate and sandstone. Allowance for thermal movement should be made for granite, slate and sandstone.
- The values listed in the table on the previous page are provided as a general guide and will vary according to the specific geological classification of the stone.
- It is advisable that most types of stone should be laid with any natural bedding plane running horizontally, to minimize the risk of splitting due to water penetration and frost.
- 'Face bedding' should generally be avoided as it often leads to delamination.

Moh's Scale of Relative Hardness*

Resistance to scratching and durability to foot traffic are largely dependent upon the hardness of the minerals that make up the stone. The hardness of a mineral is often defined by use of Moh's Scale of Relative Hardness, developed in 1822 by the Austrian Mineralogist Friedrich Moh. This scale lists 10 minerals in ascending order of scratch resistance, with 1 as the softest and 10 as the hardest:

Mineral	Equivalent everyday materials	Approximate equivalent stone		
1 Talc	Baby powder			
2 Gypsum	Fingernails			Marble
3 Calcite	Bronze	Limestone	Slate	Marble
4 Fluorspar	Iron	Limestone	Slate	
5 Apatite	Glass	Granite		
6 Feldspar	Nail file	Granite	Sandstone	
7 Quartz	Good quality steel	Granite	Sandstone	
8 Topaz	Sandpaper			
9 Corundum	Emeralds			
10 Diamond	Industrial diamonds			

Characteristics of common stone

Granite	
Colour	There are more than a hundred distinct colours with varying patterns.
Characteristics	Extremely hard, high density, high strength and resistant to weathering and abrasion. Amenable to cutting and shaping. The grain size varies from small to medium to coarse. Virtually impermeable; however has a tendency to be absorbent due to larger mineral grains or a combination of different grain sizes. Generally resistant to acid but can be affected by hydrofluoric concentrated acids such as cleaning products. Some varieties contain ferrous mineral compounds that when continuously exposed to moisture will produce discoloration which may appear as rust spots.
Finishes	Capacity to take various textural patterns plus polished and honed finish.

Sandstone	
Colour	The colour varies between red, green, yellow, grey and white. The variation is the result of the binding material and its percentage constituent.
Characteristics	Generally resistant to acids, alkalis and thermal impact; however, some sandstones can be sensitive to stain formation. Absorbs oil and water readily. Very durable but prone to becoming dirty easily and may weather less attractively. Can deteriorate when exposed to washings from limestone.
Finishes	The bedding planes in sandstones are very closely spaced and are sometimes visible. Can be polished, honed and textured.

Limestone	
Colour	The colour is generally pastel shades and is altered by the presence of impurities, which broaden the colour spectrum to include white, brown, grey, buff, yellow, red, black or mixtures of these colours.
Characteristics	Due to high absorption and susceptibility to staining, limestone is not generally used in applications where it comes into contact with soil, and it is very sensitive to acids. The flexural strength of limestone usually necessitates the use of thicker panels for cladding applications. The composition of this stone type allows for the cutting of profile by means of 'planing'. The use of a plane to shape the stone makes profile pieces more economical than in other stone types.
Finishes	Polished, honed.

Slate	
Colour	Ranges from grey to almost black, red, blue, purple, brown and dark to light green.
Characteristics	Very durable. Good resistance to acid and alkali. Absorption depends on hardness but can absorb oils and water. Has negligible moisture movement.
Finishes	Riven textures can vary from smooth to rough. Can be polished but tends to lose the finish relatively quickly.

Marble	
Colour	The purest calcite marble is white and can appear translucent. However coloured minerals and impurities often occur and give marble a variety of colours or markings: pink, reddish, yellow or green.
Characteristics	A derivative of limestone. Responds well to polishing. Can be easily scratched or etched by acids. Low porosity. May be susceptible to absorbing oils and water. Polished surfaces in exposed and polluted atmospheres can deteriorate. Discolouration can occur in damp conditions.
Finishes	Polished, honed.

Common finishes for stone

Honed	Honed stone colours are not as vibrant as polished stones and provide a smooth finish with a slight sheen produced by using a polishing head. This surface is very smooth, but often very porous, shows few scratches, and requires very little maintenance. Marble, limestone, and slate are appropriate stones for a honed finish.
Bush hammered	This is formed by a pounding action that develops a textured surface. The top surface is pneumatically tooled to produce a pitted or grooved surface finish.
Sawn	Sawn surface is coarsely polished leaving a semi-smooth, regular finish by using a gang saw.
Sand blasted	Sand blasting involves projecting a high-pressure airline of coarse-grained grit onto the surface of the stone. It is characterized by a textured surface with a matt gloss.
Polished	This provides high shine. The polish may last a long time or may be unstable depending on the type of stone. Granite, marble and limestone are frequently polished, and require varying degrees of maintenance to preserve the shine. Polished surface texture is a reflection of polished crystals. Such texture brings out the colours and grains of natural stones.
Flame texture	This provides a rough surface. This finish is used mostly for exterior applications, is labour intensive, and can be costly. The texture is achieved by heating the surface of the stone to extreme temperatures, followed by rapid cooling. Flaming is primarily carried out on granite.
Acid washed	Shiny with small etching marks (pits in surface). An acid-washed finish shows fewer scratches and appears more rustic in appearance than a honed finish. Most stones can be acid-washed but the most common are marble and limestone.
Saw cut refined	After initial cutting, the stone is processed to remove the heaviest saw marks but not enough to achieve a 'honed' finish. This produces a matt finish. Granite, marble and limestone can be purchased this way, typically on a special order basis.

Split faced	This finish provides a rough texture, less abrasive than flamed. This finish is typically achieved by hand cutting and chiselling at the quarry, exposing the natural cleft of the stone. This finish is primarily done on slate.
Tumbled	A smooth, or slightly pitted surface, finish with broken rounded edges and corners. Marble and limestone are the primary candidates for a tumbled finish.
Brushed	A worn-down look achieved by brushing the surface of the stone, simulating natural wear over time.

Source/Copyright: Materials, Alan Everett, Mitchell's Building Series.

1.2 Metals

Metals can be defined as elements which are characterized by their opacity, high thermal and electrical conductivity. Metals readily form positive ions and are often lustrous ductile solids. In pure form, metals are often very soft (e.g., lead, aluminium and iron); therefore, most metals used for construction are alloys containing controlled proportions of different metals. Metals are described as either ferrous, containing iron, or non-ferrous.

Typical properties of common metals

Non ferrous metals	Generally superior working properties and resistant to corrosion
Copper	
Properties and appearance	Three grades of copper are available for use in buildings and construction; C106, C102 and C101. Salmon red colour in ordinary atmospheres. Copper will develop a protective skin and a green patina may develop. The development of this will depend on the corrosiveness of the environment. This can be obtained more rapidly by chemical methods. Very resistant to corrosive agents particularly sea water but not to mineral acids and ammonia.
Compatibility	Washings may stain adjacent materials and corrode other materials. Contact with other metals should be avoided. May be compatible with stainless steel in dry conditions.
Joining	Can be joined by welding, brazing and soldering.
Forms	Available in rod, wire, tube, plate, sheet and strip forms.

Aluminium	
Properties and appearance	The metal can be classified as pure or as alloys. In normal atmospheres it has a good resistance to corrosion and a thin whitish film forms over the surface. Under damp conditions or external exposure, roughening of the surface may occur if not cleaned regularly. Does not require painting. Not recommended for exposure to marine atmospheres.
Compatibility	Products of corrosion do not stain adjacent surfaces. Contact must be avoided with copper and copper alloys such as brass and bare mild steel. Contact with zinc, stainless steel and lead is safe. Acids such as those found in cleaning materials or from decaying vegetable growth may attack aluminium. The metal should also be protected from fresh concrete, Portland Cement or mortar. May be prone to scratches and stains.
Joining	Can be joined by soldering and welding.
Forms	Available in rod, wire, tube, plate, sheet and strip forms.
Finishes	Finish is generally original mill or cast finished and anodized finish.*
Zinc	
Properties and appearance	Moderate strength, very ductile. Exposure to ordinary atmospheres for 3–6 months will tarnish the initial bright appearance to matt grey with the formation of a protective layer. Good resistance to inland and marine atmospheres. Liable to attack by industrial atmospheres polluted with sulphur acids. Unaffected by Portland Cement or lime mortars once they have set. Soluble salts, chlorides and sulphates may attack zinc under damp conditions and should be protected or separated by a bitumen type coating.
Compatibility	Contact with copper should be avoided. Damp timbers, particularly oak and western red cedar, may attack Zinc including any water run-off from these materials.
Joining	Available in sheet, strip, tube, wire, rods and extrusion forms.
Forms	Mainly used in the form of sheet or strip for roofing and wall cladding.
Finishes	Can be plated or stove enamelled.*

*__Finishes.__ Some steels may require an applied finish to provide appropriate protection from harsh environments to ensure longevity.

Ferrous metals	Can be worked easily compared to non-ferrous metals. With the exception of stainless steel and weathering steel, ferrous metals will require protection against corrosion.
Stainless steel	
Properties and appearance	A relatively costly ferrous metal but with high strength. Various grades are available with two principal grades used in building. It develops an invisible corrosion resistant film in contact with air and has high resistance to weak and organic mineral acids. Will not stain adjacent materials.
Compatibility	May accelerate corrosion of mild steel and other metals with the exception of copper and aluminium in protected conditions.
Joining	Can be forged, cast and be fabricated by methods including soldering, brazing and welding.
Forms	Available in tubes, rod, sheet, oval and wide range of sections.
Finishes	There are five standard mill finishes and four polished finishes ranging from dull to mirror polish finish. Can also be coloured by modifying the oxide coating.*
Mild steel	
Properties and appearance	Strong, ductile and suitable for rolling into sections, strips and sheets but not suitable for casting. Easily worked and welded. Can be used for cladding, furniture, etc. Requires galvanizing to be used externally or be similarly protected.
Compatibility	May be compatible with cast iron in dry and protected conditions.
Joining	Can be joined by welding.
Forms	Available in sections, plates, sheet and strip, tubes and rods.
Finishes	Finish is generally original mill or cast and galvanized finish. Mild steel can then be finished with a range of treatments such as paint, powder coating, etc.*

***Finishes.** Some steels may require an applied finish to provide appropriate protection from harsh environments to ensure longevity.

Cor–Ten	
Properties and appearance	Plain carbon steel with copper additions. When exposed to alternate wetting and drying it develops an oxide coating. This is a red copper colour darkening to purple brown. High strength and does not require protective treatments.
Compatibility	All corrosion products should be drained away in the first few years to avoid staining of adjacent surfaces, walls, paving, etc.
Forms	Available in sections, plates, sheet and coil.
Finishes	Unfinished. Also suitable for paint coating.
Cast iron	
Properties and appearance	Can be brittle and prone to fracturing. Very suitable for intricate casting but not for hot working. Generally grey in appearance. More resistant to corrosion than mild steel or wrought iron. Forms an adherent coat of rust therefore rarely suffers corrosion as generally used in thick sections. Does not possess the good weldability of mild steel but can be welded adequately for many purposes using suitable welding process.
Finishes	Excellent base for vitreous enamel.*
Wrought/ ductile iron	
Properties and appearance	Extremely ductile and moderately strong in tension, tough and resistant to impact. Resistance is notably better than that of mild steel.
Joining	The metal can be forged, even when cold, and joined through heating and hammering. It is the best ferrous metal for hand wrought work. Cannot be cast, tempered, gas or arc welded.

*Finishes. Some steels may require an applied finish to provide appropriate protection from harsh environments to ensure longevity.

Source/Copyright: Materials, Alan Everett, Mitchell's building series.

Common finishes for metals

Coatings	
Vitreous enamel	Can be applied to copper and aluminium and consists of powdered glass fused onto metal.
Painting	Application, appearance and service life of a paint system will depend on the quality of the metal, preparation of the surface, the coating thickness and whether the paint system is suitable for the environment.
Polyester powder coating	An electrostatically charged pigmented powder resin is applied prior to heating and curing in an oven.
Stove enamel	Enamel paint is applied and dried by a heat process (convection oven or radiant heat lamp).
Plastic coating	A thermoplastic powder developed to achieve long term adhesion to mild steel and aluminium without the need for an adhesive primer.
Metal coatings	
Electro-plating	A wide variety of metals can be used and the technique consists of applying a coating of one metal onto another. A uniform thickness of metal is applied (plated) onto another through electrolytic deposition, e.g. tin, zinc, aluminium, cadmium and chromium on steel or iron.
Galvanizing	A durable and protective coating for steel by pickling in acid to remove all impurities, drying and immersion in molten zinc which forms a protective layer of zinc iron alloy which is metallurgically bonded to the steel. The coating thickness can be varied between 50 and 150 microns. Post treatment of galvanizing is not necessary; however an additional paint, powder coat or plastic coat offers an alternative finish.
Zintec coating	This coating provides some protection against corrosion and provides a smooth finish for painting. Used on rolled flat steel sheets. A 2.5 micron coating of zinc is applied.
Sheradizing	This coating provides a protective coating of zinc alloy on steel. Zinc dust is rotated and heated in a cylinder to form an alloy of iron and zinc on the surface of varying thicknesses to provide a grey matt finish. Used on small objects such as nuts, bolts and door and window mongrey.

Mechanical treatments	
Sand blasting	Gives a matt finish which can be varied depending on the coarseness of the sand and the air pressure used.
Polishing	Can be a base for other applied finishes. The level of polish achieved can vary and be provided with progressively softer mops and finer abrasions.
Chemical treatments	
Anodizing	The protective and durable oxide film which forms naturally on aluminium is increased in thickness to improve the durability of the aluminium. The oxide film is thickened by immersing the aluminium in an electrolyte, usually sulphuric acid, and passing an electric current through it. The surface is then sealed in water. Surfaces can be dyed before sealing.

1.3 Stainless Steel

Properties and characteristics

Stainless steel is one of the most durable materials. There are many different grades of stainless steel available, each with different mechanical and physical properties and many different levels of corrosion resistance. Generally, the corrosion resistance increases with the chromium content of stainless steel.

The corrosion resistance of stainless steel arises from the passive, chromium-rich oxide film that forms on the surface of the steel. Unlike rust that forms on carbon steels, this film is stable, non-porous and adheres tightly to the surface of the steel. It is usually self-repairing and resistant to chemical attack.

If the film is scratched or broken, the exposed surface tends to react with oxygen, thereby renewing the oxide layer. The material therefore has intrinsic self-healing properties. Deposits that form on the surface of the steel can reduce the access of oxygen to the surface of the steel and therefore compromise corrosion resistance. The stability of the oxide element is dependent on factors including:

- the alloying elements present in the material.
- the corrosive nature of the environment.

The principal grades of stainless steel and their attributes

Family	EN 10088 designation	Popular name*	Attributes
Austenitic	**1.4301**	**304**	Good range of corrosion resistance and fabrication properties; readily available in variety of forms, e.g. sheet, tube, fasteners and fixings. 1.4402 (316) has better pitting corrosion resistance than 1.4301 (304). Low carbon (L) grades should be specified where extensive welding of heavy sections is required.
	1.4307	304L	
	1.4401	**316**	
	1.4404	316L	
	1.4541	321	
Duplex	1.4362	2304	Higher strength and wear resistance than standard austenitic grades with good resistance to stress corrosion cracking. Grade 1.4462 (2205) has better corrosion resistance than 1.4362 (2304).
	1.4462	2205	

The grades most widely used in architectural applications are highlighted in bold.
*The popular name originates from the, now partially superseded, British Standard and AISI (American Iron and Steel Institute) system

In identifying which stainless steel should be selected an evaluation of the following should be considered:

- site environment and weather
- finish and design
- budget and probable maintenance routine.

Suggested grades for atmospheric applications

Stainless steel grade	Location											
	Rural			Urban			Industrial			Coastal and marine		
	L	M	H	L	M	H	L	M	H	L	M	H
1.4301 (304)	√	√	√	√	√	*	*	*	x	√	*	x
1.4401 (316)	■	■	■	■	√	√	√	√	*	√	√	*
Special high alloy grades	■	■	■	■	■	■	■	■	√	■	■	√

Definitions

Rural – Rural or suburban areas with low population densities and light, non-polluting industry are included within this category.

Urban – Residential, commercial and light industrial locations with low to moderate pollution from vehicular traffic.

Industrial – Sulphur and nitrogen oxides from coal combustion and gases are released from chemical and process industry plants.

Coastal and marine – Local wind patterns determine how far sea salts are carried inland. Generally locations within 5–10 miles (8–16 km) of salt water are considered coastal. Where the material will be immersed in seawater, or regularly splashed, expert advice should be sought as this may require super duplex, super ferritic or 6% molybdenum super austenitic stainless steel.

L – Least corrosive conditions within that category, e.g. low humidity, low temperature levels.

M – Fairly typical of that category.

H – Corrosion likely to be higher than typical for that category, e.g. increased by persistent high humidity, high ambient temperatures and aggressive air pollutants.

√ – Probably the best choice for corrosion resistance and cost.

■ – Probably over specified from a corrosion point of view.

* – Worthy of consideration if precautions are taken, e.g. specifying a relatively smooth surface and carrying out regular washing.

x – Likely to suffer severe corrosion.

Factors to consider to improve the performance and prevent corrosion

Local weather patterns	• The moisture in fog, light misty rain or high humidity can combine with corrosive compounds on a surface to activate them to make corrosion possible. • Higher temperatures will increase the corrosion rate. • Light rain will not remove surface contaminants. • Storms with high rainfall rates or wind driven rain may remove corrosive deposits. • Most corrosive environments are areas with little or no rain, high temperatures, salt, aggressive pollution, moderate to high humidity or regular fog.
Salt exposure	• De-icing salt is sodium chloride or calcium chloride or a mixture. • Salt deposits can make the environment next to roadways or walkways corrosive. • Salt contamination can be carried as high as the 12th floor of buildings and as far as 200 m from busy highways dependant on traffic levels, wind speeds and climate.
Maintenance	• Encourage regular maintenance and cleaning schedule. • Design to facilitate manual washing with smooth and radiused corners.
Detailing	• Select smooth surface finishes. • Eliminate seals and crevices, slits or gaps to avoid dirt, and chemical entrapment. • Insulate at connections with other metals. • Minimize horizontal surfaces and provide clear drainage paths. • Expose components for better rain washing.

Surface finishes of stainless steel

Surface finishes may be imparted onto the material prior to fabrication or post-worked into the components after manufacture, i.e. pre-production or post-production surface finishes.

Selection of the final finish applied will have a major effect on appearance, corrosion, ease of cleaning and resistance to damage.

Finish	Characteristic/appearance	Notes
Mill finish	All hot and cold rolled material is heat treated and given a basic finish by the rolling mill. This may be an appropriate finish or be the basis for further finishing.	Good corrosion resistance can be achieved by pickling the surface with an appropriate acid solution.
(1B)	Hot rolled, heat treated with a pickled finish gives uniform matt finish.	
(2D)	Cold rolled, heat treated with a pickled finish gives uniform matt finish.	Susceptibility to finger marking. Improved smoothness and dimensional tolerances than hot rolled.
(2B)	Cold rolled, heat treated, pickled and with a skin pass (additional final light rolling process with polished rollers). Smooth, pearly, semi-lustrous appearance.	Susceptibility to finger marking.
(2R)	Cold rolled, bright annealed finish, and subsequent cold rolling using polished rollers gives highly reflective, mirror like surface.	Scratches can be removed by skilled polisher.
Embossed, three dimensional patterns	Embossed three dimensional patterns may be rolled onto or into the strip by cold rolling. May be applied to one or both sides. Designs include low reflective surfaces. Patterns are usually applied to cold rolled material bearing the basic mill finishes.	Facilities exist for rolling stainless steel in thickness of 0.1 mm. Fabrication and handling of lengths greater than 4000 mm is difficult.

Finish	Characteristic/appearance	Notes
Mechanically polished or brushed finish	The wide range of mechanically polished finishes involves cutting or polishing the surface with an abrasive medium or sequence of media.	Brushed, striated finishes and polished, reflective surfaces may be susceptible to damage. Scratches may be abraded out. Remedial polishing is possible but is more complex.
	The main classes of finishes listed in EN 10088 are:	
(1G or 2G)	Ground or coarse polish	Non-reflective. Roughness can be specified.
(1J or 2J)	Smoother (than ground)	Brushed or dull polished. Not very reflective. Roughness can be specified. Suitable for internal uses.
(1K or 2K)	Smooth with controlled cutting	Satin or fine finish. Fine, clean cut with minimal micro crevices, optimizing corrosion resistance suitable for external uses.
(1P or 2P)	Mechanically polished	Bright polished finish with high reflective qualities.
Electropolished	Enhances reflectivity of steel and provides smooth finish. Method involves the removal of the surface layer with the loss greatest at the highest spots.	Provides excellent corrosion resistance as process leaves surface smooth and free from irregularities. Vulnerable to scratches and damage. Normally carried out prior to fabrication.
Bead blasted finish	Non-directional, matt surface finish produced by the impact of hard inert medium sprayed onto the steel surface. This creates a non-directional texture with soft satin reflection in a range of coarseness dependent on the media. Similar in appearance to acid etching with low reflectivity. Various media used may include; sand, glass beads, lead bead, stainless steel shot, ground quartz, silicon carbide.	Impact can cause distortion and therefore should not be applied to stainless steel less than 0.4mm thick. Optimum corrosion performance can be achieved through use of fine media.

Finish	Characteristic/appearance	Notes
Coloured finish		
Painted	Some manufacturers provide coil coating routes to produce painted stainless steel. The coatings produce primers and pre-paint systems and finishes based upon acrylic and PVF systems.	
Chemically coloured	Coloured by immersion in a solution of chromic and sulphuric acid. Colours are bronze, blue, black, charcoal, gold, red, violet and green. Can be produced on (304) 1.4301 and (316) 1.4401 material.	Generally applied to sheet stainless steel. Can be applied to components. Difficult to repair if scratched. Can be combined with rolled, acid etched or blast finished.
Decorative finish		
Acid etched	Removes a thin layer of surface material and is used to produce standard and bespoke finishes. The area etched away becomes frosted in appearance. The un-etched area can be mirror or satin polished.	Only applied to sheet stainless steel. The pattern depth is controlled by length of exposure to the acid. Generally 0.8 mm is the thinnest material that can be etched.

Product range

Sizes and product range will differ between each manufacturer. For actual sizes and availability, refer to individual manufacturer's information.

Item	Process route	Surface finish	Approximate product dimensions	
			Thickness (mm)	Width (mm)
Sheet, strip, coil	Hot rolled		2.0–8.5	1000–2032
	Cold rolled	Soft annealed 2D	0.25–6.35	up to 2032
		Skin pass rolled 2B	0.25–6.35	up to 2032
		Bright annealed 2R	1.0–2.0	up to 1250
		Brushed	0.4–2.0	up to 1500
		Polished	0.4–5.0	up to 1524
		Pattern rolled	0.1–3.0	up to 1350
Plate	Hot rolled		3.0–140	1000–3200
	Cold rolled		3.0–8.0	1000–2000

Item	Process route	Shape	Thickness (mm)	Width (mm)	Diameter (mm)
Bar	Hot or cold finished	Rounds			2 to 450
		Squares			3 to 300
		Flats	3 to 25	12 to 150	
		Hexagons			5 to 100
Hollow sections	Seamless or welded from strip plate	Rectangular hollow sections	1.0–8.0	20 × 10 to 250 × 150	
		Square hollow sections	1.0–8.0	10 × 10 to 300 × 300	
		Circular hollow sections	0.25–60		3 to 1500
		Oval hollow sections	1.5–3.0		61 × 37 to 121 × 76
Structural sections	Hot rolled	Equal angles	2.0–20	10 × 10 to 180 × 180	
		Unequal angles	2.0–20	20 × 10 to 200 × 100	

Maintenance, cleaning and remedial repairs

Methods of cleaning stainless steel		
Requirement	**Method of cleaning**	**Comments**
Routine cleaning of light soiling	Soap, detergent or dilute ammonia (1%) solution in warm clean water. Apply with a clean sponge, soft cloth or soft fibre brush and rinse with clean water and dry.	
Oil and grease marks	Hydrocarbon solvent	
Discolouration, water marking and light rust staining	Mild, non-scratching creams and polishes. Apply with a soft cloth or soft sponge. Rinse off residues with clean water and dry.	Avoid chloride containing solutions or creams with abrasive additions.
Localized rust stains caused by carbon steel contamination	Proprietary gels or 10% phosphoric acid solution followed by ammonia and water rinses or oxalic acid solution followed by water rinse.	Carbon steel wool pads should not be used.
Adherent hard water scales and mortar/cement splashes	10–15% volume solution of phosphoric acid. Use warm, neutralize with dilute ammonia solution, and rinse with clean water and dry.	Proprietary formulations available with surfactant additions. Avoid the use of hydrochloric acid based mortar removers.
Heat tinting or heavy discolouration	(a) Non-scratching or polish. Apply with soft cloth and rinse with clean water and dry. (b) Nylon type pad.	(a) Suitable for most finishes. (b) Use on brushed or polished surfaces along the grain.
Paint and graffiti	Proprietary alkaline or solvent paint stripper depending on paint type. Use soft nylon or bristle brush on patterned material.	Apply as directed by manufacturer.

Source/Copyright: Architects Guide to Stainless Steel, 1997, SCI Publication 179. The Steel Construction Institute/Nancy Baddoo, Rana Burgan, Raymond Ogden.

1.4 Timber

Sustainable sources
Sustainability

The sustainability of forestry operations and timber supplies is an important consideration when selecting timber species. Of particular concern is the destruction of forest areas in the tropics for agricultural use, resulting in the loss of natural habitats and damage to local ecosystems. There are numerous sources of guidance and legislation which can be consulted to assist with making an informed and responsible purchase.

IUCN Red List

The International Union for the Conservation of Nature and Natural Resources (IUCN) is a worldwide conservation union. Its mission is to conserve the integrity and diversity of nature and to ensure that any use of natural resources is both equitable and ecologically sustainable. The IUCN Red List is the world's most comprehensive inventory of the global conservation status of plant and animal species. It uses a set of criteria to evaluate the extinction risk of thousands of species and subspecies. These criteria are relevant to all species and all regions of the world. With its strong scientific base, the IUCN Red List is recognized as the most authoritative guide to the status of biological diversity. The overall aim of the Red List is to convey the urgency and scale of conservation problems to both the public and policy makers, and to motivate the global community into trying to reduce species extinction. Timber species are included on this list.

CITES

The 'Washington' Convention on International Trade in Endangered Species of Wild Fauna and Flora (more commonly known as CITES) aims to protect certain plants and animals by regulating and monitoring their international trade to prevent it reaching unsustainable levels. The CITES Secretariat is administered by the United Nations Environment Programme (UNEP). CITES regulates international trade in over 33,000 species. These species are listed in three appendices. Proposals to amend the appendices, and new resolutions on the implementation of the Convention, are considered at the triennial Conference of the Parties (COP). Each Party to CITES must have a Management Authority. The Wildlife Species Conservation Division and Wildlife Habitats and Biodiversity Divisions of the Department for Environment, Food and Rural Affairs (DEFRA) together comprise the UK CITES Management Authority. The Management Authority is responsible for ensuring that the Convention is properly implemented in the UK, which includes enforcement and issuing permits and certificates for the import and export, or commercial use of, CITES specimens. In accordance with the provisions of the Convention, applications for CITES permits are referred to a designated CITES Scientific Authority for advice on the conservation status of the species concerned.

Central Point of Expertise on Timber Procurement

The Central Point of Expertise on Timber Procurement (CPET) is a service of the UK Government. CPET has been set up by the Department for Environment, Food and Rural Affairs (Defra), and is operated by ProForest, a company with wide experience in advising on responsible purchasing. From April 2009, contracts from the UK Government will require timber products to be certified as sustainable by a schedule recognized by CPET or covered by a Forest Law Enforcement, Governance and Trade (FLEGT) licence.

FLEGT – the EU Action Plan

The EU Forest Law Enforcement, Governance and Trade (FLEGT) Action Plan sets out a programme of actions that forms the European Union's response to the problem of illegal logging and the trade in associated timber products. FLEGT addresses illegal logging and links good governance in developing countries with the legal trade instruments and influence offered by the EU's internal market.

Forest Stewardship Council and the Programme for the Endorsement of Forest Certification Schemes

The Forest Stewardship Council (FSC) is an international, non-profit making association, whose membership includes environmental and social groups and progressive forestry and wood retail companies working in partnership to improve forest management worldwide. The Group aims to adopt environmental standards at least equal to legal requirements and to integrate environmental considerations into its decision-making in such areas as transport, energy usage, treatment plants, waste disposal and health and safety.

Certification Schemes

Independent verification and forest certification are convenient ways for the trade to ensure 'legal' and 'sustainable' timber. Certification schemes, notably by the FSC and the Programme for the Endorsement of Forest Certification (PEFC), offer consumers a means of ensuring that the material they are using comes from sustainably managed forests. There are many certification schemes such as CSA, MTCC or SFI.

HM Government's Timber Procurement Policy

Many contracts now stipulate that timber products must be legal as defined in the Government's Timber Procurement Advice Note. The contractor is required to ensure that the organization that felled the trees had legal use rights to the forest, held a register of all national and local laws and codes of practice relevant to forestry operations, complied with all national and local laws including environmental, labour and health and safety laws, and paid all relevant royalties and taxes. The contractor must, before delivering timber or timber products, obtain documentary evidence that the timber is both legal and legally traded. This evidence should be made available for a period up to six years after delivery. In addition, the timber must be traceable from its source in the forest and through the supply chain and verified by an appropriate third party organization whose procedures conform to

ISO Guide 65:1996. There is a variant specification for material from certified well-managed forests in accordance with ISO/IEC Guide 59: Code of Good Practice and independently verified.

Timber suppliers can offer various certifications, company policies or procurement tools to assist with environmentally responsible purchasing. The Timber Trade Federation's Responsible Purchasing Policy and Chain of Custody are examples of such verification. Such bodies can assist with specification clauses in order to place a condition on the supplier, rather than on the 'sustainability' or country of origin of a particular species to ensure that environmentally sound credentials are met.

Chain of Custody

Chain of Custody (COC) means tracking timber from the tree in the forest, to the processing plant, to the depots, and to the final customer. It is important that systems are in place at each stage to ensure identification of the material, and third party auditing of the supply chain is required to ensure that there is no contamination at any stage.

For the process to work, each company in the supply chain must have their COC system audited against a set method of working and hold a current COC certificate.

Selection of timber

Softwood is the wood of a coniferous tree. The term 'softwood' does not reflect the density of the species; however, softwoods are, in general, softer than hardwoods. Some softwoods, such as yew, are comparatively hard; while some hardwoods, such as basswood, are comparatively soft.

Hardwood is the wood of broad-leaved dicotyledonous trees. Hardwoods are, in general, harder than softwood and vary dramatically in density.

Selection of timber

The selection of a timber for a particular use is determined by:

- natural durability;
- the life service requirement of the component;
- the in-service environment in which the timber will be used;
- whether the timber will be or can be treated with preservative.

Durability – BS EN 350-1 sets out five natural durability classes for heartwood: very durable, durable, moderately durable, slightly durable, not durable. BS EN 460 gives guidance on whether a timber's natural durability alone is sufficient for the hazard class. The natural durability of the heartwood of each timber species will vary. Durability is the resistance to fungal decay of the heartwood of the species only. The sapwood of most species is not durable, or only slightly durable, and should not be used in exposed situations without preservative treatment.

Life service – The life service requirement is classified in BS 8417, which indicates 15, 30 or 60 year life service.

The in-service environment – The in-service environment in which the timber will be used is identified as the biological hazard class or use class.

The following outlines the use class and the typical service situations.

Use class	Service situation
1	Internal with no risk of wetting.
2	Internal with risk of wetting.
3	External and above the damp proof course.
4	In contact with ground or fresh water and permanently exposed to wetting.
5	Permanently exposed to wetting by salt water.

Not all timbers are equally amenable to the uptake of preservatives and, therefore, the treatability of timber varies between each species. If a timber species has been specified, care should be taken to ensure that a species is chosen appropriate to the treatment requirements.

Points to note:

- If the heartwood of the timber has sufficient natural durability, it can be used without treatment, even where a biological hazard class exists.
- Timbers of high natural durability are frequently derived from sources which are prone to be environmentally fragile or vulnerable.

Suitable timbers for use in water

Species with heartwood suitable for use, untreated, in sea water	Sustainability status	Species with heartwood suitable for use, untreated, in fresh water	Species suitable, if treated, for use in sea and fresh water
Afrormosia	CITES II/EN	All timbers which are classed as durable in BS EN 350-2.	All species in which the required combination and retention can be achieved.
Agba*	EN		
African Padauk*	EN		
Andaman Padauk	VU/EN		
Ekki*	CITES II/VU		
Greenheart*	VU		
Iroko	CITES II/LR		
Jarrah			
Opepe*	VU		
Teak			

*Species believed to be the best for marine work.

Hardwoods suitable for use in external joinery, classified according to durability of the heartwood

Less than moderately durable (treatment required)	Moderately durable or better (treatment required only if sapwood present)	Sustainability status
Dark Red Meranti	Aformosia	CITES II/EN
Red Meranti	Agba***	EN
	Idigbo*	
	Brazilian/American Mahogany	VU/EN/CITES II
	Makore	EN
	Oak – American White	
	Oak – European	
	Opepe	VU
	Sapele	VU
	Teak	
	Utile	VU
	African Walnut	VU

*The sapwood of these species is not easily distinguishable from the heartwood
**Subject to resin bleed which may be exacerbated by preservative treatment
Notes on sustainability status which may be subject to change:
CITES
Appendix I – Trading prohibited
Appendix II – Trade permitted subject to export permits from the country of origin and UK import permits from the Department of the Environment and Rural Affairs
Appendix III – Species protected within individual party states

Key to threat classification as set out by the IUCN Red List:
CR – Critically Endangered: a very high risk of extinction in the wild
EN – Endangered: a high risk of extinction in the wild
VU – Vulnerable: at risk of extinction
LR (NT) – Lower Risk (Near Threatened): close to qualifying as Vulnerable

Source/Copyright: Wood Protection Association. For further information The Wood Protection Association publishes guidance in the form of information sheets and a manual 'Industrial Wood Preservation – Specification and Practice': www.wood-protection.org.

The following table outlines some of the properties of the timbers which may be suitable for external joinery. Check verification status for sustainable and well-managed sources.

Species/origin	Type/colour	Machining/density	Texture/durability	Treatability/moisture movement	Notes
Idigbo *Terminalia ivorensis* West Africa	Hardwood/yellow light brown	Medium/ 540 kg/m³	Medium/ durable	Difficult/ medium	VU*. Also called Framire or Emeri
Iroko *Chlorophora excelsa* W and E Africa	Hardwood/from light yellow to golden brown	Medium/difficult 660 kg/m³	Medium/ very durable	Extremely resistant/ small	CITES II LR (NT). This is a hard-wearing timber which is resistant to decay
Jarrah *Eucalyptus marginata* Australia	Hardwood/pink to dark red	Difficult/ 8250 kg/m³	Medium/ very durable	Extremely resistant/ medium	
Larch *Larix decidua, Larix europaea* Europe	Softwood/pale red, brown	Medium/ 550 kg/m³	Fine/ slightly durable	Extremely resistant/ small	
Thuja plicata Western Red Cedar North America	Softwood/sapwood is pale, heartwood is rich brown	Good/ 370 kg/m³	Coarse/ durable	Extremely resistant/ small	Turns a silver grey if left to weather naturally‡

(Continued)

Species/origin	Type/colour	Machining/density	Texture/durability	Treatability/moisture movement	Notes
Mahogany, Brazilian *Swietenia macrophylla* South America	Hardwood/from reddish brown to deep reddish brown	Good/ 560 kg/m³	Medium/durable	Extremely resistant/small	CITES II
Meranti (Red) *Shorea spp* SE Asia. Due to the diversity of this species there is great variability in the physical properties	Hardwood/dark red, red brown	Good/ 670 kg/m³	Coarse/ moderate, durable	Resistant, extremely resistant/small	CR/EN/VU** depending on species. Also known as Shorea, Meranti, Seraya, Lauan dependant on its origin
Oak *Quercus spp, Quercus robur and Quercus petraea* Europe	Hardwood/yellow brown	Medium, difficult/ 670 kg/m³	Medium to fine/ durable	Extremely resistant	*
White oak *Quercus spp Quercus alba* North America	Hardwood/pale yellow to mid brown	Medium/ 760 kg/m³	Medium to coarse/durable	Extremely resistant/ medium	*‡
Douglas fir *Pseodotsuga menziesii* North America	Softwood/sapwood is pale honey, heartwood is rich brown	Good/ 530 kg/m³	Fine/moderate	Extremely resistant/small	

Padauk *Pterocarpus Soyauxii* Africa	Hardwood/vivid red toning down to dark purple-brown	Medium/ 770 kg/m³	Coarse/very durable	Moderately resistant/small	
Southern yellow pine *Pinus palustris, Pinus elliotti, Pinus echinata, Pinus taeda*	Softwood/yellowish-brown to reddish-brown	Good/ 660 kg/m³	Medium/mod-erate	Extremely resistant/small	*P. elliotii, P. echinata* and *P. taeda* LR (NT) *P. palustris* VU**
Sapele *Entandrophragma cylindricum* W. Africa	Hardwood/reddish brown	Medium/ 620 kg/m³	Medium, fine/ moderate	Extremely resistant/ medium	VU
Utile *Etrandophragma utile* W. Africa	Hardwood/fairly uniform reddish or purplish brown	Good/ 660 kg/m³	Medium/ durable	Extremely resistant/ medium	VU

*Stains in contact with iron under damp conditions

‡May corrode metal in damp conditions

**Gum/Resin exudation may be troublesome

Notes on sustainability status which may be subject to change:

CITES

Appendix I – Trading prohibited

Appendix II – Trade permitted subject to export permits from the country of origin and UK import permits from the Department of the Environment and Rural Affairs

Appendix III – Species protected within individual party states

Key to threat classification as set out by the IUCN Red List:

CR – Critically Endangered: a very high risk of extinction in the wild

EN – Endangered: a high risk of extinction in the wild

VU – Vulnerable: at risk of extinction

LR (NT) – Lower Risk (Near Threatened): close to qualifying as Vulnerable

(Continued)

Notes

Density – Timbers vary in density depending on their species and moisture content. The values quoted are averages at 15% but the increase caused by moisture can be estimated by adding 0.5% of the given weight for every 1% increase in moisture content.

Texture – Surface texture depends on the size and distribution of the wood cells and, less importantly, rays. Classification ranges from fine, through medium, to coarse.

Machining/working qualities – This refers to the ease of working and is classified as excellent, good, medium and difficult.

Moisture movement – This refers to the dimensional changes that occur when dried timber is subjected to changes in atmospheric conditions. The movement is classified as small, medium and large.

Treatability – This refers to the ease of accepting a treatment application. This is classified as extremely resistant, resistant, good, satisfactory and poor.

Drying and kilning – Kiln drying timber reduces the natural moisture in wood. The majority of timbers today are already kiln dried, except for those sold especially for external construction work, and commonly sold at an average moisture content of 12.5–15%, suitable for most internal situations bar those with continuous central heating.

North American timbers are imported already kiln dried to a moisture content varying on average 8–10%.

Sizes – The majority of imported Hardwood is in the form of Square Edged boards of random width and length. These are normally sold on the basis of 6′ (approximately 182 cm) and up in length, and 6″ (approximately 15 cm) and wider in width. However, Far Eastern timbers are more commonly 8′ (approximately 243 cm) and longer, 6″ (approximately 15 cm) and wider.

Refer to BS EN 350-2 for additional list of species.

Source/Copyright: Lathams Ltd, www.lathams.co.uk

1.5 Exterior Finishes to Timber

There are four main types of material which are suitable for the exterior treatment of wood: preservatives, varnishes, paint and exterior wood stains. Preservatives are not usually designed or expected to provide an exterior finish. Similarly, paints and exterior wood finish will not provide adequate or suitable protection to timbers in exterior locations. All timber preservatives placed on the UK market, legally, are approved by the Health and Safety Executive under the Control of Pesticides Regulations 1996.

Properties of typical finishes to timber

Finish/ Application	Appearance	Properties	Maintenance
Wood stain Brush May be organic solvent or water based	Semi-transparent. Alters tone/colour of wood but generally allows grain and texture to be visible. Build or surface film will vary from product to product. Varies from gloss to matt to high gloss finish.	Allows moisture vapour to pass in and out of timber. Stains work primarily by shedding liquid water from the surface. May reduce the effects of weathering, but not a substitute for preservative. Works better on vertical surfaces. Performs better on rough sawn finish than smooth planed surface.	Wash down to remove any contamination from weathering and any loose particles, followed by one or more coats of stain. Wood stains will fade and erode gradually rather than fail by cracking or flaking.
Paint Brush May be organic solvent borne or water borne	Opaque. Varies from gloss to matt to high gloss finish. Creates a solid film over wood surface. May disguise blemishes, knots, etc.	Primarily works by shedding liquid water from the surface. Works better on vertical surfaces than horizontal, but not a substitute for a preservative.	Clean thoroughly with slight abrasion or removal of severely degraded old paint by stripping or burning, followed by application of new paint.
Varnish Brush	Transparent. Can provide a quality natural finish.	Contains resin or modified resin with drying oils. Essentially a paint without pigments. Provides limited protection to weathering and is not a substitute for a preservative.	Long term and frequent maintenance is likely to be required in exterior applications. Clean surface, scrape all loose and flaking pieces back to the bare wood, sand back to a firm edge and stain any bleached areas. Apply one or more coats of varnish.

Preservatives		
Tar oil/creosote Pressure impregnation. Can be brush applied. Now restricted to 'professional and industrial use' and may not be used inside buildings, in toys, playgrounds, garden furniture, etc.	Semi-transparent. Alters tone and colour of wood to dark brown/black allowing the grain and texture to be visible.	Long lasting and an effective wood preservative. Suitable for use on timber to be embedded into the ground. Strong smell. Difficult to paint over. May 'bleed' creosote, particularly during periods of high temperature. Can stain absorbent materials on contact. May be harmful to plants within first few months of application. Freshly treated timber may be more flammable.	Does not require maintenance; however periodic surface applications may be required to renew the surface colour. More regular re-coatings may be necessary if the original treatment was by brush application or cold dipping.
Organic solvent borne Applied by double vacuum or pressure impregnation treatments process. Dip or applied by brush.	Does not provide a decorative surface finish to the wood or change the colour, unless a tint is added. Usually available in a water repellent grade which may interfere with the film-forming properties or application of any additional surface coatings.	Available in water repellent grade which is advantageous for exterior use. Does not change the dimensions of the timber or raise the grain. Only suitable for situations out of ground, such as cladding and joinery. Solvent may leach out over time in high moisture environments.	No maintenance is required; however may become dirty or discoloured with prolonged exposure. Re-coatings may be necessary if the original treatment was by brush application as the protection afforded by brush application is minimal.

(Continued)

Finish/ Application	Appearance	Properties	Maintenance
Micro-emulsions Pressure impregnation	Used on joinery items where the surface appearance is not of prime importance.	Suitable for internal use only. Little effect on the dimensions of the timber but may raise the grain.	
Copper organic Copper azole or Copper-quat preservatives Vacuum/pressure impregnation	Treatment imparts a greenish tint to the timber. Colour pigmentation may be added to the treatment. Treatment has no smell. Treated timber does not discolour or taint adjacent materials.	Treatment may cause the timber to swell, raise the grain or cause it to distort. Preservative treatments become permanently fixed and insoluble in the wood, creating a protective 'shell' against stain, decay, mould and insect attack. Retards the rate of natural weathering. Suitable for external use and in contact with the ground.	No maintenance is required; however, may become dirty or discoloured with prolonged exposure.

Notes: Approval for (CCA) Chromated Copper Arsenate preservative was withdrawn on 1st September 2006. Timber treated with CCA may still be available. CCA is not permitted under any circumstances for use under sea water in the UK under the regulations.

Further information – Creosote (Prohibition on use and marketing) (No. 2) Regulations 2003.

Organizations concerned with the performance of timber commodities and who may have specific requirements for the treatment of timber include: National House Building Council, Building Regulations UK, Zurich Building Guarantee, British Telecom, Highways Agency.

Source/Copyright: The Wood Protection Association

For further information The Wood Protection Association publishes guidance in the form of information sheets and a manual 'Industrial Wood Preservation – Specification and Practice'. www.wood-protection.org

1.6 Bricks and Brickwork Construction

There are many different types of bricks. However, the vast majority are clay and kiln-fired bricks. Definitions of some types of bricks are provided below.

Definitions

- **A standard brick** is defined as a masonry unit with a work (actual) size of 215 × 102.5 × 65 mm. The unit will be faced on a minimum of one header and one stretcher.
- **Facing bricks** are intended to provide an attractive appearance and are available in a wide range of colours, types and textures such as: smooth drag faced, creased, rolled, rustic and stock bricks. Bricks suitable for the full spectrum of durability classifications are available; therefore, some may not be suitable for use in areas of extreme exposure and others will have the properties of an engineering brick.
- **Calcium silicate bricks** are made from concrete and sand/lime. They are an alternative to clay and are available in a range of textures and colours. They are cost effective, but generally less attractive.
- **Engineering bricks** have no requirement for colour or texture and are not selected for appearance. They are dense bricks with a guaranteed minimum compressive strength and maximum water absorption. They are suitable for ground works, retaining walls and as a low level damp-proof course (DPC) for free-standing walls.
- **Stocks** are typically used as a facing brick with a traditional appearance. The product processes which are used result in a soft appearance and slightly irregular shape with variations in colour and texture. The bricks are machine moulded with a frog indent. The use of sand to release the bricks from the mould contributes to the soft appearance and slightly irregular shape. They are generally more expensive than wire-cut bricks.
- **Handmade bricks** are hand thrown by skilled craftsmen. Each is unique with a distinctive creased texture and will generally be more expensive than other ranges of bricks available. Handmade bricks can also be simulated by a machine thrown process which will cost less than the real thing.
- **Waterstruck** are moulded bricks released from the mould by water. Solid bricks containing no holes or frogs. Bricks have a smooth and lipped edge or arris.
- **Flettons** are made from 'Oxford' clay, contain organic impurities that burn during firing, making for interesting faces. They come in a variety of colours and textures and are fairly economical.
- **Wire-cut/Extruded** are bricks made by extruding clay through a die, then cutting it with a wire, for a smooth, regular-shaped brick. Surface textures can be applied by the addition of sand or by texturing the 'face' and there is a wide variety of colours available. Wire-cuts are the cheapest facing brick.

Brick bonding

There are a number of possible bonding patterns. The following are some of the most commonly used.

Stretcher Bond

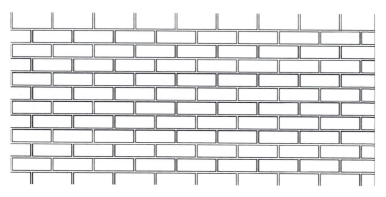

Header Bond

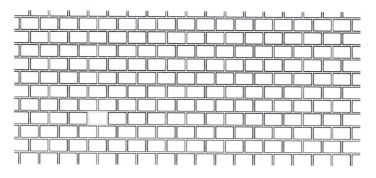

English Bond

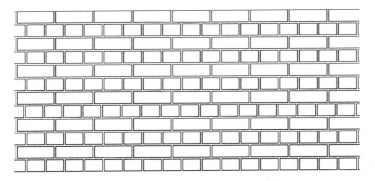

Flemish Bond

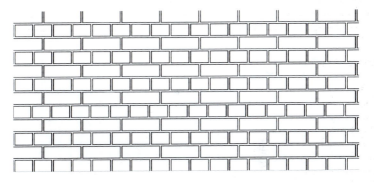

English Garden Wall Bond

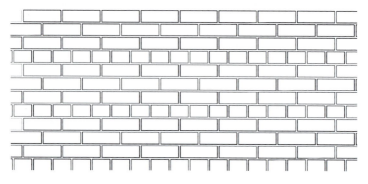

Flemish Garden Wall Bond

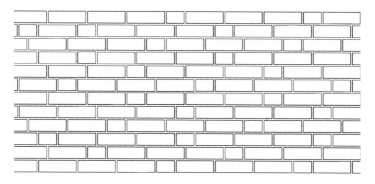

Joint profiles

The efficient shedding of water by mortar joints is essential for satisfactory long-term performance. Brickwork that remains saturated is more susceptible to frost and sulphate attack. The choice of joint profile should, therefore, be first based on performance criteria with aesthetic consideration as secondary.

Typical joint profiles

Curved recessed	(Bucket handle)	
		An efficient joint with a softer appearance
Flush	**(Raked)**	
		A common profile which is efficient in shedding water if tooled but will alter the appearance of the colour of the overall brickwork
Struck	**(Weatherstruck)**	
		An efficient and attractive joint giving the shadow effect of a recessed profile but better weathering properties.

Square recessed		
		An attractive profile which should only be used in sheltered locations. It is not recommended for free standing walls or any exposed situations. The depth of the recess should be kept to the minimum necessary to achieve the desired appearance but should not be greater than 3–4 mm. Recessed joints should not be used where there is a danger of saturation occurring.

Brickwork dimensions

Co-ordinating size is the size of the co-ordinating space allocated to a section of masonry which makes allowances for joints and tolerances.

Vertical brickwork courses dimension table, using 65 mm brick and 10 mm joints.

Course	Height (mm)
1	075
2	150
3	225
4	300
5	375
6	450
7	525
8	600
9	675
10	750

In order to calculate any alternative height: height = number of courses × 075 mm.

Horizontal brick dimensions using 215 × 102.5 × 65 mm bricks with 10 mm joints

Brickwork dimensions should be given where possible at design stage to minimize the need for cut units. The table above gives the dimensions for horizontal brickwork courses based on the standard co-ordinating size of 225 × 112.5 × 75 mm which includes 10 mm joints, this size being determined by the term 'co-ordinating size (CO)'.

Number of bricks		CO + joint	CO (co-ordinating size)	CO − joint
	½	122.5	112.5	102.5
1		235	225	215
	1½	347.5	37.5	327.5
2		460	450	440
	2½	572.5	562.5	552.5
3		685	675	665
	3½	797.5	787.5	777.5
4		910	900	890
	4½	1022.5	1012.5	1002.5
5		1135	1125	1115
	5½	1247.5	1237.5	1227.5
6		1360	1350	1340
	6½	1472.5	1462.5	1452.5
7		1585	1575	1565
	7½	1697.5	1687.5	1677.5
8		1810	1800	1790
	8½	1922.5	1912.5	1902.5
9		2035	2025	2015
	9½	2147.5	2137.5	2127.5
10		2260	225	2240

Source/Copyright: Ibstock Technical Information Sheet 9

Clay bricks

Each brick type will have different properties and technical specification in relation to its performance. BS EN 771-1 is the sole product standard for clay bricks, or clay masonry units in accordance with European standards.

Some of the properties set out the technical specification in accordance with BS EN 771-1 which may be applicable in relation to selecting a brick are set out below:

- Facing description (appearance)
- Dry brick weight (kg)
- Manufacture, e.g. Wire-cut
- Brick dimensions (L × W × H mm): 215 × 102.5 × 65
- Dimensional tolerances mean and range: T2, R1
- **Masonry Unit Group:** LD or HD

- Category: e.g. I or II
- Configuration: e.g. Vertically perforated
- Voids (%): 23–28
- **Compressive strength** (N/mm^2)
- **Active soluble salts**: e.g. S2
- Water absorption (% weight)
- **Durability**: e.g. F0, F1, F2
- Gross dry density (sound insulation) (Kg/m^3): 1640 (where applicable for intended use)
- Initial rate of absorption (suction rate) (Kg/m^2/min): 0.60 (where applicable for intended use)
- Water vapour permeability
- Thermal conductivity
- Bond strength (in combination with the mortar) N/mm^2
- Fire reaction e.g. A1 (where applicable for intended use)
- Equivalent thermal conductivity 'K' value (where applicable for intended use)
- Density tolerance: e.g. D1 (acoustic).

Some of these highlighted properties are described below. The classifications for each should be declared by the manufacturer with reference to the performance.

Density	Masonry unit group
LD	Clay masonry unit with low gross dry density less than or equal to 1000 kg/m^3 for use in protected masonry such as internally or where protected by impervious cladding.
HD	Clay masonry unit for unprotected masonry with high gross dry density greater than 1000 kg/m^3.

Freeze/thaw resistance should be declared by the manufacturer with reference to performance under passive, moderate or extreme exposure.

Freeze/thaw resistance	Durability
F0	Suitable for passive exposure. Bricks liable to be damaged by freezing and thawing. Such bricks are only suitable for internal use or behind impervious cladding.
F1	Suitable for moderate exposure. Bricks durable except in situations where they are in a saturated condition and exposed to repeated freezing and thawing.
F2	Suitable for severe exposure. Bricks which are durable even when used in situations where they will be saturated and exposed to repeated freezing and thawing.

No requirement for completely protected walls otherwise when sampled and tested in accordance with EN 772-5, the content of water soluble salts should be no greater than tabled.

Active soluble salt content	Active soluble salts	Total % by mass not greater than:	
		Na$^+$+ K$^+$	**Mg**
Category S0	Not subject to any limits on specified soluble and intended for use where total protection from water penetration is provided.	No requirement	No requirement
Category S1	Bricks which have limits on soluble salts, e.g. sodium, magnesium and potassium	0.17	0.08
Category S2	Bricks which have lower limits than category S1 bricks.	0.06	0.03

Na$^+$ – Sodium, K$^+$ – Potassium, Mg – Magnesium

Compressive strength should be declared and recorded by the manufacturer in N/mm^2.

Compressive strength	
Category I	Masonry units with a probability of failure to reach their declared compressive strength of not exceeding 5%.
Category II	Masonry units with a probability of failure to reach their declared compressive strength greater than 5%.

Source/Copyright: BS EN 771-1 – European Standard Specification for Clay Masonry compared to BS 3921 British Standard Specification for Clay Bricks by Ibstock, Oct 2003.

Engineering bricks

Engineering bricks are not included in EN 771-1, but are referenced instead in the UK National Annex 771-1. In BS 3921, Engineering Bricks are classified as A or B based on minimum compressive strength and maximum water absorption not falling below 70 N/mm^2 – 4.5% and 50 N/mm^2 – 7%, respectively. The appropriate equivalents are indicated in the following table.

		Compressive strength N/mm^2	Water absorption %	Net dry density kg/m^3	Freeze/ thaw resistance category	Active soluble salts content category
BS 391	Class A	≥70	≤4.5	NA	NA	NA
	Class B	≥50	≤7	NA	NA	NA
BS EN 771	Class A	≥125	≤4.5	≥2200	F2	S2
	Class B	≥75	≤7	≥2100	F2	S2

Facing bricks undergo a different test method involving a 24-hour soak. The quoted water absorption for facing bricks should not be confused with the requirements for engineering bricks. Clay engineering bricks must be frost resistant (categorized as F2). Also, although it was not included as a requirement in BS 3921, UK clay engineering bricks conformed to the L category of soluble salts content. This is now S2. Under the National Annexe, limits are also set for net dry density for engineering bricks as shown above, to emphasize their resistance to abrasion.

Source/Copyright: Ibstock Building Products Ltd, BS EN 771-1, Technical Information Sheet

Selection of bricks and mortars for durability

Areas where bricks are likely to remain saturated for long periods of time include free-standing walls, retaining walls, copings, sills and cappings, near ground level, below DPC and in foundations. These are vulnerable locations; therefore, particular attention should be paid to the choice of brick and mortar (see table opposite).

Application	Suitable categories of bricks	Suitable mortar strength class/ designation
Planting boxes	F2, S1	M12[1] (i)
Planting boxes should be waterproofed on the inner face for the full depth of earth fill, and be provided with drainage.	F2, S2	M12 (i)
Work below or within 150 mm above ground level Brickwork near external ground level is vulnerable to frost action and sulfate attack, particularly one course (75 mm) below and two courses (150 mm) above ground level. In this area, brickwork will become wet and remain so for long periods. The degree of saturation will mainly depend on the climatic exposure of the building, the nature of the soil, and site drainage. Care should be taken to ensure that paved surrounds are held back from face of bricks in order to avoid splash back and channelling water into brickwork.	Low risk of saturation – well drained site F1/F2, S1/S2 High risk of saturation – poorly drained site: without freezing.[3] F1/F2, S1[4]/S2 High risk of saturation poorly drained site: with freezing. F2, S1[4]/S2	M12 (i), M6 (ii), M4[2] (iii) M12 (i), M6 (ii) M12 (i), M6 (ii)
Sills, copings and cappings Purpose-made sill and coping units may be preferred, but their specification is not included in this table. The requirements for brick-on-edge and similar cappings of clay bricks is indicated.	Standard format bricks and standard[5] and purpose made special shapes F2, S1/S2	M12 (i) N.B. Mortar strength class M12 should be used for bedding associated dpcs in clay brickwork.

(Continued)

Application	Suitable categories of bricks	Suitable mortar strength class/ designation
Facing brickwork to concrete retaining walls (see note*)	Low risk of saturation F1/F2, S1 F1/F2, S2 High risk of saturation F2, S1 F2, S2	M12 (i), M6 (ii)[1] M12 (i), M6 (ii) M12 (i), M6[1] (ii) M12 (i), M6 (ii)
Earth-retaining walls (excluding the coping or capping) Because of the possibility of contamination from the ground and saturation by ground waters, in addition to severe climatic exposure, these walls are particularly prone to frost and sulfate attack, if not protected. It is strongly recommended that such walls are back-filled with free-draining material to prevent a build-up of water pressure, and are waterproofed on the retaining face.	Waterproofed retaining face Effective coping. F1/F2, S1/S2 Waterproofed retaining face F2, S1 F2/S2 No waterproofing of retaining face (staining may occur if this is omitted). F2/S2 NB. Clay engineering brick can be used for this application.	 M12 (i), M6 (ii) M12[1] (i) M12 (i) M12 (i)
Free-standing walls (excluding the coping or capping) Free-standing walls are likely to be severely exposed, irrespective of climatic conditions, and an effective coping will protect the brickwork from saturation.	Effective coping used F1/F2, S1 F1/F2, S2 Flush capping used F2, S1 F2, S2	 M12 (i), M6 (ii) M12 (i), M6 (ii), M4(iii) M12 (i), M6[7] (ii) M12 (i), M6 (ii)

Application	Suitable categories of bricks	Suitable mortar strength class/ designation
NB. In areas of severe driving rain, class M12 and M6 mortars are preferred and, if class M6 is specified with (F1/F2, S1) clay bricks, the use of sulphate resisting Portland cement should be considered.		
Rendered external walls of buildings (other than parapet walls and chimney stacks, and excluding brickwork sills, copings and cappings)	All exposures F1/F2,S1 F1/F2,S2	M12 (i), M6 (ii), M4 (iii)[1] M12 (i), M6 (ii), M4 (iii)
Unrendered external walls of buildings more than 150 mm above ground level (other than parapet walls and chimney stacks, and excluding brickwork sills, copings and cappings). The risk of saturation of walls will be greatly reduced by roof overhangs and by other projecting features that incorporate a drip groove. However, these details may not give adequate protection from saturation in some exposed buildings where there are exceptional driving rain conditions. The omission of protective features may consequently increase the risk of frost damage.	Low risk of saturation Walling well protected by roof overhangs, sills and cladding designed to shed water clear of brickwork F1/F2, S1/S2 High risk of saturation. Brickwork inadequately protected and saturated by water run-off. F2, S1 F2, S2	 M12 (i), M6 (ii), M4 (iii) M12 (i), M6 (ii)[7] M12 (i), M6 (ii)

(*Continued*)

Clay brick damp-proof courses	Suitable mass categories of bricks	Maximum water absorp tion% by	Suitable mortar strength class/ designation
Certain low water absorption clay bricks with good frost resistance properties may be used for the construction of damp-proof courses. Such DPCs can resist rising damp, although they will not resist water percolating downwards. They are particularly appropriate in positions where the DPC is required to transmit flexural tension, e.g., free-standing and retaining walls. Guidance on the laying of brick damp-proof courses is given in BS 74315. Two categories of damp-proof course bricks for use in buildings and external works are now specified in BS EN 771-1:20034. The manufacturer declares the water absorption. The National Annex to BS EN 771-14 relates the number to traditional applications.	Damp proof courses in buildings DPC1	4.5	M12 (i)
	Damp proof courses in external works DPC 1 DPC 2	 4.5 7	 M12 (i) M12 (i)

Notes:

1. Sulfate-resisting Portland cement is recommended.

2. Strict supervision of batching is particularly important to ensure that the requisite amount of cement is incorporated in mortar strength class M4.

3. Where brickwork is (at least 150 mm) below finished external ground level, most category F1 clay bricks will be suitable, although the manufacturers' recommendations should be sought.

4. Where S1 units are used in class M6 mortar, sulphate-resisting Portland cement should be used in the mortar.

5. To BS 472913.

*For work above the DPC near to ground level, mortar strength class M2 may be used when it is known that there is no risk of frost during construction

7. Sulfate-resisting Portland cement is recommended with class M6 mortar.

Source/Copyright: BDA Design Note 7, Brickwork durability, Brickwork Development Association

1.7 Concrete

Concrete is a mixture of cement, sand (fine aggregate), small stone or gravel (coarse aggregate) and water. It has many applications, from foundations to pavement or motorway bases and, because of this, there are many different ratios in which to mix the constituents. Concrete will contain aggregates with dimensions greater than 5 mm.

Making concrete

Most concrete is now ordered from ready-mixed plants so the most commonly used mixes are designated mixes. These are quality assured mixes supplied by ready-mixed concrete plants. A designated mix or designed mix is a mix selected from a restricted range, where the producer must hold a current accredited product conformity certification. Where designated mixes cannot be supplied, standard mixes can be used. For most applications there is a standard mix equivalent to the quality assured designated mix.

Selection of concrete

The concrete should be selected by reference to the British Standard Code of Practices:

- BS 8500-1:2006 Concrete. Complementary British Standard to BS EN 206-1. Method of specifying and guidance for the specifier.
- BS 8500-2:2006 Concrete. Complementary British Standard to BS EN 206-1. Specification for constituent materials and concrete.
- BS EN 206-1:2000 Concrete. Specification, performance, production and conformity.

Typical application	Concrete designated mix	Standard prescribed mix	Min strength class
Un-reinforced foundations and associated works requiring DC-1 concrete			
General purpose applications: kerbs, backing, bedding	Gen 0	ST1	C6/8
Blinding concrete, footings and foundations, mass concrete, drainage works	Gen 1	ST2	C8/10
Mass concrete, general purpose, reasonable quality	Gen 2	ST3	C12/15
Un-reinforced foundations, e.g. garage floors	Gen 3	ST4	C16/20
Un-reinforced foundations and associated works requiring DC-2 and DC-3 concrete			
DC-2	FND 2	N/A	C25/30
DC-3	FND 3	N/A	C25/30
DC-4	FND 4	N/A	C25/30
Reinforced concrete			
	RC 20/25	N/A	C20/25
	RC 25/30	N/A	C25/30
	RC 28/35	N/A	C28/35
	RC 30/37	N/A	C30/37
	RC 32/40	N/A	C32/40
	RC 35/45	N/A	C35/45
	RC 40/50	N/A	C40/50
Roads and footways			
Exposed in-situ paving and drives (no de-icing)	Gen 4	ST 5	C20/25
Exposed in-situ paving and domestic drives subject to de-icing salts.	PAV 1	N/A	C25/30
Heavy duty exposed in-situ paving and drives subject to de-icing salts	PAV 2	N/A	C28/35

Site mixed concrete

The mix proportions, when mixing on site to produce concrete equivalent to standard prescribed mixes.

Equivalent to:	ST2	ST3	ST4	ST5
Site mixed by volume				
Cement	4 parts	3 parts	3 parts	3 parts
Damp concreting sand	9 parts	6 parts	5 parts	4 parts
20 mm aggregate	15 parts	10 parts	9 parts	7 parts

Notes:

- Site mixes are for site aggregate particle size maximum 20 mm. 20 mm aggregate is sufficient for all in-situ and pre-cast members unless a special finish is required. Mass concrete will normally contain 40 mm aggregate.
- Use medium workability (75 mm slump, wetness) for all concrete except where variations are indicated.
- 40 mm aggregate may be used in mass concrete or large foundations. High workability (125 mm slump, wetness) concrete may be used for trench fill foundations.
- Where concrete is subject to even occasional de-icing salt, designated mix PAV 1 is recommended. Not applicable for site mixing.
- Acids may be present in soils contaminated by industrial waste, therefore, an acid-resisting concrete mix should be used.

Definitions

- DC – designed chemical class used to classify the resistance of concrete to chemical attack.
- GEN identifies a designated mix, usually used for housing and similar applications.
- FND – designation used for a series of designated concretes that are used in foundation applications.
- PAV – designation used for series of designated concretes that are used in paving applications.
- RC – designation used for a series of designated concretes that are used in reinforced and pre-stressed concrete applications.

Environmental and ground conditions are classified as 'Exposure Classes'. These classes are set out in BS 8500. These conditions should be considered when selecting a suitable reinforced concrete and in relation to the nominal.

Source/Copyright: British Cement Association.

1.8 Mortar

Mortar is essentially a bonding and bedding material used throughout the construction industry. It is used for a variety of purposes, including brick-laying, bedding of small components, for bedding certain types of paving, rendering and plastering.

Components of mortar. Mortar consists of sand, a binder (cement, lime or hydraulic lime) and water. Admixtures, additions or pigments can be added to enhance performance characteristic or appearance. Mortar is a cementitious material containing aggregates with dimensions less than 5 mm. This is in contrast to concrete, also a cementitious material, which will contain aggregates with dimensions greater than 5 mm.

Making mortar

Mortars can be either site mixed or factory produced ready-to-use. Factory produced mortars are delivered to site ready-to-use in every respect and require no further mixing; no further constituents should be added. They have guaranteed mix proportions. For prescribed mortars the mix proportions by volume or by weight of all the constituents shall be declared by the manufacturer. In addition, the workable life, compressive strength and, where relevant, the bond strength, water absorption and density shall be declared.

Selection of mortar mix

The mortar should be selected by reference to the British Standard Code of Practice for Use of Masonry BS 5628.

Common mortar types

Lime mortar. Lime mortar is created by mixing sand, slaked lime and water. The vast majority of pre-1900 masonry buildings are built from lime mortar. Lime mortar is a soft, porous, flexible and breathable material. The limited strength is compatible with the solid, heavy, low stressed character of traditional masonry.

Portland Cement mortar. This is often referred to as cement mortar and is created by mixing Portland cement with sand and water. This mortar was developed in order to produce stronger mortars in the mid-nineteenth century suitable for thinner, higher stressed brickwork construction, economizing on materials and with the ability to accommodate flexural stress. Using Portland Cement provided a material of consistent quality and a mortar of more predictable performance. Portland Cement mortar began to supersede lime mortar. Portland Cement mortar sets hard and quickly and it allows less flexibility.

Terminology

Non-hydraulic and hydraulic. The main difference is in the way that each of these two different mortars set and the way in which they attain their final strength. In the context of cement, the term 'hydraulic' means 'to harden under water'; therefore, a hydraulic mortar will set by combining with water. A non-hydraulic mortar will not harden under water but 'goes off' by drying out.

Standards and guidance

- BS 5628 outlines mortar designations with regard to prescriptive mixes for each mortar type.
- In BS EN 998-2 the mortar designation is performance related.
- BS EN 459-1 outlines the definitions, specifications, conformity and test methods criteria for building lime.

Equivalent common mortar mixes

Mortar designation to BS 5628-3	cement: sand (plasticized)	Air entrained Portland cement: sand	Masonry cement: sand	Cement: lime: sand	Hydraulic lime: sand	Equivalent BS EN 998-2 mortar class (Compressive strength N/mm²)
(i)	1:03	1:3		1:¼:3		M12
(ii)	1:3 to 4	1:3 to 4	1:2½ to 3½	1:½:4–4½		M6
(iii)	1:5 to 6	1:5 to 6	1:4 to 5	1:1:5 to 6		M4
(iv)	1:7 to 8	1:7 to 8	1:5½ to 6½	1:2:8 to 9	1:2 to 3	M2

The proportion of sand depends on whether it is Type S (0/2 category 2) or Type G (0/2 category 3). In the case of the latter use the lower proportion of sand.

- Designation (iii) mortars are identified as general purpose suitable for most applications.
- BS 5628-3 recommends the use of designation (i) mortars 1:¼:3 (cement: lime: sand or equivalent) should be used in coping and capping courses.
- For bricks with low strength and high absorption designation (ii) (1:½: 4½) would be more appropriate.
- In wet locations consider a level (i), high durability, mortar at and below DPC.
- Mortar mixes for cast stone – it is usual to use designation (iii) (1:1:6) cement:lime:sand.
- High durability mortar should be used for resistance to severe weather conditions. Designation (ii).
- Low permeability mortar should be used to resist water penetration. Designation (i).

Mortars for stone masonry will depend on the type of stone being used as well as the durability requirement. Generally the requirement for external stone walls, above the DPC, will be:

- Stone, cast stone or flint – Designation (iv)
- Sandstone or granite – Designation (iii)
- Very dense granite – Designation (i).

Stone can be relatively dense and rigid and will require the use of closely spaced movement joints to reduce the risk of random cracking. Alternatively they can be laid in a soft flexible lime mortar.

Source/Copyright: Reproduced from 'Mortars for masonry: Guidance on Specification, Types, Production and Use (CS159). Published by The Concrete Society and available to purchase from The Concrete Bookshop. www.Concretebookshop.com.

Lime mortar

Properties   Lime mortar is not as strong in compression as ordinary Portland cement mortar, nor does it adhere as strongly to the masonry. The mortar is softer; therefore, it can accommodate movement and is less prone to cracking. These properties are beneficial when used with old bricks or masonry which tends to be softer than modern bricks and prone to damage by harder mortars.

Types of lime mortars

High calcium lime   This is traditional lime mortar. It is non-hydraulic and referred to as 'lime putty'. Lime putty is produced by 'slaking' (mixed with water) a highly reactive calcium oxide to form lime milk. This is allowed to settle and mature resulting in lime putty. This is then mixed with an aggregate (usually sand) to produce a mortar suitable for pointing or rendering. Other materials have been used as aggregate instead of sand. A traditional course plaster mix also had horse hair added for reinforcing. This kind of lime mortar, also known as non-hydraulic, sets very slowly through reaction with the carbon dioxide in air.

Natural hydraulic lime or hydraulic lime mortar   Natural hydraulic lime (NHL) and hydraulic lime (HL) can be considered, in terms both of properties and manufacture, as part-way between non-HL and cement mortar. It is manufactured by the addition of impurities such as clay or silica. The limestone may contain quantities of this. The resultant properties of the product mean that it is hydraulic and hardens once it is combined with water.

There are three strength grades for NHL in accordance with BS EN 459-1. They are designated on the basis of compressive strength of greater than or equal to 2, 3.5 or 5 (N/mm^2).

Grade to BS EN 459-1:	Equivalent mortar classification of:
NHL2	Feebly hydraulic
NHL3.5	Moderately hydraulic
NHL5	Eminently hydraulic

Cement lime sand mortar   This is a hybrid mortar comprised of cement, lime and sand. These mortars tend to have a low durability, due to the low cement content. Some well-designed traditional high calcium lime (HCL) or a natural NHL can have increased durability compared to this group of mortars.

Typical hydraulic lime (HL) mortar mix proportions

Mortar class	Lime: sand	Equivalent natural hydraulic lime designation to BS EN 459-1	Mortar mix durability designation to BS 5628	Equivalent BS EN 998-2 mortar durability class	Typical compressive strength (N/mm² at 91 days)
Feebly hydraulic	1:2¾	HLM1	(v) at 28 days (iv) at 91 days	3–4	1
Moderately hydraulic	1:2¼	NHL2.5	(iv) at 28 days (iii) at 91 days	5–6	2.5
Eminently hydraulic	1:2	HLM5	(iii) at 28 days (ii) at 91 days	7–8	5

Source/Copyright: Lime Technology Ltd, www.limetechnology.co.uk

1.9 Damp-proof Courses

Purpose

A damp proof course (DPC) is a strip of impervious material the same width as brickwork or a block work wall. Its purpose is to keep out moisture. Historically, DPCs were also made of impervious bricks or slates.

DPCs must act as a barrier to the passage of moisture or water either upwards, downwards or horizontally. The DPC must form a continuous horizontal DPC above ground in walls where the foundations are in contact with the ground.

The DPC should be continuous throughout the length and thickness of the wall and be sandwiched in mortar. It must project about 5 mm beyond any external face and must not be covered with mortar, pointing or rendering.

Notes on DPCs above ground

High level DPCs

Should be capable of delivering a high bond with mortar and be flexible. Bitumen polymer materials or equivalent are preferred. Slates or tiles can also be used. A continuous sheet DPC should be provided beneath jointed copings and cappings, in order to prevent downwards percolation of water into the wall should the joints fail. The DPC will normally be positioned immediately underneath a capping. With a capping, in order to obtain greater mass above the DPC, it may be positioned one or more courses lower down. The risk of a coping or capping being displaced will be minimized by the use of a DPC designed to give a good bond with the mortar. DPCs may be omitted if coping is jointless. A DPC should not be used if it is incapable of providing adhesion across the joints.

Low level DPCs

Should be at least 150 mm above ground level.

Brick DPCs are used extensively in free-standing and retaining walls where it is required to resist tension and shear. Although it is unlikely that such walls will become saturated by rising damp, the DPC does form a barrier against soluble salts from the ground and groundwater. DPCs are required near the base of walls to prevent rising damp. In the case of buildings, the DPC will normally be a flexible material, although slate or brick DPCs can be used.

DPC clay bricks are classified as DPC1 and DPC2 bricks having maximum water absorption values of 4.5% and 7.0% by mass, respectively. DPC1 bricks are recommended for use in buildings, while all DPC bricks are acceptable for use in external works. If the wall is constructed with frost-resistance bricks or material near ground level, a DPC is unlikely to be required. A low level DPC should not be used unless it has been accommodated within the structural design.

Four principles to consider when selecting a DPC material

Resistance to stress: The material should withstand any compressive stress (direct loading) shear stress (tendency to slide) or flexural strength (tendency to overturn) placed upon it.

Durability: This should match the life of the building.

Pliability: A material that is easy to shape may be more suitable if there are many changes of direction or level in the DPC to be accommodated on site.

Compatibility: A material may need protection against corrosion.

Note:

In cavity walls the outer edge of a DPC is two brick courses lower than the inner edge, to prevent entry of driving rain, and both edges are built into the bed joints.

Physical properties and performance of various materials suitable as DPCs

Material/ installation	Minimum mass/ thickness	Durability/notes
Flexible DPCs		
Sheet lead Laid and lapped at least 100 mm or the width of the DPC at running joints and intersections.	19.5 kg/m² 1.8 mm	Can suffer distortion due to settlement without damage. To avoid corrosion in contact with fresh lime or cement mortar, coat with bitumen on either side of the surface and on the corrosion producing surface. Expensive material. Ductile material which can be worked to form shapes.
Sheet copper (C104 or C106) Spread on an even bed of mortar and lapped at least 100 mm or the width of the DPC at running joints and intersections.	2.28 kg/m² 0.25 mm	Can suffer distortion due to settlement without damage. May stain surfaces due to oxide that forms. Highly resistant to corrosion. If soluble salts are present, protect as for lead. Expensive material and difficult to work.

Material/ installation	Minimum mass/ thickness	Durability/notes
Bitumen – Hessian based Laid in rolls on an even bed of mortar and lapped at least 100 mm and at intersections. Sealed with cold applied roofing felt.	3.8 kg/m² –	Economical, durable, flexible and convenient. Reasonably flexible and can withstand moderate settlement in walls without damage. The hessian or fibre may decay but efficiency is not affected if the bitumen remains undisturbed. Bitumen/sheet metal composites are best if structure is to have a long life expectancy or there is a risk of movement. Refer to manufacturer's instructions for installation and refer to British Standard.
Bitumen – fibre based Installation as above.	3.3 kg/m² –	Cheaper but less durable than the Hessian. Bituminous felt damp proof courses are vulnerable to being squeezed out slightly under pressure, especially in hot weather, but the amounts exuded are usually insufficient to compromise their performance and durability. Bituminous felt damp proof courses are also relatively ineffective against horizontal displacement, providing a slip plane on which the walling can move with relative ease.
Bitumen/sheet metal composite – Hessian based and lead Installation as above and joined with soldered joints.	4.4 kg/m² –	Creates deep mortar joint.

(Continued)

Material/ installation	Minimum mass/ thickness	Durability/notes
Bitumen/sheet metal composite – fibre based and lead Installation as above.	4.4 kg/m^2 –	Creates deep mortar joint.
Polymer-based sheets: Bitumen polymer and Pitch polymer Laid on fresh mortar bed with laps sealed with adhesive, min 100 mm, in accordance with manufacturer's recommendations.	1.5 kg/m^2 1.1 mm	Accommodates considerable lateral movement. Pre-formed cloaks should be used where cavity trays are required. Higher performance damp proof courses are often formulated from a blend of pitch and polymer and these have good resistance to squeezing. Prone to damage by sharp particles during installation. Creates thin mortar joint.
Polythene – low density polythene Laid on fresh mortar bed with laps sealed at least 100 mm and at intersections with appropriate jointing tape in accordance with manufacturer's recommendations.	0.5 kg/m^2 0.46 mm	Cost effective damp proof course for domestic construction. Compatible with other building materials. Can suffer distortion due to settlement without damage. Plain sheet can have very low shear bond. Available embossed products assist with mortar adhesion, improve shear and flexural bonds. Remains flexible – even at low temperatures. Safe and clean to handle. Suitable for use in horizontal and vertical applications throughout domestic construction. Difficult to use as a cavity tray. Prone to damage by sharp particles during installation. Creates thin mortar joint.

Material/ installation	Minimum mass/ thickness	Durability/notes
Semi-rigid DPCs		
Mastic asphalt Spread hot in one coat. To provide mortar key add up to 35% grit into asphalt immediately after application and leave proud of surface or score surface while still warm.	– 12 mm	No deterioration. To be laid on a fully supporting rigid substrate. Moderate settlement in a wall may fracture the seal. Relatively expensive. Creates deep mortar joint.
Rigid DPCS		
Slate Laid in two courses laid breaking joint in mortar.	– 2 courses	No deterioration. Expensive material. Cannot accommodate settlement in a wall without fracture. Creates deep mortar joint
DPC brick DPC appropriate bricks can be used, laid as a minimum of two bonded courses and jointed in mortar strength class M12/designation (i). Laid to break joint.	– 2 courses DPC 1 or DPC 2.	Particularly suitable if DPC is required in free standing wall. Cannot resist water under pressure.

Standards and guidelines

- BS 743:1970 Specification for materials for damp-proof courses (partially replaced).
- BS EN 772-7:1998. Methods of test for masonry units.
- DD 86-3:1990 Damp-proof courses. Guide to characteristic strengths of damp-proof course material used in masonry.
- BS EN 13969:2004 Flexible sheets for waterproofing. Bitumen damp proof sheets including bitumen basement tanking sheets. Definitions and characteristics.
- BS 6515:1984, Specification for polyethylene damp-proof courses for masonry.
- 08/30179055 DC, BS 8215 AMD1. Code of practice for design and installation of damp-proof courses in masonry construction.
- BS EN 14909:2006, Flexible sheets for waterproofing. Plastic and rubber damp proof courses. Definitions and characteristics.
- 08/30176739 DC, BS 6398 AMD 1. Specification for bitumen damp-proof courses for masonry.

Structural considerations affecting selection

Material	Resistance to stress					
	Compressive strength – N/mm² (loading)				Shear stress	Flexural stress
	High >2.5 (walls higher than 10 storeys)	Medium 0.5–2.5 (walls 4–10 storeys)	Low 0.1–0.5 (walls up to 4 storeys)	Minimal <0.1 (copings, parapets, etc.)		
Sheet lead	×	•	•	•	×	•
Sheet copper (C 104 or C 106)	•	•	•	•	×	•
Bitumen – Hessian based	×	×	•	•	×	×
Bitumen – Fibre based	×	×	•	•	×	×
Bitumen – Hessian base and lead	×	×	•	•	×	×
Bitumen – Fibre base and lead	×	×	•	•	×	×
Polythene – Low density polythene	•	•	•	×	×	×
Bitumen polymer and Pitch polymer	•	•	•	•	•	•
Mastic Asphalt	×	• (up to 0.65)	•	•	•	•
Slate	•	•	•	•	•	•
DPC Brick	•	•	•	•	•	•

• = Acceptable
× = Unacceptable

Source/Copyright: BRE Digest, Concise reviews of building technology, Digest 380, Building Research Establishment.

1.10 Damp-proof Membranes

Damp-proof membranes should be impermeable to water, either in a liquid or vapour form caused by capillary action and be suitably tough to avoid potential damage during installation. Damp-proof membranes can be used to waterproof the rear of brickwork retaining walls. This will prevent soluble salts within the retained substance (earth, concrete etc.) from washing through to the surface of the brickwork where it would be deposited as efflorescence.

Common types of damp-proof membranes

Sheet membranes may be: polythene, bituminous felt, copper sheet. They are useful in retaining walls where earth is likely to rest against the wall. They can be fixed to battens which are then fixed to the wall to create both an impermeable layer and an air gap.

Liquid forms may be: brush or spray applied materials. They come as a bitumen or tar coating, usually in a fairly thick liquid form. They are normally spread within the first one or two courses and are built up to a certain depth or applied to smooth surfaces to form a waterproof layer.

1.11 Lighting

Choices of lights available to the designer

Light Type	Colour Temp in Kelvins (K) 3000 – warm 4000 – cool	Wattage (W)	Colour Rendering (Ra)	Yeild in Lumens/ Watt (lm/w)	Lamp life (Hours) 100h/lm	Application	Advantages/ Disadvantages
Typical Daylight	5500 – 6000 White daylight	–	–		–	–	
Sunrise	3000 – warm	–	–		–	–	
Incandescent – Electrical current passed through tungsten wire that becomes white hot and produces light	3000 – warm	5–100	100	20-Oct	1–2,000 (1 year)	Residential garden/inte- rior	Expensive to operate, low efficiency and short life span
Halogen – Incandescent bulbs filled with halogen gas	3000 – warm	200–500	100	25	2,000 (>1 year)	Garden, park, plaza	25% more efficient than incandescent lamps with a 25% increased lifespan
Flourescent – Electricity passed through a gas enclosed tube	3200 – warm 4200 – white 5000 – white daylight 6500 – daylight	6–110	60–88	40–80	8–15,000 (3 years)	Signage	Not used extensively outdoors. Good colour rendition

Metal Halide – Electricity passed through gas	3000 – warm 6500 – white	70–150 70–3500 70–400 1000/2000	60–85	70–100 lm/w	9–12,000 (3–4 years)	Sports stadia floodlighting	Good natural colour rendering available in cool, medium and warm appearance. Lamp colour is not so stable over a life time and has a lower efficacy and a shorter life span. Expensive to maintain and install.
Metal Halide with Ceramic Burner	3000–4200	35–250 70–150	81–92	>90 lm/w	9,000 (3 years)	Residential streets and City Centre	Stable over a life time with good white light natural colour rendering. Compact lamps allow for reduced light spillage. Shorter lamp life, poorer lumen maintenance and higher cost.
Sodium lamps – Gas discharge lamps with sodium. 2 Types: High Pressure Sodium (HPS) include mercury Low Pressure Sodium Oxide (SOX)	Orange	50–1000 150–400 70–400 35–100	20–65	100–150 lm/w	20,000 (6 years)	Streets and parking	Poor colour rendering but suitable where a warm colour appearance is required. Very high efficiency, long life time and increased resistance to vibration. Output does not decline with age.

(Continued)

Light Type	Colour Temp in Kelvins (K) 3000 – warm 4000 – cool	Wattage (W)	Colour Rendering (Ra)	Yeild in Lumens/ Watt (lm/w)	Lamp life (Hours) 100 h/lm	Application	Advantages/ Disadvantages
White Son –White light version of sodium lamp	Warm White	Max 100	85	48 lm/w	4,800 h (2 years)	Residential streets and parking	Better colour rendering than normal sodium lamp but decreased efficiency and life expectancy. However fewer lamps required due to higher output.
LEDs Light Emitting Diodes Solid state semi conductor devices that produce light				30 lm/w	50–60,000 h	Feature lighting in urban areas	High efficiency/output per watt. Cannot produce point source light. Colour changing LEDs can produce many colours across the spectrum from a single fitting. High heat producers.
Fibre optics	Expensive and not efficient. LEDs will take over in the future. Currently used for feature lighting of objects and also good in water. Can direct light but lose effect over a length as they rely on a transmitter. Maximum length, if end emitting, 20 m; slightly longer if side emitting.						

Colour Rendering	Colour rendering is a property of a given light source which decides on how the particular colour appears to our eyes in comparison with an ideal or natural light source. The colour rendering of lamps is measured by a colour rendering index (Ra). The lower the number the poorer the colour rendering. The maximum of 100 is excellent colour rendering. Each type of lamp as shown in the table above has a different colour rendering which is the way the output of a lamp affects human perception of colour. Incandescent Lamps, Fluorescent and Metal Halide all have excellent colour rendering. High Pressure Sodium has poor colour rendering, with objects appearing yellow or orange.				
Light fittings: Degree of protection **IP ratings (EN 60529)** NB Check with manufacturers before specifying as some IP ratings are quoted only for fittings in a certain orientation, e.g. glass pointing downwards, and if orientated another way they are not protected.	Levels of protection are identified using IP classifications which are indicated after the product reference. • The 1st number indicates the protection of the luminaire with respect to the penetration of dust/dirt and protection for people against contact with moving parts. • The 2nd number indicates the protection of the luminaire with respect to the ingress of moisture/water.				
	Degree of protection against solids		**Degree of protection against penetration of liquids**		**Application**
	0	Not protected	0	Not protected	Suitable for internal use only
	1	Protected against the penetration of solid objects >50 mm or hand	1	Protected against dripping water	
	2	Protected against the penetration of solid objects not greater than 80 mm length and 12 mm diameter or fingers	2	Protected against vertically dripping water when tilted to 15°	
	3	Protected against the penetration of solid objects or tools/wires >2.5 mm	3	Protected against sprayed water	
	4	Protected against the penetration of solid objects >1 mm	4	Protected against splashed water	
	5	Protected against the penetration of dust that would interfere with the operation of the equipment	5	Protected against water projected form a nozzle	IP 56 Suitable for external use depending on location
	6	Completely protected against the penetration of dust	6	Protected against heavy seas, or powerful jets of water	
		Sealing effectiveness is not specified against mechanical damage, explosions, condensation, vermin, etc	7	Protected against immersion (<1.0 m)	
			8	Protected against complete, continuous submersion in water	

(Continued)

Inground fittings: Water ingress	Water is present usually in the form of condensation, not penetration from the top. This is caused by the capillary action of the product heating up and cooling down, drawing moisture in through the supply cable. To avoid this, specify a recessed product that has a different wiring chamber from the rest of the product.

Light fittings: Shock resistance IK ratings

Levels of protection against shock are identified using IK classifications which are indicated after the product reference.

Degree of protection against impact – shock resistance according to CEI EN 50102

Code	Height of luminaire in cm	Protected against impact/shock measured in Joules of energy (point loading)	Uses
IK00	Not protected		
IK01	7.5	Protected against 0.15 Joules of shock	Suitable for indoor use only
IK02	10	Protected against 0.2 Joules of shock	
IK03	17.5	Protected against 0.35 Joules of shock	
IK04	25	Protected against 0.5 Joules of shock	
IK05	35	Protected against 0.7 Joules of shock	
IK06	20	Protected against 1 Joule of shock	Suitable for outdoor use but protected
IK07	40	Protected against 2 Joules of shock	
IK08	30	Protected against 5 Joules of shock	
IK09	20	Protected against 10 Joules of shock	Suitable for inground light fittings
IK10	40	Protected against 20 Joules of shock	

If vehicles are present, products should be chosen to take the right loading from 0.5 tonnes (500 kg) to 5 tonnes (5000 kg).

Light fittings: Touch surface temperature	**Maximum of 60–65°C**

Adoptable lighting	Lighting which will be installed in public areas that will be adopted by the local authority must be approved by that authority's lighting department. They will usually have a standard list of suppliers or fittings to enable them to undertake long term maintenance easily. Alternatives can be suggested by well known lighting manufacturers, provided the control mechanisms and luminaires have similar life spans and outputs and are as easily available as those already used.

Lighting design	**Colour effects** General rule of thumb in lighting is if you wish to highlight a colour then use the same colour of light: A blue bridge can be highlighted using blue light or a cool source of light, e.g. 4000K. For foliage use a green lamp or green filter or a light from the warm end of the light spectrum e.g. 3000K. **Lighting objects – How much light?** This is dependent on how much light is present in the area you are going to be lighting. This can be described as high (town centre), medium, or low (rural) district brightness. The general rule of thumb to make something stand out is that it needs to be three times brighter than the ambient level. Buildings or objects with detailing may be better lit to create depth, rather than flattening with high light levels.
Light pollution	Limitation of light pollution that causes night glow, obtrusive (spill) light, glare, light trespass and reflected light is starting to appear in national and international standards. (Refer to ILE (Institute of Lighting Engineers) Guidance Notes on the Reduction of Light Pollution 2000.) Luminaries are required to achieve better control of lights through advanced optical systems, use of reflectors, shields, baffles and louvres and maximizing the distance between luminaries.
Energy and maintenance	Two aspects need to be considered in the approach to lighting design and the issues associated with energy use and maintenance. **Life cycle costing** • Capital cost of equipment • Cost of installation (including electrical supply) • Annual energy cost • Annual maintenance cost (cleaning, re-lamping) • Product life • Replacement costs and frequency (lamps, gear, luminaire) and ease of access for maintenance. **Minimizing energy consumption** • Use energy efficient light source • Use high performance optic • Optimize scheme design • Minimize waste light.

(Continued)

Relevant legislation and Codes of Practice	**BSEN 60598: Luminaires**
	The European Standard specifying requirements for mechanical and electrical construction, classification and making of luminaires. The standard is concerned primarily with the safety aspects of manufacturing luminaires which are fit for purpose in their intended installation location, to ensure safe operation and to provide protection for the public.
	BS5489-1:2003 – Lighting in Urban Centres and Public Amenity Areas
	Part of the British Standard is for lighting of urban centres and public amenity areas and gives guidance on the objectives of lighting of urban areas as well as general advice on the lighting of Conservation areas, security and safety and visual appreciation.
	Chartered Institute of Building Services Engineers (Society of Light and Lighting) CIBSE (SLL) Lighting Guide 6 – The Outdoor Environment (1992)
	Advice on technical and aesthetic aspects of lighting in outdoor environments.
	ILE (Institute of Lighting Engineers) Guidance Notes on the Reduction of Light Pollution 2000
	Provides notes on acceptable and unacceptable practice with regard to reducing obtrusive light, upward light, sky glow and glare.
	ILE/CIBSE Lighting the Environment – A Guide to Good Urban Lighting

Source: iGuzzini Illuminazione UK Ltd
Urbis Lighting
Cameron McDougall

1.12 Drainage

Gradient limits for surfaces	Different surfaces need minimum falls to shed water and leave a dry surface to prevent ponding and possibly icing. This usually relies on falls in two directions (crossfall or camber and longfall) Where only one is available the fall should not be less than the figure specified for each material

Material	Crossfall
Paving Slabs	1 in 70
Bricks	1 in 50
Insitu Concrete	1 in 48
Asphalt and Bituminous surfaces	1 in 40 – 1:48
Gravel/Bound Gravel	1 in 30
Granite Setts	1 in 40
Cobbles	1 in 40

Gradient limits for paved areas	Each local Roads Authority or Trunk Roads Authority has minimum gradient limits required for a road or footpath to be to an adoptable standard. The following are an example:

Gradient	Access road	Paved areas	Footpaths
Long Fall	1 in 20 max.	DDA compliant	DDA compliant
Crossfall	1 in 40–48 normal	1 in 60 min	1 in 30 max. 1 in 40 min.

DDA = Disability Discrimination Act

(Continued)

Gulley spacing for carriageways

Gulley spacing for carriageways of varying widths including 2 no 2.0m wide footpaths and based on rainfall intensity of 50mm/hour and a width of channel flow of 600mm.

Gradient (Longfall)		1/150 0.66%	1/100 1.0%	1/80 1.25%	1/60 1.66%	1/40 2.5%	1/30 3.33%	1/20 5.0%
Cross Section:	Carriage width (m)	Gully spacings in metres						
Camber	5.5	30	35	40	45	55	60	75
	6	25	30	35	40	50	60	70
	7.3	20	25	30	35	40	45	55
Crossfall	5.5	15	17	20	22	27	30	37
	6	12	15	17	20	25	30	35
	7.3	10	12	15	17	20	22	27

Regardless of the above a gulley should always be positioned:

- Upstream of the tangent point at road junctions;
- At any low point;
- At traffic calming measures where necessary.

Drainage design of adopted roads and footpaths will be subject to approval of the local Roads Authority or Trunk Road Authority

Gulley spacing for paved areas

For large irregular shaped areas the empirically derived formulae of one gulley for each 200m² of catchment can be used.

Additional gulley's will be required where:

- gradients are steeper that 1 in 20;
- gradients are flatter than 1 in 150;
- and where surface water draining from adjacent area may be anticipated.

Footpath gulley's should be avoided as footpaths can be constructed with a fall either to the adjacent road or with a flush kerb to flow into adjacent soft landscape.

Falls and sizes for drainage pipes	Rules of Thumb for minimum falls

- Footpath Drainage:100 mm Drains – 1 in 40
- Road Drainage: 150 mm drains – 1 in 60
- Road Drainage: 225 mm drains – 1 in 90.

Note: When designing drainage in a local authority adopted area all works will be to the design standards of that Roads Authority or Trunk Roads Authority.

Load classes for manhole covers

FACTA Class (*1)	BS EN 124 1994 Class	SMWL (*2)	GLVW (*3)	Application
A	A15	0.5 tonne	1 tonne	Pedestrians and cycles only
AA	N/A	1.5 tonne	5 tonne	Slow moving private cars
AAA	N/A	2.5 tonne	10 tonne	Slow moving vehicles >10 tonnes GLV
B	B125	5.0 tonne	38 tonne	Slow moving HGV
C	C250	6.5 tonne	38 tonne	Carriageways of fast moving traffic of all types but located within 0.5 m of kerb line
D	D400	11 tonne 7.5 tonne fork lift truck	38 tonne	Carriageways, hard shoulders and parking areas for all types of fast moving road vehicles
E	E600			Extra heavy vehicles for special applications e.g. runways.
F	F900			

(*1) FACTA– Fabricated Access Covers Trade Association

(*2) SMWL – Slow Moving Wheel Load

(*3) GLVW – Gross Laden Vehicle Weight

1.13 Sustainable Urban Drainage Systems (SUDS)

Ahh .... SUDS

What are SUDS?	Sustainable Urban Drainage Systems are an alternative approach to conventional drainage design that replicates natural drainage and deals with run-off where it occurs, thereby reducing environmental impact from surface water drainage. It is now increasingly a requirement by Local Authorities in authorising developments particularly with global warming and the increased risk of flooding in the UK
Benefits of using SUDS	• Reduction in pollution • Reduction in risks of flooding • Improvements to the environment • Reduction in costs.

SUDS techniques	The following methods of control can be used to manage surface water run-off and prevent pollution: • Filter Strips and Swales • Filter Drains and Permeable Surfaces • Infiltration Devices • Basins and Ponds. These systems of control should be positioned close to the source of run-off to provide maximum attenuation by reduction in flow and prevention of erosion and flooding. Each one can also provide varying degrees of treatment for surface water through the natural processes of sedimentation, filtration, absorption and biological degradation. The decision to use the following systems will be based on available land, nature of the site – rural or urban, use of the site and its long term management.
Filter strips and swales	**Form/design** • Filter strips consist of vegetated gently sloping areas of ground. • Swales are formed as vegetated long channels. **How they work** They copy natural drainage patterns by permitting rainwater to run as sheet flow through vegetation off impermeable areas, consequently slowing the flow and filtering any polluting solids through sedimentation. **Where used** They are effective in small residential developments, parking areas and roads. They can easily be incorporated into public open space areas and road verges. The introduction of wild grass/flower species adds amenity and ecological value. Choice of species is important to ensure a consistent drainage flow is maintained but this does not preclude the introduction of tree and shrub species. A design can accommodate this by a wider area and reduced angle of slope. **Maintenance** Minimal – regular mowing, litter removal, periodic removal of silt and erosion repair.

| Filter drains and permeable surfaces | **What are they?**
• Filter Drains are linear systems draining water off impermeable surfaces in a diffuse way.
• Permeable surfaces intercept and control the rainwater where it falls.

Form/design
Filter drains and permeable surfaces are devices that allow storage of surface water in an area of permeable material below ground flowing via a permeable surface which can include:

• Un-trafficked grass or reinforced grass
• Gravel
• Paviors with vertical holes filled with soil or gravel
• Paviors with gaps between the units
• Porous paviors with voids within the unit
• Continuous surfaces with an inherent system of voids.

How they work
The rainwater run-off drains through the surface to the permeable fill which then also allows the storage, treatment and infiltration of water. Both the surface and the sub base material must allow the water to flow through to ensure this system will work. The volume of water stored will depend on the plan area, depth of fill and the ratio of voids to fill. Water can be disposed of by infiltration, underdrain or pumping out.

Where used
Can be used for car parks, residential driveways, paths and patios. Not currently used for adoptable roads and footways.

Maintenance
Surfaces should be kept clear of silt and cleaned twice a year to keep voids clear and the system operational. |

Infiltration devices	**What are they?**
	Infiltration devices drain water directly into the ground and can be used at the source of the rainfall, or the runoff can be conveyed in a pipe or swale to the infiltration area.
	Design/form
	• Soakaways and infiltration trenches store water in lined underground chamber filled with course crushed stone.
	• Infiltration basins and swales can store water on the ground but are dry except in periods of heavy rainfall.
	How they work
	The infiltration technique works by enhancing the natural process of rain percolating through soil to dispose of surface run-off. This process is heavily dependent on the permeability of the soil and the location or quality of the water table. Runoff is treated by filtration to remove solids, absorption of particles by the material in the soakaway, or by biochemical reactions with micro-organisms growing on the fill or in the soil.
	Where used
	Infiltration devices vary in size from soakaways serving individual houses to basins that collect run-off from entire developments. They can be integrated into playing fields, recreational areas or public open space. Basins can be planted with trees and shrubs, which also improves their amenity and ecological value.
	Maintenance
	Periodic inspections to remove silt.

Basins and ponds	**Form/design** Basins store surface run-off in wet weather but they are free from water under dry weather conditions. Ponds contain water in dry weather and are designed to hold more when it rains. The two systems can be mixed. **How they work** Basins and ponds store water at the ground surface either as temporary flooding or as permanent wetland features. They are designed to manage water quantity and quality through settlement of solids in still water, absorption of particles by aquatic vegetation, or biological activity. Flow rates are slowed by storing water and releasing it slowly, or allowing it in areas to filtrate into the surrounding soil. **Where used** Basins can be incorporated into sports and recreational areas and amenity spaces. Ponds offer the advantage of improving habitats and landscape amenity as part of public open space. **Maintenance** Access for maintenance inspections is required for both basins and ponds. This will include cutting of grass, annual clearance of aquatic vegetation and silt removal as required. **Basin types** Basins are areas for storage of surface runoff that are free from water under dry weather flow conditions. These structures include: • Flood plains – dry most of the time but will store water briefly after severe storms • Detention basins or balancing ponds – principally dry but store water until a flood has passed • Extended detention basins – hold storm water for up to 24 hours. This also allows for both attenuation and treatment. At other times the site will be dry.

Basins and ponds (continued)	**Pond types** Ponds are permanently wet even in dry weather but water depth fluctuates as they are designed to hold more when it rains. They can attenuate flows and treat pollutants. They include:
	• Balancing and attenuation ponds – only store run-off until the flood peak has passed and so have little treatment capacity.
	• Flood storage reservoirs – only store run-off until the flood peak has passed and so have little treatment capacity.
	• Lagoons – provide still conditions for settlement but offer no biological treatment.
	• Retention ponds – have detention periods of up to 3 weeks. They provide a greater degree of treatment than extended detention basins.
	• Wetlands – have permanent water flowing slowly through aquatic vegetation. Wetlands have detention periods of up to 2 weeks and can be more efficient than retention ponds at treating pollutants.
	Basins and ponds can even be mixed, including both a permanently wet area for wildlife or treatment of the run-off and an area that is usually dry to cater for flood attenuation. Basins and ponds tend to be found towards the end of the surface water management train, so are used where:
	• Source control cannot be fully implemented.
	• Extended treatment of the runoff is required.
	• They are required for wildlife or landscape reasons.

1.14 Sustainability of Materials and Life Span

The new landscape architect caused quite a stir when she turned up for the sustainable landscape meeting.

The table opposite is based on the British Research Establishment: Environmental Assessment Method (BREEAM) ratings for material specification which enables users to assess materials on their overall environmental impact based on 12 environmental parameters. These include climate change, fossil fuel depletion, ozone depletion through to freight transport, waste disposal, water and mineral extraction. The impacts are amalgamated into three categories which indicate low, medium or high environmental impact over a 60 year life cycle. In addition, the recyclability of the material is rated in the same way.

Element	Impact rating	Estimated life span	Ability to recycle
Hard surface materials(over prepared sub base)			
Asphalt	High	30	Medium
Brick pavers	Medium	30	High
Precast concrete pavers	Medium	25	High
Precast concrete slabs	Medium	25	High
Insitu concrete	High	25	High
Granite setts	Medium	40	High
Stone paving	Medium	40	High
Gravel	Low	10	Medium
Recycled glass aggregate	Low	10	High
Treated softwood timber decking	Low	20	High
Soft landscape Materials			
Bark or wood chip mulch	Low	5	Low
Grass (incl mowing)	Low	30	High
Low maintenance planting	Low	15	High
Separating elements			
Brick wall (1 brick thick)	High	45	High
Drystone wall	Low	60	High
Stone and mortar wall	Medium	60	High
Galvanized steel railings	Medium	45	High
Galvanized chainlink fencing	Low	30	High
Plastic coated chainlink with galvanized steel posts	Low	20	Low
Pre-treated timber close board	Low	20	Medium
Pre-treated timber post and rail	Low	20	Medium
Hedges	Low	60	High

Copyright granted by BRE Press, *Green Guide to Housing Specification* BR 390, 2000

1.15 Recycled Materials and Products

Why use recycled products?

To help achieve sustainability through more efficient use of materials and the avoidance of waste going to landfill.

Some materials which can be recycled and used in landscape applications include the following:

- Glass
- Plastic
- Aggregates
- Wood
- Fly ash
- Blast furnace ash
- Garden waste
- Tyres and Rubber
- Bitumen products
- Paper
- Polystyrene
- China clay by-products.

Glass

Processed sand is made form 100% recycled glass. This can be used as top dressing or in cement, or in planting pits.

Decorative surfacing material, either in the form of recycled glass chips or a bound surface, provides different colour solutions (Ref: Sureset Ltd).

Plastics and polythene

Furniture, gates, fencing, geotextiles and paving in external applications. Useful as the material is robust and does not rot. (Ref: Plaswood Ltd, Mamax Products Ltd, Netlon (reinforced grass products)).

Aggregates can be recycled from inert construction waste (concrete, blocks, bricks, etc.). Recycled aggregates can be used in the formation of paths and roads or as a drainage layer (Ref: aggregain.org.uk).

Wood can be used as woodchip or play bark in rural play areas, rural or domestic path surfaces, as a mulch or in decking and railings (Ref: Tracey Timber Products, Kindawood Ltd).

Fly ash and **blast furnace slag** can be used in the formation of paths and roads, blocks or bricks or concrete (Ref: Ibstock Brick Ltd, Marshalls Plc, Cemex UK).

Garden Waste can be turned into compost for soil improvement in accordance with PAS 100, turf establishment top dressing, planting or topsoil manufacture.

Rubber is used within play surface surface applications (Ref: Island Leisure Products. Playtop Ltd).

Bitumen products are used as part of a bound path surface (Ref: Tarmac 'Toptreck').

Paper can be used as mulch.

Polystyrene in fencing and decking (Ref: XPLX Ltd).

China clay by-products in paving materials (Ref: Formpave Ltd, Charcon Ltd).

Source/Copyright: WRAP.

Refer to **WRAP** (Waste and Resources Action Programme) for more information on recycled products and their uses and a comprehensive listing of suppliers, www.wrap.org.uk/lcproducts.

1.16 Typical Footpaths

Pedestrian Paving (Stone or Concrete Slabs)

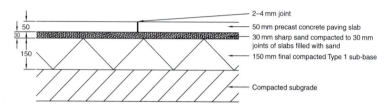

2–4 mm joint
50 mm precast concrete paving slab
30 mm sharp sand compacted to 30 mm joints of slabs filled with sand
150 mm final compacted Type 1 sub-base
Compacted subgrade

Bitmac

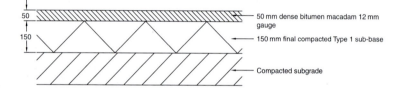

50 mm dense bitumen macadam 12 mm gauge
150 mm final compacted Type 1 sub-base
Compacted subgrade

Asphalt

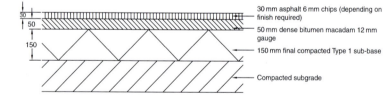

30 mm asphalt 6 mm chips (depending on finish required)
50 mm dense bitumen macadam 12 mm gauge
150 mm final compacted Type 1 sub-base
Compacted subgrade

Concrete Slabs

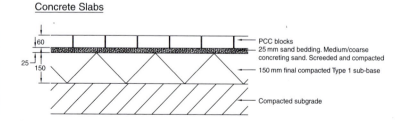

PCC blocks
25 mm sand bedding. Medium/coarse concreting sand. Screeded and compacted
150 mm final compacted Type 1 sub-base
Compacted subgrade

Gravel surface

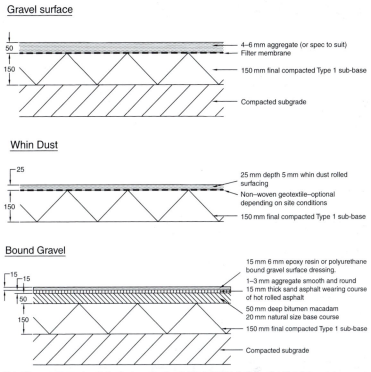

50 · 4–6 mm aggregate (or spec to suit)
Filter membrane

150 · 150 mm final compacted Type 1 sub-base

Compacted subgrade

Whin Dust

25 · 25 mm depth 5 mm whin dust rolled surfacing
Non–woven geotextile–optional depending on site conditions

150 · 150 mm final compacted Type 1 sub-base

Bound Gravel

15 mm 6 mm epoxy resin or polyurethane bound gravel surface dressing.

15 · 1–3 mm aggregate smooth and round
15 mm thick sand asphalt wearing course of hot rolled asphalt

50 · 50 mm deep bitumen macadam 20 mm natural size base course

150 · 150 mm final compacted Type 1 sub-base

Compacted subgrade

Note: These are examples of standard construction details only. The designer should satisfy himself of site conditions and vary the details and dimensions to suit

1.17 Typical Footpath Edging

Edging - PCC Blocks

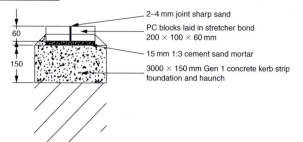

60

150

2–4 mm joint sharp sand

PC blocks laid in stretcher bond
200 × 100 × 60 mm

15 mm 1:3 cement sand mortar

3000 × 150 mm Gen 1 concrete kerb strip
foundation and haunch

Edging - Timber

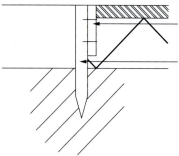

Treated timber edge 200 × 35 mm. 2 m
lengths depending on situation

Treated tiner pegs 50 × 50 × 450 mm,
pointed at one end. Fixed every 15 m c/s
using galvanised nails

Edging-Concrete Flush Pin Kerb

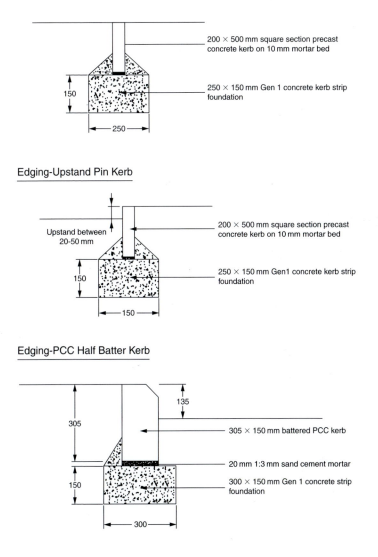

200 × 500 mm square section precast concrete kerb on 10 mm mortar bed

250 × 150 mm Gen 1 concrete kerb strip foundation

150

250

Edging-Upstand Pin Kerb

Upstand between 20-50 mm

200 × 500 mm square section precast concrete kerb on 10 mm mortar bed

250 × 150 mm Gen1 concrete kerb strip foundation

150

150

Edging-PCC Half Batter Kerb

305

135

305 × 150 mm battered PCC kerb

20 mm 1:3 mm sand cement mortar

300 × 150 mm Gen 1 concrete strip foundation

150

300

Edging-Stone Kerb

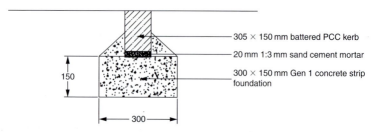

305 × 150 mm battered PCC kerb

20 mm 1:3 mm sand cement mortar

300 × 150 mm Gen 1 concrete strip foundation

150

300

Note: These are examples of standard construction details only. The designer should satisfy himself of site conditions and vary the details and dimensions to suit

2 Soft Landscape

2.1 Definition and Specification of Tree Sizes

The National Plant Specification, prepared by the Horticultural Trades Association, is an important vehicle to aid the specification and delivery of reliable plant material throughout the landscape industry.

The regularly updated National Plant Specification provides a comprehensive and accurate level of information to aid the production of rigorous plant schedules. By stipulating supply under the National Plant Specification, buyers can be sure that plants are supplied to their exact specification and that different nurseries will provide like-for-like quotations and a consistent level of quality.

The Nursery and Contractors Certification Schemes complement the National Plant Specification. The Nursery and Contractors Certification Schemes set out the level of quality to be attained by nursery staff and contractors including workmanship, delivery and planting of stock. Members of both of these schemes are rigorously policed and are subject to regular independent audit.

The table on the following page outlines the information and specification requirements for trees, as set out in the National Plant Specification. The table indicates some of the categories.

The table in section 2.2 outlines the information and specification requirements for shrubs.

Specification Requirements for Trees

Name	Form	Age (year)	Girth (cm)	Height (cm)	Clear stem (cm)	Root	Containment	Breaks
Species	Seedling	1 + 0 or 1/0		30–40		B		
	Seedling	1 + 0 or 1/0		40–60		B		
	Transplant	1 + 1 or 1/1		60–80		B		
	Transplant	1 + 1 or 1/1		80–100		B		
	Transplant	1 + 2 or 1/2		125–150		B		
	Whip	2X		125–150		B		1
	Feather	2X		175–200		B		5
	Feather	2X		200–250		C	15	5
	Standard-light	2X	6–8	250–300	150–175	B		3
	Standard-light	2X	6–8	250–300	150–175	C	25	3
	Standard	2X	8–10	250–300	175–200	B		3
	Standard	2X	8–10	250–300	175–200	C	25	3
	Standard-selected	2X	10–12	300–350	175–200	RB		4
	Standard-selected	2X	10–12	300–350	175–200	C	25	4
	Standard-heavy	3X	12–14	350–425	175–200	RB		5
	Standard-heavy	3X	12–14	350–425	175–200	C	75	5
	Standard-extra heavy	3X	14–16	425–600	175–200	RB		
	Standard-extra heavy	3X	16–18	400–450	min 200	RB	60	

Standard-extra heavy	3X	18–20	450–500	min 200	RB	70	
Standard Semi-mature	4X	20–25	500–550	min 200	RB	80	
Standard semi-mature	4X	25–30	min 450	min 200	RB		
Standard semi-mature	4X	30–35	600–650	min 200	RB	100	
Multistem	3X	200–250			RB		2 stems
Multistem	4X	250–300			RB		3 stems

Notes:

Name. Each tree must be specified by giving its full botanical name.

Age. Within these definitions the following conventions are followed: ' + ' or '/' indicates transplanting, 'u' or ' = ' indicates undercutting.

Root. Rootballed trees are indicated by the letters 'RB'. Bare root (bagged) are indicated by the letter 'B'. Container or pot grown are indicated by the letter 'C'. Cell grown trees are indicated by the letters 'CE'.

Containment. Container grown plants are defined by 'C' followed by a number indicating the volume in litre, e.g. C5. The volume of cell grown plants is indicated in cubic centimetres (cc).

Breaks. The minimum number of breaks/branches/lateral growth may be included in the specification.

Other details or criteria specified may include:

- Origin/Provenance, e.g. British Grown, British Provenance, Local Provenance.
- Top/Bottom worked.
- Shape, e.g. Pleached, Pollard, Parasol, Espalier, Fan.

Copyright: Horticultural Trades Association. Refer also to www.gohelios.co.uk.

2.2 Definition and Specification of Shrub Sizes

The following table outlines the information and specification requirements for shrubs, as set out in the National Plant Specification. The table indicates some of the categories.

Age/condition × transplanted	Height/spread in cm*	Root condition†	Container size (min size in litres)	Habit	Min no of breaks/ branches	Comments
1 + 0 or 1/0	10–15, 15–20, 20–25, 25–30, 30–40, 40–50, 50–60, 60–80	B				
1 + 0 or 1/0	15–30, 10–20, 20–40, 40–60, 60–90	Ce	50, 100, 150 or 200cc			
0/1	40–50, 60–80, 80–100, 100–125	B				
0/2	60–80, 80–100, 100–125, 125–150	B				
1 + 1 or 1/1	30–40, 40–50, 60–80, 80–100, 100–125	B or C	1, 2 or 5			
1u1	25–30, 30–40, 40–50, 50–60, 60–80, 80–100	B				
	20–30, 30–40, 40–50, 60–80, 80–100, 100+	B			3, 4 or 5	Compact, low, medium and vigorous species
	15–30, 30–50, 50–80	B				Transplants
	25–40, 40–70, 70–90	B			2 or 3 depending on height and vigour	Light shrubs

Height or spread in cm		RB		Habit	Number	Species
10–15, 15–20, 20–25, 25–30, 30–40, 40–50, 50–60, 60–70, 70–80, 80–100, 100–125, 125–150, 150–175, 175–200, 200–225, 225–250 and above 250 in 50 cm steps, above 400 in 100 cm steps		RB		Branched; bushy	2, 3/4, 5/7, 8/12 depending on heights, age and growth habit	Low/compact species, e.g. Cotoneaster 'Coral Beauty'
Height or spread in cm 15–20, 20–30, 30–40, 40–60, 60–80, 80–100, 100–125, 125–150, 150–175, 175–200, 200–225, 225–250 and above 250 in 50 cm steps, above 400 in 100 cm steps		RB		Branched; bushy; leader and laterals; Several shoots; single leader	2, 3/4, 5/7, 8/12 depending on heights, age and growth habit	Medium species, e.g. Berberis thunbergii
Height or spread in cm 20–30, 30–40, 40–60, 60–100, 100–150, 150–200, 200–250, 250–300, 300–400, and above 400 in 100 cm steps		RB		Branched; bushy; leader and laterals; several shoots; single leader	2, 3/4, 5/7, 8/12 depending on heights, age and growth habit	Vigorous species, e.g. Cotoneaster 'Cornubia'
Spread in cm 10–15, 15–20, 20–(25), (25)–30, 30–40, 40–50, 50–60, 60–80				Branched; bushy; several shoots	2, 3/4, 5/7, 8/12 depending on heights, age and growth habit	Ground Cover species, e.g. Cotoneaster dammeri
Height or spread in cm 10–15, 15–20, 20–25, 25–30, 30–40, 40–50, 50–60, 60–70, 70–80, 80–90, 90–100–120				Branched; bushy	4, 5/7, 8/12 depending on height, age growth and habit	Low compact and medium Rhododendrons

Age/condition × transplanted	Height/spread in cm*	Root condition†	Container size (min size in litres)	Habit	Min no of breaks/ branches	Comments
	Height or spread in cm 30–40, 40–50, 50–60, 60–70, 70–80, 80–90, 90–100, 100–120, 120–140, 140–160, 160–180, 180–200, 200–225, 225–250, 250–275, 275–300 above 300 in 50 cm steps	RB		Branched; bushy	4, 5/7, 8/12 depending on height, age growth and habit	Vigorous Rhododendrons
	Height in cm 30–40,40–50, 50–60, 60–70, 70–80, 80–100, 100–125, 125–150, 150–175, 175–200, 200–250, 250–300	RB		Branched; bushy	4, 5/7, 8/12 depending on height, age growth and habit	Deciduous Azaleas
	Spread in cm 15–20, 20–25, 25–30, 30–40, 40–50, 50–60, 60–70, 70–80, 80–90, 90–100, 100–120, 120–140,	RB		Branched; bushy	4, 5/7, 8/12 depending on height, age growth and habit	Japanese Azaleas
	Height in cm 10–15, 15–20, 20–30, 30–40, 40–60, 60–80, 80–100	C	0.5, 1, 2, 3, 4, 5, 7.5, 10.15, or larger sizes for specimen shrubs	Branched; bushy; leader and lateral; several shoots; single leader	Branched, several shoots; 2–3: bushy 3–6; depending on height, age and growth habit Rhododendron: 4–10	Typical container grown shrubs specified by over-all height

*(D) + Diameter; †B, bagged; Ce, cell grown; RB, root ball; C, container.
Copyright: Horticultural Trades Association. Refer also to www.gohelios.co.uk.

2.3 British Native Trees and Shrubs

Species	Latin name	Soil type	Native location	Exposure	Height (m)	Wildlife value	Evergreen	Flowers/ fruit	Autumn colour
Trees									
Alder	Alnus glutinosa	Wet/alka-line	UK		6–15	*		Catkins	
Ash	Fraxinus excelsior	Most	UK	*	16+			Keys	
Aspen	Populus tremula	Heavy/acid	NW UK	*	16+				
Beech	Fagus sylvatica	Dry/acid	UK		16+			Nuts	*
Birch (Downey)	Betula pubescens	Wet	UK		16+				
Birch (Silver)	Betula pendula	Wet/acid	UK	*	16+	*			*
Cherry (wild)	Prunus avium	Heavy acid	North UK		6–15+	*		Flowers/ cherries	*
Charry (bird)	Prunus padus	Wet	North UK		6–15	*		Flowers/ cherries	
Crab apple	Malus sylvestris	Moist, not wet	South UK		6–15	*		Flowers/ apples	

Species	Latin name	Soil type	Native location	Exposure	Height (m)	Wildlife value	Evergreen	Flowers/fruit	Autumn colour
Elm (Wych)	Ulmus glabra	Heavy	NW UK	*	16+	*			
Hornbeam	Carpinus betulus	Heavy/alkaline	South UK		16+				*
Lime (small leaved)	Tilia cordata	Heavy/alkaline	Not Scotland		16+	*			*
Maple (field)	Acer campestre	Heavy/alkaline	UK/S. Scotland		6–15	*			
Oak (common)	Quercus robur	Heavy/alkaline	UK	*	16+	*		Acorns	
Oak (Sessile)	Quercus petrea	Acid	UK lowlands		16+	*		Acorns	
Pear (wild)	Pyrus pyraster	Alluvial	UK lowlands		6–15			Flowers/pears	
Pine (Scots)	Pinus sylvestris	Dry/acid	Scotland	*	16+	*			
Poplar (black)	Populus nigra	Alluvial	South England		16+				
Rowan	Sorbus aucuparia	Light/acid	UK	*	6–15	*		Flowers/berreis	*
Whitebeam	Sorbus aria	Dry/chalk	South England		6–15			Flowers/berries	*

Willow (Crack)	Salix fragilis	Wet	South UK	*	16+	*		
Willow (Goat)	Salix caprea	Wet	UK	*	6–15	*		Catkins
Willow (Grey)	Salix cineria	Wet	UK	*	6–15	*		Catkins
Willow (Purple)	Salix purpurea	Wet	UK	*	0.5–5	*		
Willow (White)	Salix alba	Wet	South UK	*	16+	*		
Yew	Taxus baccata	Dry/alkaline	UK		16+	*		
Shrubs								
Alder buckthorn	Frangula alnus	Wet/alkiline	UK		4–5			
Bilberry	Vaccinium myrtillus	Acid	UK	*	0.6	*		Berries
Blackthorn	Prunus spinosa	All soils	UK		1–4	*		Flowers/berries
Bramble	Rubus fruticosa	All soils	UK		1.5	*		Berries
Bog myrtle	Myrica gale	Acid/wet	UK		1–2			Flowers/fruits

Species	Latin name	Soil type	Native location	Exposure	Height (m)	Wildlife value	Evergreen	Flowers/ fruit	Autumn colour
Broom	Cytisus scoparius	Dry/acid	UK	*	1–2			Flowers	
Butchers broom	Ruscus aculeatus	Alkaline	South England		0.5	*		Flowers/ berries	*
Dogwood	Cornus sanguineum	All soils	South UK		2–5	*	*		*
Gorse	Ulex europeus	All soils	UK	*	2.5			Flowers	
Guelder rose	Viburnum opulus	Heavy/wet	South UK		4	*			
Hawthorn	Crateagus monogyna	Not acid	UK		6–15	*		Flowers	*
Hazel	Corylus avellana	Heavy	UK		10			Catkins	
Heath	Calluna vulgaris	Acid	UK	*	0.5			Flowers	*
Heather (bell)	Erica cinerea	Acid/dry	UK	*	0.5			Flowers	*
Heather (cross leaved)	Erica tetralix	Acid/wet	UK	*	0.5			Flowers	*
Holly	Ilex aquifolium	Not wet	UK		16+			Berries	*

Honeysuckle	Lonicera pericly-menum	All soils	UK		6–15	*		
Ivy	Hedera helx	All soils	UK		6–15			
Juniper	Juniperus communis	Light dry/acid	UK uplands	*	0–11		Berries	*
Midland hawthorn	Crataegus laevigata	Heavy/alkaline	South England		2	*		
Purging buckthorn	Hyppophae catharticus	Calcareous	South UK		4–6	*	Berries	
Privet	Ligustrum ovalifolium	Dry/alkaline	UK		3–4	*		
Sea buckthorn	Hyppophae rhamnoides	Light dry/acid	UK coasts	*	3			
Travellers joy	Clematis vitalba	Chalk/limestone	South UK		6–15			
Tutsan	Hypericum androae-mum	All soils	West UK		1			
Wayfaring tree	Viburnum lantana	Calcareous	South UK		2–6	*	Berries	

Column header: Flowers

Source/Copyright: *Planting Native Trees and Shrubs* by Kenneth and Gillian Beckett from more information.

2.4 Plants for Encouraging Wild Life

Bee-loving plants	When grown in suitable conditions the flowers of plants listed in the table below are visited by bees for nectar and pollen	
Trees	ACER campestre	MALUS in variety
	Negundo	MESPILUS germanica
	Platanoides	NOTHOFAGUS antarctica (pollen)
	'Royal Red'	POPULUS nigra (pollen)
	Pseudoplatanus	PRUNUS avium
	AESCULUS carnea 'Briottii'	Padus 'Grandiflora'
	Hippocastanum	Sargentii
	Indica	'Shirotae'
	Plantierensis	Subhirtella
	AILANTHUS altissima	Pendula Rubra'
	ALNUS glutinosa (pollen)	Tai-Haku'
	Incana and forms (pollen)	'Ukon'
	BETULA in variety (pollen)	'Umeniko'
	CARAGANA arborescens	Yedoensis
	CASTANEA sativa	QUERCUS in variety (pollen)
	CATALPA bignoniodes	ROBINIA pseudoacacia
	CRATAEGUS prunifolia	SALIX alba
	FAGUS (pollen)	SORBUS aria forms
	FRAXINUS excelsior (pollen)	Aucuparia and forms
	KOELREUTERIA	Intermedia
	LIQUIDAMBAR styraciflua	TILIA euchlora
	LIRIODENDRON tulipifera	
Shrubs	AESCULUS parviflora	PHYSOCARPUS
	ARBUTUS	POTENTILLA
	BERBERIS darwinii	PRUNUS laurocerasus
	x irwinii	forms
	x stenophylla	PYRACANTHA
	Thunbergii and	RHAMNUS frangula
	'Atropurpurea'	RHUS
	Wilsonae	RIBES sanguineum
	BUDDLEIA globosa	Speciosum
	BUXUS	SALIX caprea
	CEANOTHUS	Repens 'Argentea'
	CERCIS siliquastrum	SENECIO 'Sunshine'
	CHAENOMELES speciosa	SKIMMIA
	forms	

Bee-loving plants	When grown in suitable conditions the flowers of plants listed in the table below are visited by bees for nectar and pollen	

Shrubs (continued)	CISTUS
	COLUTEA arborescens
	CORNUS
	COTONEASTER
	CYTISUS
	DAPHNE mezereum
	ELAEGNUS
	ESCALLONIA
	FUCHSIA
	HYPERICUM androsaemum;
	  forrestii
	ILEX
	LAURUS nobilis
	OLEARIA
	PEROVSKIA
		SPIRAEA
		STAPHYLEA
		STEPHANANDRA
		SYMPHORICARPUS
		SYRINGA
		TAMARIX pent. 'Pink Cascade'
		ULEX europaeus
		VIBURNUM opulus
		  Tinus
		WEIGELA

Butterfly loving plants	**Shrubs** BUDDLEIA LAVANDULA LIGUSTRUM RHAMNUS frangula SYRINGA	**Perennials** ACHILLEA ASTER (Michaelmas Daisies) CENTRANTHUS ERIGERON HELENIUM SCABIOSA SEDUM spectabile SOLIDAGO

Berries and fruit for birds
 	
The peak period of interest is September/ October
	TREES
	AESCULUS hippocastanum
	AILANTHUS altissima
	ALNUS cordata
	AMELANCHIER lamarckii
	CASTANEA sativa
	CATALPA bignonioides
	CRATAEGUS x grignonensis
	  x lavallei (carrierei
	  Prunifolia)
	GLEDITSIA triacanthos
	JUGLANS regia
	KOELREUTERIA paniculata
	MALUS coronaria varieties
	MESPILUS Nottingham 'Medlar'
	MORUS nigra
	PLATANUS hispanica
	PTEROCARYA fraxinifolia
		SORBUS
		Aucuparia
		  'Asplenifolia'
		  'Cardinal Royal'
		  'Ghose'
		  'Sheerwater Seedling'
		  'Xanthocarpa'
		Cashmiriana
		  'Columbia Queen'
		Commixta
		  'Embley' (discolour)
		Essertauiana (conradinae)
		Matsumarana
		Vilmorinii
		SORBUS aria
		Lutescens'
		  x 'Magnifica'
		Intermedia
		  'Leonard Sprenger'
		  X thuringiaca 'Fastigiata'

Bee-loving plants	When grown in suitable conditions the flowers of plants listed in the table below are visited by bees for nectar and pollen	

Berries and fruit for birds (continued)	**Shrubs**
	AMELANCHIER lamarckii
	ARBUTUS unedo
	ARCTOSTAPHYLOS uva-ursi
	AUCUBA japonica
	BERBERIS. Var
	CALLICARPA 'Profusion'
	CHAENOMELES
	CLERODENDRON trichotomum
	COLUTEA arborescens
	CORNUS. Var
	CORYLUS avellana
	  Maxima "Purpurea'
	COTONEASTER. Most forms
	  berry prolifically
	DAPHNE mezereum
	DECAISNEA fargesii
	DORYCNIUM hirsutum
	ELAEGNUS
	EUONYMUS europaeus
	  'Intermedia'
	  'Red Cascade'
	  Sachalinensis
	  Yedoensis
	GAULTHERIA procumbens
	HIPPOPHAE rhamnoides
	HYPERICUM androsaemum
	  forrestii
	ILEX. Most forms berry freely
	MAHONIA
		OSMANTHUS decora
		PERNETTYA mucronata forms
		PONCIRUS trifoliate
		PYRACANTHA. All berry prolifically
		RHAMNUS frangula
		RHUS typhina
		RIBES odoratum
		RUBUS calcycinoides
		  X 'Betty Ashburner'
		  'Darts Ambassador'
		RUSCUS aculeatus
		SAMBUCUS. Red or black berries
		  in clusters
		SKIMMIA female variety
		  Japonica 'Foremanii'
		  Laureola
		STAPHYLEA
		SYMPHORICARPUS
		VIBURNUM davidii
		  Lantana
		  Opulus
		  – 'Compactum'
		  –'Fructo Luteo'
		  –'Notcutt's Variety'
		  Rhytidophyllum
		VITIS. 'Vine'

2.5 Common Poisonous Plants

The lists below show some examples of poisonous plants. Please note that this is not an exhaustive list, and the landscape architect should consider very carefully the choice of plant in relation of the use and location of the site.

Poisonous to humans

Toxic of eaten	Harmful if eaten	Skin allergy/ irritation
Horse chestnut fruits	Daffodils bulbs and foliage	Crysanthemum
Daphne berries	Euonymus	Daffodils bulbs and foliage
Digitalis/Foxglove leaves	Lysichton/Skunk Cabbage	Daphne
Euphorbia/Spurge	Polygonatum/ Solomon's Seal	Echium/ Viper bugloss
Gaultheria	Rhamnus	Euphorbia
Iris underground stem	Robinia pseudocacia 'Frisia'	Iris
Kalmia	Sambucus racemosa	
Laburnum seeds	Scilla	Lupins
Lily of the Valley	Snowberries	Ruta
Lupinus	Wisteria seed pods	
Rhus		
Solanum		
Oleander leaves and branches		
Laurels		
Rhododendron		
Azalea		
Jasmine berries		
Yew berries		
Wild cherry twigs and foliage		
Apple seeds and pips		
Autumn crocus		
Azalea		

Poisonous to animals

Apple seeds and pips	Common stonecrop	Leyland cypress
Autumn crocus	Daffodil	Lupin
Azalea	Daphne	March marigold
Black locust	Deadly nightshade	Mistletoe
Black walnut	Delphinium	Daffodils
Bluebell	Elderberry	Oak
Box wood	Ivy	Poppy
Buckthorn	Foxglove	Primrose
Buttercup	Holly	Ragwort
Cherry	Honey suckle	Red clover
Cherry laurel	Horse chestnut	Rhododendron
Chrysanthemum	Hyacinth	Senecio
Clematis	Iris	Wysteria St. Johns Wort

The Horticultural Trades Association has a list of Potentially Harmful plants which is divided into three categories depending on their severity. Refer to HTA 'Potentially Harmful Plants'. www.the-hta.co.uk.

2.6 Grass Seed Mixes

Grass seed should comply with BS 3969 and be from a certified and approved source, reaching prescribed standards of purity and germination as set out in the Fodder Plant Seed Regulations 1985 (S1 975) and the Seeds Regulations 1982 (S1 844). The landscape architect should check certificates of purity, germination, and total weed content.

Major Species – General characteristics

	Fast establishment	Wear Tolerance	Shade tolerance	Saline tolerance	Dry soil	Wet	Poor fertility	Close mowing	Alkaline soil	Acid soil
Chewings fescue										
Slender creeping red fescue										
Strong creeping red fescue										
Hard sheeps fescue										
Browntop bent										
Creeping Bent										
Smooth stalked meadow grass										
Rough stalked meadow grass										
Wood meadow grass										
Perennial rye grass										
Timothy										
Crested Dogstail										

Poor
Average
Good

Common grasses

Common name	Latin name
Perennial ryegrass	Lolium perenne
Strong creeping red fescue	Festuca rubra rubra gunuina
Slender creeping red fescue	Festuca rubra rubra litoralis
Creeping bent	Agrostis stolonifera
Browntop bent	Agrostis tenuis
Chewings fescue	Festuca rubra commutate
Hard/sheeps fescue	Festuca longifolia
Smooth stalked meadow grass	Poa pratensis
Hard stalked meadow grass	Poa rigida
Timothy	Phleum pretense
Crested dogstail	Cynosurus cristatus

Grasses for particular uses

Sports mixes

Rye grassed base for hard wearing.
Bents and fescues to fill out the base with rhyzomes.

Golf course mixes

Golf greens – these need to be fine dense grasses, i.e. brown top bent grass are better than fescues, they are more aggressive and provide an all year round colour.

Golf tees and fairways – Rye grass for hard wear and Creeping red fescue for close knit base growth.

Dry Shade

Bent grasses best.
Poa supina good under trees.
Do not use rye grass or smooth stalked meadow grass.

SUDs areas and wet areas

Crested Dogstail, Timothy, Cocksfoot and Meadow foxtail will tolerate infrequent flooding and are low maintenance.

Lawns

Fine, short lawn.
80% fescue (slender or chewings).
20% bent.

Road verges

Flattened meadow grass and slender fescue are salt tolerant.
Creeping bent but will only tolerate sandy soils and not clay.

Low maintenance/hard wearing Rye grass is slow growing.

Reclamation mixes Should include clover which aids with nutrient establishment.

Tolerance to drought Slender creeping red fescue. Cultivar 'Helena' is one of the most suitable.

Sowing methods

Generally 30–35 g/m^2.
Ensure seed is covered by soil with a light raking.
One-way sowing only is required.

Cutting heights

Rye grass – no lower than 6 mm.
Bent grass – to 3 mm.
Fescues – not below 5 mm.

Source/Copyright: British Seed Houses and Rigby Taylor.

Refer to growers for up to date correct mix for specific conditions. More information on seed quality can be found in the British Standard.

2.7 Wild Flower Mixes

Seeds

Key to success:

- Checking soil types
- The correct seed mix and sowing
- Subsequent maintenance (cutting regime)

Components of the seed mix
Usually contain:

- 80% Nurse crop – open growing non competitive grass seed mix
- 20% Main crop – wild flowers

Sowing rates
- 4 g/m^2 non-competitive grasses
- 1 g/m^2 wild flowers

Sowing times
May to September (except when very hot and dry)

Plugs

Types – normally in trays as in follows:

No. of plugs/tray	Approx. volume of plug (ml)
400–600	<5
200–400	<5–15
100–200	<14–40
50–100	<40–50
30–50	>50

Planting rate 6–15 plants/m^2.

Pots

Season for planting: March–April and August–September.
Planting: with trowel or dig a hole.

Maintenance

To aid seedling development and maintain a balanced composition.

General rule of thumb: First cut. If cut sward exceeds 10 cm in late March or early April reduce to 40–70 mm. Second cut. If re-growth exceeds 100 mm by April/end of May. The more fertile the soil the more cuts required.

All mixes ex. Cornfield annuals

		Autumn establishment	Spring establishment	Autumn establishment	Spring establishment
All mixes inc. cornfield annuals.	First year	Cut 1: March. Cut to 4–7 cm Cut 2: Early May. Cut to 4–7 cm Cut 3: September. Cut to 4 cm Leave tidy through winter. Remove cuttings	Cut 1: approx 6 weeks after sowing. Cut to 4–7 cm Cut 2: May, when height exceeds 10 cm. Cut to 4–7 cm Cut 3. Sept/October. Cut to 4–7 cm Remove all cuttings	Cut 1: Spring cut to 7 cm April Cut 2: August/September. Cut to 4–7 cm to prevent dense canopy of annuals competing with perennials Remove all cuttings	August/September/October. Cut to 4–7 cm. Remove all cuttings
	Future years	Cut 1: Cut to 4–7 cm March/April Final cut: 4–7 cm End September/October Additional cuts required on fertile soils Spot weed	Cut 1: Cut to 4–7 cm March/April Final cut: 4–7 cm End September/October Additional cuts required on fertile soils Spot weed	Cut 1: Cut to 4–7 cm March/April Final cut: 4–7 cm End September/October Additional cuts required on fertile soils Spot weed	Cut 1: Cut to 4–7 cm March/April Final cut: 4–7 cm end September/October Additional cuts required on fertile soils Spot weed

Refer to growers for suitability of specific mixes for specific uses and situations.

2.8 Topsoil

There was nothing Monty liked better than showing off his new topsoil trick.

Relevant British Standard: BS 3882: 2007

Definitions
Topsoil: natural topsoil or manufactured topsoil in which plants can grow healthily.

Manufactured topsoil: material produced by combining mineral matter and organic matter to provide the same function as natural topsoil.

Topsoil characteristics
Refer to British Standard for characteristics of specific types of soil.

Parameter	Multipurpose topsoil
Soil texture %m/m Clay content % Silt content % Sand content	 5–35 0–65 30–85
Soil organic matter content %m/m Clay 5–20% Clay 20–35%	 3–20 5–20
Maximum course fragment content %m/m >2 mm >20 mm >50 mm	 0–30 0–10 0
pH	5.5–8.5
Available plant nutrient content Nitrogen 5 m/m Extractable phosphorus mg/l Extractable potassium mg/l Extractable magnesium mg/l	 0.15 16–100 121–900 51–600
Carbon:Nitrogen	<20:1
Exchangable sodium % (need not measure if soil electrical conductivity <2800 μcm^{-1})	<15
Visible contaminants %m/m >2 mm	 <0.5
of which plastics of which sharps	<0.25 Zero in 1 kg air-dried soil

(%m/m = %mass)

Angle of Repose of soils	Degrees
Firm earth	50
Loose earth	28
Firm clay	45
Wet clay	16
Dry sand	38
Wet sand	22

Hand test for texture if it is:

- gritty and fails to soil the fingers – SAND
- gritty but soils the fingers and can be pressed into a ball – SANDY LOAM
- sticky and easily moulded in the fingers and quickly polished by sliding between the finger and thumb – CLAY LOAM
- sticky, stiff and plastic enough to be rolled into long flexible worms – CLAY
- not sticky nor can be polished but feels silky or soapy and can be moulded but is non-cohesive – SILTY LOAM
- neither gritty, sticky nor silky – MEDIUM LOAM

Stones

Maximum size of stones in any direction 50 mm

35% by dry weight of which a fraction 2 mm–5 mm must be under 20% dry weight.

Phytotoxic elements (not normally hazardous to health)

Threshold trigger concentrations for any uses where plants are to be grown. A pH of 6.5 is assumed. If pH falls the toxic effect and uptake of elements will increase.

Total copper (Cu)	<135 mg/kg
Total nickel (Ni)	<70 mg/kg
Total zinc (Zn)	<200 mg/kg
Total nitric acid (Ni)	<75 mg/kg
Water soluble Boron (B)	<3 mg/kg

Zoo toxic elements (hazardous to health)

Threshold trigger concentrations for use in parks, playing fields and open space.

Total arsenic (As)	<40 mg/kg
Total cadmium (Cd)	<15 mg/kg
Total Chromium (Cr)	<1000 mg/kg
Total Lead (Pb)	<2000 mg/kg
Total Mercury (Hg)	<20 mg/kg

Refer to the British Standard for information on use, sampling, handing and storage of topsoil.
Source/Copyright: British Standards Institute.

British Standards can be obtained in PDF or hardcopy formats from BSI online shop: www.bsigroup.com/shop or by contacting BSI Customer Services for hard-copy only.

Textural classification (limiting percentage of sand, silt and clay
sized paticles for the mineral texture class)

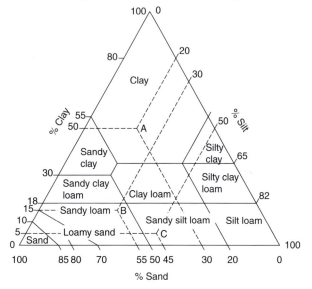

NOTE: Examples of textural classification:

Soil A with 30% sand, 20% silt and 50% clay is in the clay textural class

Soil B with 55% sand, 30% silt and 15% clay is in the 'sandy loam' textural class

Soil C with 45% sand, 50% silt and 5% clay is on the 'sandy silt loam' textural class

2.9 Times of Year for Planting

Deciduous trees and shrubs: late October to late March.

Conifers and evergreens: September/October or April/May

Herbaceous plants, including marginal: September/October or March/April

Dried bulbs, corns and tubers: September/October

Colchicum: July/August

Green bulbs: After flowering in spring

Wildflower plugs: Late August to Mid November or March/April.

Aquatic plants: May/June or September/October

Container grown plants: at any time if ground and weather conditions are favourable.

Cold storage, root balling and local weather conditions may extend planting period.

2.10 Tree Planting

What does a girl have to do for a drink and decent haircut in this goddamn place?

Planting season

The tree planting season in the northern hemisphere is generally late October to late March.

Cold storage, root balling and local weather conditions may extend this period from early October to late March.

Tree planting preferences

Half hardy species – preferably spring.

Hardy, deciduous – preferably between October and December.

Hardy, evergreens – early or late in the planting season.

Container-grown trees – all year round. However, the preceding guidelines will give better results.

Points to note

Avoid planting in frosty, cold or windy, hot, sunny or drying weather.

Choose cloudy and drizzly weather if possible.

If planting in late spring or summer, plants should be watered during dry spells for the first growing season.

Pre-planting care

It is essential to:

- prevent drying of the roots. Heel the trees in or, for short periods of storage, put them in plastic bags. Keep them shaded and out of the wind
- keep as much fibrous root on the trees as possible
- avoid damaging the roots, breaking the stem tops or stripping the bark from stem or roots
- prevent heating, by maintaining air circulation around the stems and foliage of trees in storage or transit. Heat is generated by bacteria and micro-organisms on the plants, especially on the leaves of evergreens. Plants are seriously weakened and may be killed if the roots become warm to the touch at any stage between lifting and planting.

Storage

Ideally, plants should be lifted, transported and re-planted without interruption. Often, however, they need to be held for some weeks or even months before planting. Therefore:

- Root balled plants – place close together and cover root balls with sand, moist compost, soil or wet straw

- Bare root plants – the traditional storage method is to heel-in for longer periods. Dig a trench in fresh moist soil which will not dry out or become waterlogged. Dig the trench deep enough for the tree's roots to be completely covered. For shorter periods of time they can be stored in strong plastic bags in a cool location.

Trees in bundles should be separated and spaced along the trench to keep the plants in the centre of the bundles from drying out; or – in the case of evergreens – from heating up. It is convenient to place a marker stick every 50 or 100 plants to save counting later.

Where it is necessary to lift the plants in very frosty weather, the roots should be covered in a thick layer of straw to prevent the soil freezing to them.

Notes

Hardy species are robust and capable of surviving unfavourable conditions such as cold weather and lack of moisture.

To heel in (to press the soil down around the roots of the tree). This will ensure root to soil contact.

Planting Methods
Small trees
Notch planting
Notch planting, L, T or V shaped, is the quickest method, but not the most reliable. The method consists of making a notch in the ground and inserting the roots of the plant into the cut. It is generally suitable for the mass planting of bare-rooted transplants and whips under about 90 cm (3') high. It should not be used in wet soil or for large or expensive trees or where failures must be minimized.

Mound and ridge planting
For poorly drained sites where the turf is difficult to cut, mound planting provides extra inches of freely draining soil for the roots. In some cases it may be possible to arrange the ploughing of the site to create ridges and furrows to assist drainage. In exposed sites, plant on the leeward side of the furrow, the direction in which the wind is blowing.

Large trees
Pit planting
Pit planting is the slowest method but one which ensures plenty of room for the roots. It should be used for trees over about 90 cm (3') tall and where failures would be expensive or difficult to replace.

Pit dimensions: Allow at least 150 to 300 mm, and up to 600 mm, greater than the diameter of the root ball for the initial root growth.

Support

There are two methods for supporting a tree: either above-ground by timber stake(s) or below-ground by taut cables. Support is generally required if the tree is over 1.5 m. Stakes should be softwood, peeled chestnut or larch, free from projections and large edge knots, with one end pointed. Stakes should not be more than 1/3 of the height of the tree.

Tree size	Staking height	Overall length of stake (mm)	Cross-section of stake (mm)
Light standard up to heavy standard	At approximately 1/3rd height of tree above ground level	1800	75–100
Light standard up to heavy standard	At a point immediately below the lowest branch	2700	75–100
Extra heavy standard and above	At approximately 1/3rd height of tree above ground level	1800	100
Extra heavy standard and above	At a point immediately below the lowest branch	2700	100

Further sources of information and reference:
BS 4428: 1989 Code of practice for general landscape operations.
BS 4043: 1989 Recommendations for transplanting root balled trees.

Tree root ball sizes and tree weights

The following information is approximate and will depend on species, soil type and the moisture content of the soil.

Girth (cm)	Root ball diameter (cm)	Ball height (cm)	Weight in Kg
14–16	45–50	40	150
16–18	50–60	40	200
18–20	60–70	40–50	270
20–25	60–70	40–50	350
25–30	80	50–60	500
30–35	90–100	60–70	650
35–40	100–110	60–70	850
40–45	110–120	60–70	1100
50–60	130–140	60–70	1600
60–70	150–160	60–70	2500
70–80	180–200	70	4000
80–90	200–220	70–80	5500
90–100	230–250	80–90	7500
100–120	250–270	80–90	9500

Source/Copyright: Practicality Brown. www.pracbrown.co.uk.

2.11 Plant Protection

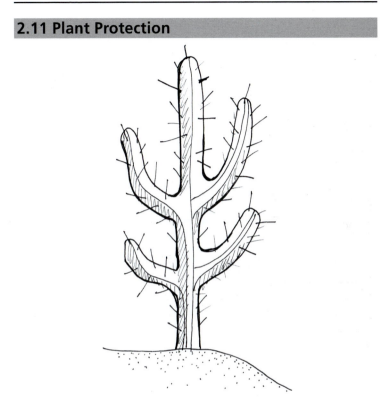

Plant protection

Tree shelters

Uses:

- To create a greenhouse environment, stimulating rapid height and growth of slow growing broadleaves
- Small/young plants
- Rabbit protection
- Aids weed control by screening from sprays and marking location of plant

Spiral shelter

- Wound around single stemmed plant
- Must be tall enough to provide the necessary browsing protection
- Expands as tree grows
- Supported by bamboo cane attached with nylon tie (external or internal)

Shelter guards

- Tubes of plastic netting and polythene lining
- The polythene degrades leaving a free draining netting
- For shrubs and trees, varying dimensions to suit types and sizes of plant

Grow cones

- Preformed tubes
- Brown tinted reinforced plastic with view of young plant
- Slightly conical in shape to enable rapidly growing stems to split the tube
- Supported by timber stakes, bamboo cane or steel rod, tied at top and bottom
- Varying sizes to suit types of predator, i.e. 1.2 m for roe deer, 30 cm for rabbits

Tree guards

Uses:

- To protect against damage or predators, i.e. stock, voles, rabbits, deer
- Tree guards do not stimulate plant growth
- Larger plants and trees – metal or timber tree guards supplied by many street furniture manufacturers mainly to prevent damage by vehicles or people

Stock netting

Also known as sheep netting, pig netting, 'Rylock'.

Hinged joint fencing. Continuous horizontal wires are joined by lengths of vertical wires which are wound around horizontal wires to form hinged joints. Joints give flexibility but are liable to concertina if erected badly.

Knotted Joint fencing. Continuous horizontal and vertical tensile wires, joined with a knot of wires. Used for deer netting, which requires height and further strength achieved by the continuous verticals and non-slip knots.

Ringlock joints. Continuous horizontal and vertical wires are joined with a ring.

Fence coding

Stock fencing is coded as follows:

- Grade of netting
- HT – high tensile
- Number of horizontal wires
- Height of netting
- Spacing of vertical wires

E.g. HT8/80/15

HT – high tensile, 8 horizontal wires, 80 height of netting, 15 spacing of vertical wires (cm).

High tensile wire

High tensile requires fewer intermediate posts and strong straining posts. Grades:

- Heavy – Industrial, coastal, high stocking rates
- Medium – Normal use
- Light – Economy

Wire netting

Chicken wire or hexagonal wire mesh to BS EN 10223–2:1998
Should not be strained. Hung on high tensile wire with netting rings

13 mm Fruit cages
19 mm Thatching (keeping out small sparrows)
25 mm Chicken runs
28 mm Rabbit proof
50 mm Poultry, game proof
75 mm general purpose
100 mm sheep proof.

Deer fencing

Netting options:

- High tensile hinged joint deer netting
- Lightweight hexagonal mesh netting
- High tensile plastic mesh netting most suitable due to light weight, range of mesh sizes and re-rolling ability

Line wires:

- 2 mm diameter zinc coated
- At top and bottom but more tin at the bottom half where pressure from deer may be more.

Posts:

- Timber or metal
- Straining and corner posts – full length 2.4 m
- Minimum height to top of netting – 1.8 m

Rabbit fencing

- Minimum height 800 mm to top of netting

Line wires:

- At top and bottom (ground level)
- 2–4 mm diameter

Netting:

- 31 mm hexagonal 18 gauge mesh netting
- 150 mm netting to go under ground or on the surface but covered with turves and turned inwards towards rabbits

Posts – timber or metal:

- Straining and corner posts – Full length 2.13 m

2.12 Composts, Mulches and Manufactured Soil

Compost
Benefits of compost use
- Nutrient supply, e.g. nitrogen and phosphate in a slow release form; potash in a readily available form; primary nutrients such as such as calcium, magnesium, sulphur; and trace elements such as zinc, copper, manganese and boron.
- Reduced nutrient losses and improved cation exchange capacity – enables soil to retain nutrients more easily.
- Better plant survival and growth – added organic matter will improve soil structure and nutrients for healthy growth.
- Reduction on soil compaction – organic matter improves the strength of soils making them more penetrable and workable.
- Improvement in soil water holding capacity and infiltration of water.
- Control of erosion and weeds (through mulching with compost) – physical barrier which degrades over time, reduces chances of wind erosion of light soils.
- Micro-organisms increase soil aggregation, recycle nutrients and suppress soil borne diseases.
- Cost benefits. Possibly reduce the requirements for fertilizers and (as mulches) save in need for herbicide treatments.

Product specification

Soil improvement for general landscape works
Planting beds, trees, shrub and herbaceous planting and turf establishment.

Horticultural parameters	Reported as (units of measure)	Recommended range
pH	pH units (1:5 water extract)	6.5–8.7
Electrical conductivity	μs/cm or mS/m (1.5 water extract)	3000 μs/cm or 300 mS/m max
Moisture content	% m/m of fresh weight	35–55
Organic matter content	% dry weight basis	>25
Particle sizing	% m/m of air dried sample passing the selected mesh aperture	95% pass through 25 mm screen 90% pass through 10 mm screen
C:N ratio		20:1 maximum

Top dress and grass maintenance

Horticultural parameters	Reported as (units of measure)	Recommended range
pH	pH units (1:5 water extract)	7.0–8.7
Electrical conductivity	μs/cm or mS/m (1.5 water extract)	2500 μs/cm or 250 mS/m max
Moisture content	% m/m of fresh weight	35–55
Organic matter content	% dry weight basis	>25
Particle sizing	%m/m of air dried sample passing the selected mesh aperture	100% pass through 10 mm screen
C:N ratio		20:1 maximum

Topsoil manufacturing

Horticultural parameters	Reported as (units of measure)	Recommended range
pH	pH units (1:5 water extract)	7.0–8.7
Electrical conductivity	µs/cm or mS/m (1.5 water extract)	2000 µs/cm or 200 mS/m max
Moisture content	% m/m of fresh weight	35–55
Organic matter content	% dry weight basis	>25
Particle sizing	% m/m of air dried sample passing the selected mesh aperture	99% pass through 25 mm screen 99% pass through 10 mm screen
C:N Ratio		20:1 maximum

Mulch

Horticultural parameters	Reported as (units of measure)	Recommended range
pH	pH units (1:5 water extract)	6.0–9.0
Electrical conductivity	µs/cm or mS/m (1.5 water extract)	3000 µs/cm or 300 mS/m max
Moisture content	%m/m of fresh weight	35–55
Organic matter content	% dry weight basis	>30
Particle sizing	% m/m of air dried sample passing the selected mesh aperture	99% pass through 75 mm screen >25 pass through 10 mm screen

The British Standards Institutions Publically Available Specification for Composted Materials Safety Related Parameters and Limits. (PAS 100 specification) PAS sets out the minimum quality criteria for composted products.

Contaminant parameters	Reported as (units of measure)	Limits
Chemical		
Cadmium (Cd)	mg/kg (ppm) dry matter	<1.5
Copper (Cu)	mg/kg (ppm) dry matter	<200
Chromium (Cr)	mg/kg (ppm) dry matter	<100
Lead (Pb)	mg/kg (ppm) dry matter	<200
Nickel (Ni)	mg/kg (ppm) dry matter	<50
Mercury (Hg)	mg/kg (ppm) dry matter	<1
Zinc (Zn)	mg/kg (ppm) dry matter	<400
Biological		
Salmonella spp.	MPN/25 g	Absent
Eschericha coli	CFU g^{-1}	<1000CFU g^{-1}
Weed seeds	Viable propagules/litre	<5 maximum
Phytotoxicity	Score % of control	80% minimum
Physical		
Glass, metal, plastic of which plastic	% m/m air dried sample >2 mm	<0.5*
	% m/m air dried sample >2 mm	<0.25*
Stones and other consolidated mineral contaminants	% m/m air dried sample	<7*

*It should be noted that the target limit for these specific contaminants should be zero or near zero.
%m/m = %mass.

For all contracts, the contractor should be able to provide a sample and certificate for approval by the Contract Administrator.

Applications can vary depending on the requirement:

- For use on the surface as a topdressing
- For use on the surface as a mulch
- For use to mix in with soil at a certain ratio depending on the type and quality of soil for backfill of tree pits or planting beds

Mulches

Uses:

- Aesthetics – to make planting area look neat and tidy
- To suppress weed growth
- Informal path surface – domestic situations
- Erosion control
- To conserve soil moisture
- Reduces effects of ground freezing

Materials

Mulches are mostly bark based, wood based or composted plant residue but can also be straw, shredded paper or biodegradable matting.

Bark Mulches – specification

- Bark mulches are from the conifer species generally and are graded into nominal bark particle sizes from 1–125 mm
- The pH should be between 4.5 and 5.5, there should be minimal fines
- Where possible they should be fire tested to BS 4790:1987
- For ground cover and amenity shrub planting a minimum layer of 50 mm should be spread over the topsoil. Elsewhere for larger shrubs and trees the depth should be 75 mm
- Wood content varies according to the product but should be specified as a percentage
- All should be pest and weed free and should not have been treated with Methyl Bromide or any additives
- Excess volatile products should have been driven from the product during the maturing process
- Colour should also be specified

Urban tree soil

Made up of a mix of selected and graded silica sand and green waste to add organic matter, urban tee soil is sometimes known as 'Amsterdam Tree Soil' because it was first formed through research carried out between the Dutch University of Wageningen and the Mechanics Department of the City of Amsterdam. The concept came about in Holland during the 1970s when the optimum growing medium for urban trees in terms of particle size, shape, compaction, levels of clay, organic content, pH values and nutrient status was studied.

A mix of selected and graded silica sand and green waste to add organic matter.

Advantages:

- It replaces costly imported topsoil and has consistent quality and availability
- Offers more structural stability and better drainage
- Improves access of water and oxygen to the root system

Application:

- Mainly urban situations where good quality topsoil is not readily available and structural stability is required
- As backfill around the rootball in a tree pit

Manufactured soil

All manufactured topsoil should be in accordance with BS 3882 2007 Specification for topsoil.

Where grass/turf or landscape planting is to occur, it is suggested that any manufactured topsoil contains a minimum of 5% organic matter (as measured by loss on ignition) and a 2–2–1 P–K–Mg (and ideally 3–3–2) nutrient index. The minimum nutrient index levels will usually be surpassed when compost is used as a component in the manufactured topsoil; therefore, additional fertilization will not typically be necessary.

Source/Copyright: Heicom.

Compost Specifications for the Landscape Industry – developed by WRAP in conjunction with the Landscape Institute, BALI and NBS. Melcourt Industries.

2.13 Soft Landscape Maintenance

Anally retentive? What makes you think that Edith?

Soft landscape maintenance

Component	Objective	Task	Time of Year	Frequency
Trees	To ensure that trees remain in a healthy, attractive and safe condition	Inspection of mature trees	March–September	Annually
		Selective felling of over mature/declining specimens	October–February	As required
		Selective thinning of plantings	October–February	Every 10 years
		Pruning and repair of wounds	October–February	As required
		Removal/adjustment of stakes and ties	As necessary following inspection	As required
		Watering	As necessary depending on weather condition-largely May–August	As required-daily in dry spells
		New planting to broaden/supplement diversity of tree stock	October–March	Annually or as required
		Review of tree survey information and tagging	March–September	Every 5 years
		Other works – removal of debris trapped in branches, etc.	As necessary following inspection	As required
Riparian Woodland	To ensure woodland remains in a healthy, attractive and safe condition.	Remove all self-set seedlings from all naturally riparian woodland areas.	January	Annually

Riparian Woodland (*Continued*)		Selective thinning and pruning to be undertaken to ensure that there is sufficient light through the tree canopy to enable healthy growth of the under-storey planting.	As necessary	As required
Shrubs				
Ornamental shrubs and herbaceous material	To create healthy, attractive shrub mixes. Beds should be kept weed-free and any pernicious weed such as dock and thistle removed immediately	Pruning to encourage best display of given species, taking account of natural habit and form		
		• Winter flowering	Prune Spring	Annually
		• Shrubs flowering between March and July	Immediately after the flowering period	Annually
		• Shrubs flowering between July and October	Prune back to old wood in Winter	Annually
		Coppicing (dogwood)	February	Annually
		Chemical weed control	Spring and Summer and only where other methods of control have failed	As required
		Manual weed control	Throughout. Spring	Monthly October–March
		Fertilizing		Annually

(Continued)

Soft landscape maintenance (*Continued*)

Component	Objective	Task	Time of Year	Frequency
Shrubs (*Continued*)		New planting	Bare root stock October–March. Containerized stock all year	As required
		Litter/debris removal	Throughout	Daily
		Turn over soil – break up ground	April	Annually
		Watering	As necessary depending on weather condition – generally May–August	As required
		Re-mulching	March after turning over soil and when soil is moist	Annually
		Trimming edges to beds	May–September after grass cutting	Weekly
		Half Moon edging	March–April	Annually as required
		Staking of herbaceous planting. Other works – removal of dead plants, thinning of plants, etc.	June–October	As required
		Deadheading herbaceous planting	Spring	As required
		Dividing herbaceous plants	Winter, open weather	Annually if required

		Trimming	April–October	5 times
Hedges:	To maintain a healthy, attractive manicured hedges			
		Reshaping	Hard prune Oct-Feb	Annually if required
		Chemical Weed Control along baseline	In Winter and Summer and only where other methods of control have failed.	Annually
		Manual Weed Control	Throughout	Monthly
		Fertilising	Spring	Annually
		New Planting	October–March	Annually, if required
		Litter/Debris	Throughout	Daily
		Watering	As necessary depending on weather condition – largely May–August	As required – daily in dry spells
Bulbs: Within ornamental planted areas	Display to best advantage	Cut off dead heads	Check twice weekly during flowering period	As required
		Tie up dead leaves neatly when flowering is over	Throughout according to flowering time	Annually
		Remove dead leaves when completely brown	Throughout according to flowering time	Annually as required
		Replanting if failed	According to species & flowering time	Annually as required
		Check for need to split and replant	Just after flowering while still green	Annually
		Split and replant	According to species & flowering time	Annually, as required

(Continued)

Soft landscape maintenance (*Continued*)

Component	Objective	Task	Time of Year	Frequency
Climbers	Ensure healthy growth according to species	Treat as for shrubs but also check they are attached to support	Throughout	As required following inspection
Amenity Grass	Good sward of even colour and smooth gradients. Height maximum 50 mm	Eroded areas: repair, rotovate to 150 mm, 100 mm topsoil if required, seed with BSH mix 19	May–September	As required
		Litter/debris removal	Throughout	Daily
		Grass cut, leave arisings, trim edges and collect trimmings - remove	April–October	Every 2 weeks
		Fertiliser – Spring	April	Annually
		Fertiliser – Autumn	October	Annually
		Scarification	March	Annually
		Spiking	Autumn	Twice annually
		Reforming of edges to paths and planting	Autumn	Annually

Long Grass with Bulbs:	Good sward of even colour and smooth gradients.	Eroded areas: repair, rotovate to 150 mm, 100 mm topsoil if required, seed with BSH mix 19	May–September	As required
	Height maximum 100 mm	Litter/debris removal	Throughout	Weekly
		Grass cut after bulbs have flowered remove arisings, trim edges and remove trimmings-	June–October	Every 4 weeks
		Fertiliser – Spring	April	Annually
		Fertiliser – Autumn	October	Annually
Wildflower Areas		Eroded areas: repair, rotovate to 150 mm seed with BSH mix WFG 13	May–September	As required
		Litter/debris removal	Throughout	Weekly
		Cut to 40–70 mm All arisings – remove from site	March/April depending on species in mix	Twice Annually
		Cut to 40 mm after flowering. All arisings – remove from site	September/October, depending on species in mix	Annually

2.14 Soft Landscape Maintenance Programme – Routine Operations

Below are examples of maintenance programmes and schedules. These will require amending, depending on the degree of maintenance required for the particular situation.

Operation	January	February	March	April	May	June	July	August	September	October	November	December	Quantity
GRASS													
Cut (litter collection prior)													16–20
Fertilizer			1							1			2
Weedkiller					1								1*
TREES													
Prune		1											1
Refirm		1											1
Check ties and stakes		1											1
Hand Weed						1	1	1	1				4
Weedkiller				1						1			2*
Fertilizer					1								1
Replacements													1*

SHRUBS, CONIFERS AND HEDGES											
Prune	1										1
Refirm	1										1
Replacements	1										1*
Fertilizer			1		1	1	1		1			6
Hand weed			1						1			2*
Weedkiller		1										
LITTER COLLECTION												
Shrub areas												52
Grass												52
POST AND WIRE FENCING												
Routine operations												26
WATERING												*

*Only if required.

2.15 Green Roofs

Why have green roofs?	**Benefits** • Reduces flow of run-off into drainage systems • Improves the climatic environment • Increases the waterproof membrane's life expectancy by protecting it • Reduces noise and harmful environmental factors in the atmosphere • Improves the thermal insulation properties of the roof • Can provide amenity spaces with wildlife benefits
Types of green roof systems	• Extensive • Intensive • Semi Intensive

Extensive green roof systems	• Lightweight systems with shallow substrate depths of 50–150 mm that can be installed on almost any roof deck
	• Extensive substrate
	• Access is for maintenance only, i.e. inaccessible for amenity or recreation
	• Hardy, low maintenance plants only (drought and frost resistant) such as:
	  – Moss + Sedums
	  – Sedums + Moss + Herbs
	  – Sedums + Grasses + Herbs
	  – Grasses + Herbs
	• No integrated irrigation systems – the water is stored in the growing medium which evaporates slowly and reduces run off
	• Can be used on flat roofs (minimum fall of 1 in 60) and sloping roofs with a pitch of up to 25%

Intensive green roof systems	• Intensive substrate has higher organic content to support a variety of plants and is laid to depths of 150–1500 mm • Full access available for recreational and leisure use with hard and soft landscape. NB Roof structure must be designed for access by people and heavy loading of landscape features (e.g. substrate, lawn, hedges, trees, small and large shrubs, walls, water features and hard surfaces) • Greater drainage depth provides greater storage of water • Drainage medium also acts as sub base to support hard landscape features • Irrigation system required • High maintenance • Not suitable for pitched roofs

Semi-intensive green roof systems	• Lightweight with shallow substrate depth of 100–200 mm
	• Semi-intensive substrate with some irrigation
	• Limited access – e.g. from patio areas and for maintenance
	• Will support a wider variety of plants than intensive but still requiring minimal maintenance:
	  – Grass + Herbs
	  – Shrubs + Woody Plants
	  – Woody Plants

Design considerations	There are a number of design considerations when proposing a green roof system:
	  • Proposed use of the roof – high access or limited access
	  • Structural load bearing capacity of the roof
	  • Roof build up proposed by the Architect – is it Warm, Cold or Inverted (this relates to the location of the insulation layer and will affect the type of membrane specified)
	  • Roof falls/pitch
	  • Height of building and effects of wind and wind uplift
	  • Maintenance and safety
	  • Fire prevention – extensive green roofs require specific design features to make them fire resistant such as gravel or concrete fire breaks every 40 m or a minimum width of 1 m or height of 300 mm; a minimum 30 mm depth of substrate with no more than 20% weight organic soil; gravel safety strips around roof penetrations and in front of walls with openings

Make up of green roofs	Green roofs are constructed in layers and the complexity of the layers depends on your design considerations: • **Carefully selected plants** – see over • **Growing medium** – see below • **Filter membrane** – to prevent fine particles being washed out of the substrate into the drainage medium • **Drainage element** – designed to retain water even on sloping roofs • **Moisture mat** – retains moisture and nutrients and provides mechanical protection to the root barrier and waterproof membrane • **Root barrier** – prevents roots from affecting the waterproofing. The type thickness and method of installation depends on the nature of the landscape and the shape and slope of the roof • **Waterproof membrane** – requires to be durable and have a long lifespan • **Thermal insulation** – location depends on whether the architect has chosen a warm, cold or inverted roof design • **Structural roof deck** – designed to support the weight of the green roof and any live loads • **Vapour control** – layer situated between the structural deck and insulation to prevent the formation of condensation
Green roof substrate	The mix and structure of the substrate will depend on the plants specified and their requirement for water retention, aeration and nutrients. Many companies specializing in waterproof membranes and green roof systems have their specified mixes of substrate depending on whether it is for an extensive or intensive system.
Extensive substrate	Suitable only for hardy plants such as Sedums: • Coarse grain size • Low water retention capacity • High air volume • Low nutrient reserves • Fire retardant to DIN 4102

Semi-intensive substrate	Intensive substrate mixed with some organic matter which increases the range of hardy plants that can be specified • Medium Grain size • Medium water retention capacity • Medium air volume • Medium nutrient reserves
Intensive substrate	Greater percentage of organic material enables a full range of plants to be specified • Fine grain size • High water retention capacity • Low air volume • High nutrient reserves
Roof drainage	Landscaped roofs retain a high percentage of the rainwater that falls on the roof but there is always an excess of water that needs to be drained. This can be in the form of roof outlets, gutters and water spouts. All companies specializing in waterproof membranes for green roofs have purpose designed integrated systems for roof drainage and can offer design advice on the number of outlets and sizes proposed based on: • Area of green roof • Local rainfall intensity • Building life and safety factor • Frequency and size of outlets and downpipes There should always be a minimum of two outlets, or one outlet and one overflow, for safety reasons. Outlets must be kept clear of vegetation by installing inspection chambers or grills Minimum roof falls for drainage are: • Extensive roofs – 1:60 to 1:40 • Intensive roofs – 1:80 to 1:40

Plant selection extensive green roof	Sedum Carpet on min 50 mm depth of growing medium	Rockery type plants on min 80 mm depth of growing medium
	Sedum album (different varieties)	All Sedums as per 50 mm depth substrate
	Sedum ewersii	Achillea tomentosa
	Sedum floriferum 'Weilhnstephaner Gold'	Allium senescens sp montanum
	Sedum hispanicum var. minus	Dianthus cathusianorum
	Sedum hybridum 'Immergrunchen'	Dianthus deltoids
	Sedum sexangulare	Dianthus plumarius
	Sedum spurium – pink, white, red	Hieracium aurantiacum
	Sedum reflexum	Hieracium pilosella
		Koeleria glauca
		Petrorhagia saxifrage
		Potentilla neumanniana
		Saponaria ocymoides
		Saxifraga paniculata
		Sempervirens – hybrids
		Thymus serpyllum
Plant selection semiintensive green roof	Herbs, grasses and sedums on 100–150 mm growing medium	
	All sedums as above Allium tuberosum	Helianthemum nummularium
		Helicotrichon sempervirens
	Aster amellus	Lavandula angustifolia
	Carex humilis	Melica ciliate
	Carex ornithopoda	Oenothera missouriensis
	Dianthus carthusianorum	Origanum vulgare
	Dianthus deltoids	Pennisetum alopecuroides 'Compressum'
	Dianthus gratianopolitanus	Prunella grandiflora
	Festuca gratianopolitanus	Saxifraga paniculata
		Sedum telphium 'Herbstfreude'
		Tecrium chamaedrys
		Thymus vulgaris
Plant selection for intensive green roofs	These can include any climbers, shrubs, perennials, grasses and small trees species suitable for amenity planting schemes	

Source: Alumasc Green Roof Systems. www.alumasc-exteriors.co.uk

2.16 Geotextiles

What are geotextiles?

Geotextiles are made of synthetic fibres and are woven or non-woven to produce a flexible blanket like product.

Landscape uses

- Prevention of weed growth – bark mulch
- Moisture conservation
- A filter layer, i.e. beneath a vegetated roof
- A weed control layer, i.e. beneath a gravel path
- Erosion control
- Root barriers
- Sediment entrapment

Civil engineering uses

- Construction materials can be adversely affected by soils if allowed to intermix. For example the load bearing capacity of a road will be greatly reduced if fine grained subgrade soil particles intermingle with the roads granular sub base. Geotextiles prevent this
- Ease of spreading granular material over soft areas
- Minimize the need for excavation and replacement of the original ground
- Allow work to continue during bad weather
- Aid in filling of layers without the risk of construction vehicles getting 'stuck in the mud'
- Large scale erosion control and sea defences
- Prevention of contamination

Materials used in geotextiles

- Jute matting – biodegradable
- Straw or coir (coconut fibre)
- Wire
- Plastic
- PVC coated mesh
- Polymer matting

Laying

In rolls and pinned to substrate if required.

'Non-woven' textiles for ground stabilization

The overall stabilization function can be divided into three fundamental components:

- Separation component – the geotextile prevents the intermixing of the granular layer and soft subgrade
- Filtration component – the geotextile allows controlled passage of excess water from the subgrade
- Confinement component – restrains the lateral movement of the material at the bottom of the granular layer

Where the subgrade is very soft (CBR $\leq$ undrained sheer strength $\leq 10 \, \text{kN/m}^2$) it may be prudent to use grades of geotextile which have a higher tensile strength to aid constructability. Example – over soft peat or sledge capping layers.

Design and selection of non-woven geotextile

- Determine the thickness of the granular layer above the geotextile
- Select the appropriate grade of geotextile to be used

The thickness of the sub-base and/or capping should be derived from appropriate national standards. Construction is largely dependant on the strength of the subgrade which is dictated by its moisture content. Field data should provide the subgrade CBR values. The grade selected must be sufficiently robust to resist the installation of the stabilized structure. The lower the subgrade strength and the larger the stones in contact with the geotextile, the more robust the geotextile must be.

Refer to Terram Ltd 'Ground stabilization' guidelines for more detailed information on laying of Terram non-woven products.

3 Planning and Legislation

3.1 Planning and Development Control

Legislation	• Town and Country Planning Act 1990.* • Planning and Compensation Act 1991. • Planning and Compulsory Purchase Act 2004. • The Planning etc (Scotland) 2006. • Planning (Northern Ireland) Order 1991 and Amendment 2003. • Detailed interpretation of development is given in the General Permitted Development Order (GPDO) 1995, revised in 2003. In Scotland, the current GPDO dates from 1992.
The need for Planning Permission	Permission is required for any development of land under current legislation. Development is defined as: • The carrying out of building operations, engineering operations, mining operations or other operations in, on, over or under land or the making of any material change of use of any buildings or other land.
Is Planning Permission Always Required?	**NO** • Development before 1947. • Certain activities not considered as development. • Permitted development. • Other developments including Annex 2 Environmental Impact Assessments (EIA). • 'Changes of use' that always require consent. **YES** • Designated/bad neighbour development. • Projects likely to have significant environmental effects, i.e. Annex 1 EIA.

*NB: The New Planning Reform Bill is due out in early 2009.

Activities not Considered to be Development	• Works that do not affect a building's external appearance. • Local authority and statutory undertaker work to highways and services. • Uses within the curtilage of a dwelling incidental to its enjoyment as a house. • Forestry and agriculture. • Formation of hard-standings or access except in Conservation Areas. • Change of use within a Use Class (refer to use Class Orders). • The formation of hard-standings, except in Conservation Areas. • The formation of a means of access to a road which is not a trunk or classified road, except in Conservation Areas. • The installation of solar panels and velux windows on up to 10% of a roof area, except in Conservation Areas. • Developments in Enterprise Zones, Special Protection Zones (SPZs) and Special Development Orders.
Permitted Development	Limited enlargement or improvement of a dwelling. Forming access to a minor road. Painting the exterior of a building except for advertisement. 31 Classes of permitted development (refer to GPDO). Class 1: Development within the curtilage of a dwelling. Class 2: Gates, fences below 1.0 m high by a vehicular highway; less than 2m elsewhere. Class 4: Temporary buildings and uses. Classes 6 and 7: Agricultural and forestry buildings and works.

Changes of Use that Always Require Consent	• Separation of a building into two or more separate dwelling houses. • Deposit of refuse or waste material on land already used for this purpose which enlarges the surface area of or increases the height above the land adjoining the site. • Display of advertisements on any part of a building not normally used for that purpose. • Fish farms.
Planning Permission Types	• **Full**: All details approved. Conditions may be imposed. • **Outline**: Consent in principle. Reserved matters to be agreed. • **Approval of Reserved Matters**: Approval of, for example, siting, design, external appearance, access, landscape. • **Variation of Planning Consent**: Insignificant changes to an approval already given. • **Notice of Intention to Develop (NID)**: Procedure to publicise local authority developments.
Planning Permission Application	• **Application form**: Details about the applicant or their agents; detail of the purpose, location, timing and cost of the development; Certification of neighbour notification; Agricultural status of the land; Confirmation that the plans are available for view for 21 days; Ownership certificates. • **Advertisements**: Required for developments in Conservation Areas and for designated developments/bad neighbour developments. • **Plans**: Location plan; Site plan; Drawings including floor plans; Elevations; Section drawing. • **Fee**: Depends on size and type of development (refer to guidance note in LPA application forms). • **Possible additional information**: Environmental statement; Design statement; Access statement; Transport assessment; Draft travel plan; Flood risk assessment/drainage strategy; Affordable housing statement; Open space; Sustainability appraisal; Landscaping; Tree survey; Noise impact assessment; Air quality assessment; Assessment for treatment of foul sewage; Utilities statement; Energy statement.

Planning Permission Procedure	**Person applies for planning permission**: • Full, outline, reserved matters, variation or notice of intention to develop. **Local Planning Authority (LPA)**: • Considers landscape design. • May call in further information. • Undertakes consultations. • Complies with guidelines. • May require EIA. • May require bond and or Planning Obligation. **Local Planning Authority decides to**: • Grant unconditional permission. • Grant permission with conditions. • Refuse permission.
Dealing with Refusal	• With the client's approval accept the refusal. • Recommend amendments to the proposals to suit LPA's reasons for refusal and resubmit. • Appeal. • Request judicial review.
Duration of Planning Permission	• Full planning permission – 3 years. • Outline planning permission – 3 years with 2 years for details and reserved matters to be resolved.

3.2 Listed and Protected Areas for Heritage, Amenity, Landscape Quality, Cultural and Natural Habitat

Protected Site/Item	Legislation	Application	Purpose	Governing Body
Tree Preservation Orders	Town and Country Planning Act; The Town and Country Planning (Trees) Regulations 1999; The Planning and Compensation Act 1991; The Forestry Act 1967	UK	Protects individual/groups of selected trees and woodlands if their removal would have a significant impact on the environment and its enjoyment by the public. Prevents harming trees covered by an order unless consent is obtained from the local authority. Secures the replanting of trees the felling of which has been permitted.	Local Planning Authority
Conservation Areas	Town and Country Planning Act 1990 and Planning (Listed Buildings and Conservation Areas) Act 1990. (Listed Buildings and Buildings in Conservation Areas) (Amendment) (Scotland) Regulations 2006.Town and Country Amenities Act 1974 Planning (NI) Order 1993 and The Planning (Conservation Areas) (Consultation) Regs 2006	UK	Protects areas of special architectural or historic interest, the character or appearance of which is desirable to preserve or enhance under a Conservation Area plan. Includes trees if not already protected by a TPO. Consent required for any alteration.	Local Planning Authority

(Continued)

Protected Site/Item	Legislation	Application	Purpose	Governing Body
Buildings of Special Architectural or Historic Interest – Listed Buildings	Town and Country Planning Act 1990 and Planning (Listed Buildings and Conservation Areas) Act 1990. (Listed Buildings and Buildings in Conservation Areas) (Amendment) (Scotland) Regulations 2006 Town and Country Amenities Act 1974 Planning (NI) Order 1991	UK	Protects buildings which have been listed for the contribution their exterior makes to the architectural or historic interest of a group of buildings or preserves any feature fixed to the building or contained within its curtilage (can include the landscape). Consent required for any alteration.	English Heritage; CADW (Welsh Historic Monuments); Secretary of State and Historic Scotland; DOENI – Built Heritage Local Planning Authority
Ancient Monuments and Archaeological Areas	Ancient Monuments and Archaeological Areas Act 1979 Historic Monuments and Archaeological Objects (NI) order 1995	UK	Protects scheduled monuments, that are of national importance. Scheduled monument consent is required for any alterations or works affecting the site. The legislation also enables rescue archaeological investigations/records to be made on sites deemed to be of archaeological interest.	English Heritage; Secretary of State and Historic Scotland; CADW (Welsh Historic Monuments) DOENI – Built Heritage: Local Authority

Historic Gardens and Designed Landscapes	Town and Country Planning Act Planning (NI) Order 1991	UK	Presumption against development, likely to have an adverse effect on the integrity, landscape setting or distinctive character of gardens and designed landscapes listed in the inventory by the governing body.	English Heritage; Secretary of State and Historic Scotland; CADW (Welsh Historic Monuments) DOENI – Built Heritage: Local Authority
Environmentally Sensitive Areas (ESA) Agri-Environment Schemes	Agriculture Act 1986

EU Common Agricultural Policy through the Rural Development Programme | UK

EU | Outstanding ecology, landscape, archaeology, architecture or historical interest threatened by changing agricultural practice. | DEFRA SEERAD; Welsh Assembly; Agriculture Department; Department of Agriculture for NI |
| Green Belt | London Home Counties Green Belt Act 1938 Town and Country Planning Act 1947 | Home Counties UK | Protect urban and rural amenity. | Local Planning Authority |

(Continued)

Protected Site/Item	Legislation	Application	Purpose	Governing Body
Areas of Great Landscape Value (AGLV)	Town and Country Planning Act 1947	UK	Rural amenity.	Local Planning Authority
Country Parks	Countryside Act 1981, Countryside Sctoland Act 1968	UK	Pleasure grounds.	Local authority
Areas of Outstanding Natural Beauty(AONB)	National Parks and Access to the Countryside Act 1947; Countryside and Rights of Way (CROW) Act 2000	England and Wales	Enhance, promote, protect natural beauty and character.	CCW; CA; ES Local authority
National Scenic Areas (NSA), National Heritage Areas (NHA)	SO Circular 1980; National Heritage (Scotland) Act 1991	Scotland	Protect outstanding flora, fauna, geology and physiology.	SNH Local authorities
Hedgerows	Environment Act 1995; Hedgerow Regulations 1997	Act: England/Wales; EU Regulations: UK	UK: Protect important hedgerows; EU: Protect linear features for their role helping biodiversity.	Local authorities; DEFRA; SEERAD
Badgers and Setts	Wildlife and Countryside Act 1981, B 1973, 92	UK	Protect badgers/setts.	MAFF; SO-AFD
Bats and Bat Roosts	Wildlife and Countryside Act 1981	UK	Protect bats/roosts.	EN; CCW; SNH
Limestone Pavements	Wildlife and Countryside Act 1981	UK	Protect limestone pavements.	EN; CCW; SNH; Local authority

Site of Special Scientific Interest	National Parks and Access to the Countryside Act 1949; Wildlife and Countryside Act 1981, 1985; Countryside (Scotland) Act 1981; Countryside and Rights of Way Act 2000; National Conservation (Scotland) Act 2004	UK	Protect flora, fauna, geology, physiography.	EN; CCW; SNH Land owner, occupier, lessee, third parties
Nature Reserves (NR)	National Parks and Access to the Countryside Act 1947	UK	Study of flora, fauna, geology and physiography.	EN; CCW; SNH Local authority Occupier, owner, lessee
National NR	Wildlife and Countryside Act 1981	UK	As above but of national importance.	EN; CCW; SNH; ES and or RSPB, etc.
Marine NR	WC Act 1981	UK	As above, marine	EN; CCW; SNH
UK Species and Habitats	Wildlife and Countryside Act 1981; Countryside and Rights of Way Act 2000; National Conservation (Scotland) Act 2004; Conservation on International Trade to Endangered Species (CITES)	EU	Protection of species and habitats; conservation of biodiversity.	EN; CCW; SNH Local authoritiesLand owner, occupier, lessee, third parties, all.

(Continued)

Protected Site/Item	Legislation	Application	Purpose	Governing Body
Ramsar Sites	Ramsar Convention 1971	World	Protect wetland ecology, botany, zoology, limnology, hydrology.	IUCN; EN; CCW; SNH; ES
Special Protection Areas (SPA)	EC Act 1972 EC Directive 79/409	EC	Protection of wild birds and their habitats.	EN; CCW; SNH; ES
World Heritage Sites	Convention 1972	World	Protect man-made treasures.	UNESCO; ES
Habitats and Species	WC Act 1981, ECD 92/43	UK	Protect wildlife habitats and species in general and listed species with additional protection.	EN; CCW; SNH; NI

In addition to the national designations described above, many local authorities have undertaken landscape assessments, habitat surveys, access reviews and the like as a foundation for Structure Plans, Local Plans and Inter-District habitat and amenity management strategies.

When dealing with a particular area or site, a prudent Landscape Architect would check with the local authority, region or county for information on such designations as these may materially affect applications for development consent, provision of grants and inter-agency co-operation.

3.3 Tree Preservation Orders

"That's not quite what we at the council had in mind Mr. Smith …"

Background	• Local Planning Authorities (LPAs) are required to make appropriate provision for the planting and preservation of trees under The Town and Country Planning Act. Planning Policy Guidance also states that LPAs should seek to protect trees where they have natural heritage value or contribute to the character or amenity of an area.
Legislation UK	• Planning and Compensation Act 2004. • Town and Country Planning (Scotland) Act 1997. • The Town and Country Planning (Trees) Regulations 1999. • Planning (Northern Ireland) Order 1991 Part 2 TPOs.
Purpose	• To prevent the felling, mutilation and harming to the health of a tree or woodland covered by an order unless consent is obtained from the LPA. • Protects selected trees and woodlands if their removal would have a significant impact on the environment and its enjoyment by the public.
Types	• Individual • Groups • Woodland.

Who Makes a TPO	• LPA • Special arrangements exist for National Parks, The Broads, Enterprise Zones and Urban Development Areas (UDAs).
Exemptions to an Order	• Hedges, bushes, shrubs • Trees on Crown Land (without consent) • Forestry Authority interest in land (unless consent is obtained).
Exemptions to Obtaining Consent	• Dead, dying or dangerous trees. • Preventing/abating a nuisance. • Trees on airfields/defence installations. • Ornamental fruit trees and orchards. • Forestry Authority plans of operation. • Trees on/adjacent to Ancient Monuments or churchyards. • Work by a statutory undertaker but not utility co's (except in certain situations, e.g. safety). • Work permitted as part of planning permission.
Procedure for Making a TPO	• A TPO must be in the form of the model order contained in the Regulations. • The Order must define the position of the trees, the number, species and location, using an OS map at 1:1250 or 1:2500 for woodlands. • A copy of the Order and map and grounds for it being made is served to the occupiers of the land and also at a place where it can be inspected. • Objections may be made to appropriate authority within 28 days. • Copy of the Order is served to the Conservator of Forests. • LPAs are advised to inform affected neighbours and provide a site notice if the TPO will affect the interests of the neighbourhood.
Penalties	• On summary conviction, to a fine up to £20,000.00 – Magistrates Court. • On conviction on indictment, to an unlimited fine – Crown Court.

3.4 Hedgerow Legislation

George spent many a sunny afternoon plotting the demise of Arthur and his hedge …

Legislation	Key Facts
• **The Environment Act 1995 (Part V)** • **The Hedgerow Regulations 1997** **Covers England and Wales only**	Important 'hedgerows may be protected if they are: • In the countryside (not garden hedges). • Over 20 m length and more than 30 years old. • Of significant historic, landscape or wildlife value. • Amendments considered for holly, elm and willow and hedges that form habitat for protected species. • Designated by local planning authority and confirmed by the Secretary of State for the Environment and the Department of the Environment, Food and Rural Affairs (DEFRA).

Legislation	Key Facts
• **Article 8 of the Habitats Directive** • **Government Circulars 06/2005** **UK wide coverage**	• Requires member states to encourage management of linear features used by wildlife for migration, dispersal or genetic exchange. This covers hedges and traditional field boundaries, rivers, ponds and small woods.
• **Antisocial Behaviour Act 2003 Part 8**	• Local Planning Authority, Landscape Architects and Tree Preservation Officers are required to adjudicate on high hedge difficulties between feuding neighbours. • High hedges are classified as barriers to light or access and must be predominantly evergreen. • The Local Planning Authority can serve a Remedial Notice that requires the owner of the hedge to reduce the height (not below 2.0 m above ground level) or remove the hedge.

3.5 Notifiable Weeds

Relevant Legislation	Definitions and Actions
THE WEEDS ACT 1959	• Defines and lists 'Notifiable Weeds'. • Gives powers to the Government to order occupiers of land to prevent the spread of 'Notifiable Weeds'.
'Notifiable Weeds'	Include the following species: • Curled and broadleaved docks – both reduce the purity and value of arable crops. • Field thistles – reduces the purity and value of arable crops. • Ragwort (*Senecio jacobaea*) – poisonous to horses, cattle and goats as it contain pyrrolizidine alkaloids which remain in hay and silage and reduces the value of arable land.
Eradication – Best Practice	• Docks and thistles – spot treat with herbicide treat or dig out. • Ragwort – treat with Glyphosate and leave for 2 weeks before animals are allowed back to graze.
WILDLIFE AND COUNTRYSIDE ACT 1981 Schedule 9 Section 14	Lists species by which it is an offence under the legislation to plant or otherwise cause these species to grow in the wild.
Listed Species	This includes the following: • Japanese Knotweed • Giant Hogweed.
Effects	Plants take over native vegetation, create a monoculture and reduce biodiversity.
Eradication – Best Practice	Japanese Knotweed • In situ Herbicide Treatment – Glysophate or Picloram (if using near watercourse) apply early on in growing season, during growing season, and as the plant is dying back. Requires 4 years treatment.

	• Excavation and removal to landfill (contaminated soil is classified as controlled waste). Required to excavate a minimum area of 7.0 m laterally from the stand and 2.0 m depth which will relate to the extent of the rhizomes. • Excavation and burial on site: Excavate the stand plus 7.0 m laterally and 2.0 m depth and cover with a minimum 5.0 m depth capping layer of soil. • Excavation and Bunding – excavate infected soil and lay on non-penetrable root barrier and treat with herbicide. Cover with capping layer of soil. • Giant Hogweed – treat with herbicide. NB: furocoumarins in the sap can sensitize skin to ultraviolet rays from the sun and cause burning when cutting back of plant.
Notification	Notify Environment Agency and Scottish Environment Protection Agency of intention to use herbicides adjacent to water courses or if digging/cutting Japanese Knotweed as rhizomes can travel down water and re-establish elsewhere.
ENVIRONMENTAL PROTECTION ACT 1990	Japanese Knotweed is classified as 'Controlled Waste' and must be disposed of safely at a licensed landfill site in accordance with EPA Duty of Care Regulations 1991.
Case Law	• Giles v Walker 1890 – owners and occupiers have a duty of care to prevent weed spreading to adjacent land (classified as negligence) and thereby creating a nuisance. • Contractors may commit trespass if they allow weeds to spread from one site to another.

3.6 Environmental Impact Assessment (EIA)

Source Legislation	The EC Directive on 'The Assessment of the Effects of Certain Public and Private Projects on the Environment' adopted on 27 June 1985.
UK Legislation	The Environmental Impact Assessment Directive was amended in March 1997 (EC Directive 97/11/EC amending Directive 85/337/EEC) UK Legislation brought the EC Directive into force: • The Town and Country Planning (Environmental Impact Assessment) (England and Wales) Regulations 1999. • The Environmental Impact Assessment (Scotland) Regulations 1999. • The Planning (Environmental Impact Assessment) Regulations (Northern Ireland) 1999.
When is an Environmental Impact Assessment (EIA) needed?	The Regulations require that certain types of projects which are likely to have significant environmental effects should not proceed until these effects have been systematically assessed. The regulations apply to two separate lists of projects. • Annex/Schedule 1 projects – EIA is required in every case. • Annex/Schedule 2 projects – for which EIA is required only if the particular project in question is judged likely to give rise to *significant* environmental effects (includes scale, sensitivity of location, any complex of adverse effects).
Screening	• The regulations allow a procedure which enables a developer to apply to the planning authority for an opinion on whether an EIA is needed prior to applying for a planning permission. • For all Schedule 2 development the local planning authority (LPA) must adopt its own formal determination of whether or not EIA is required (screening opinion) and provide a written statement as to their reasons for an EIA being required.
Environmental Statement (ES)	ES is submitted alongside the planning application and comprises a document providing 'specified information' (refer to Schedule 4) to enable the assessment of the likely impact upon the environment of the proposed development.

Specified Information	<ul><li>Description of the development.</li><li>Alternatives studied and reasons for choosing the development.</li><li>Data necessary to identify and assess the effects of the development.</li><li>Description of the significant effects on the environment of humans, flora, fauna, soil, water, air, climate, landscape, material assets, cultural heritage.</li><li>Mitigating measures.</li><li>Non-technical summary.</li></ul>
Scoping	Regulation 10 allows developers to obtain a formal (scoping) opinion from the LPA on what should be included in the ES. This ensures that the LPA and the relevant consultees can consider the project and the likely impacts at an early stage and to focus the EIA process on those that are relevant.
Submission Process	<ul><li>LPA receives request from developer for an opinion on need for EIA and carries out screening exercise.</li><li>If EIA is necessary LPA notifies developer within 3 weeks of the date of the receipt of the request, if sufficient information is provided and gives reason.</li><li>LPA puts details on public record.</li><li>Developer notifies LPA in writing that he will produce EIA and scope of EIA is agreed with LPA.</li><li>LPA informs statutory consultees listed in the Regulations who are required to provide relevant information to developer if requested.</li><li>Specialist team assembled and consults statutory and relevant consultees. Environmental Statement (ES) prepared and submitted alongside planning application.</li><li>Applicant publishes notice in press, posts site notice and information on where ES can be inspected for 21 days.</li><li>ES placed on planning register and copies sent to Secretary of State.</li><li>LPA consults statutory consultees who have 14 days to comment.</li><li>LPA considers representations from third parties and statutory consultees and gives decision. It must not be made in less than 21 days but must be within 16 weeks.</li><li>When determining an EIA application the LPA or Secretary of State must inform the public of their decision to grant or refuse the application and their main reasons for it.</li></ul>

Consultees	<ul><li>Principal council (if not LPA).</li><li>Conservancy Councils – (English Nature, Scottish Natural Heritage, Countryside Agency, CC for Wales, Environment Service NI).</li><li>Environment Agency/SEPA/Northern Ireland Environmental Service for Pollution (special waste or pollution).</li><li>Highways Authority.</li><li>Secretary of State.</li><li>Anybody that a planning authority would normally be required to consult as part of a planning application.</li><li>In certain circumstances: HSE – for hazardous operation; Coal Authority – for mining; English Heritage/Historic Scotland/NI Environment and Heritage Service/Welsh Historic Monuments; CADW for listed buildings, DEFRA, SDEFRA for loss of agricultural land, FA for loss of forestry.</li><li>NB: The LPA has discretionary powers to consult beyond the statutory bodies, e.g. specialist interest groups.</li></ul>

3.7 Landscape and Visual Assessment

Legislation	Landscape and Visual Impact Assessment forms part of the Environmental Impact Assessment Regulation requirements under Schedule 4: • The Town and Country Planning (Environmental Impact Assessment) (England and Wales) Regulations 1999. • The Environmental Impact Assessment (Scotland) Regulations 1999. • The Planning (Environmental Impact Assessment) Regulations (Northern Ireland) 1999.
Guidelines	The Landscape Institute and the Institute of Environmental Management and Assessment have produced 'Guidelines for Landscape and Visual Impact Assessment' 2002. The Guidelines set out an outline methodology that should be flexible to suit modifications required during early stages of the project.
Methodology	<u>Baseline studies</u> Review existing landscape and visual resource through: • research and survey work; • classification of landscape into character types; • analysis of information. <u>Description of the proposed development</u> A general description of the siting, layout and characteristics of the proposed development. <u>Consideration of alternatives</u> Description of the main alternatives considered including environmental effects. <u>Stages in the project life cycle</u> A description of the development at each stage in the life cycle and the landscape and visual impacts at: • construction stage; • operational stage; • decommissioning and restoration stage. <u>Identification and assessment of landscape and visual effects</u> • Identify the sources of effects throughout the project life cycle.

	• Identify the nature of the effects *direct* (as a result of the development) and *indirect* (as a result of an associated development secondary to main development) *cumulative*. • Identify the landscape effects in relation to the sensitivity of the landscape; the scale and magnitude. • Identify the visual effects in relation to sensitivity of visual receptors; the scale or magnitude. • Identify the significance of landscape and visual effects. <u>Mitigation</u> Proposals to address likely negative effects on the environment arising from the development through: • avoidance • reduction • remediation • compensation • enhancement. These should be considered for all stages in the project life cycle.
Consultation	<u>Consultation</u> Consultation with the local community and special interest groups is vital during this stage of the assessment and can be carried out through: • correspondence • face to face discussions • presentations and internal public meetings • exhibitions • workshops • leaflets and mailings.

3.8 Landscape Character Assessment

Guidance	'Landscape character assessment: guidance for England and Scotland' Prepared for the Countryside Agency and Scottish Natural Heritage (2002). See also www.countryside.gov.uk/cci/guidance.
Definition	Landscape character assessment is regarded as a tool for identifying features that give a locality its sense of place and distinctiveness. Landscape character has been defined as a 'distinct and recognizable pattern of elements that occur consistently in a particular type of landscape. Particular combinations of geology, landform, soils, vegetation, land use, field patterns and human settlement create character'.
When used	Landscape character assessment may be used as a part of and to guide local plan development policies; studies of development potential and landscape capacity; environmental impact assessment and landscape management proposals. It is different from visual assessment, but may be closely linked to it, for instance when assessing landscape capacity.
Stages in the assessment process	There are six main stages in landscape character assessment: • Define the scope and geographical scale of the study (this is critical to successful completion by the researcher and for the practical use of the study to the client) • Desk study • Field survey • Classification and description • Making judgements – deciding on the approach • Making judgements – drawing conclusions.
England	'The Character of England' (1995) was produced by the Countryside Commission and English Nature in association with English Heritage. The map charts the character and wildlife character of the whole country. Hundred and fifty-nine separate 'character areas' give a concise summary of a region's historic character, landscape and natural history. Twenty-two maritime areas have also been identified. The data base also holds the results of local landscape character assessments including information about the owner, extent and context of landscape character assessment studies, the methodology employed and how it has been applied to inform policy and strategy. The database is accessible via www.ccnetwork.org.uk.

| Scotland and Wales | The landscape character of Scotland and Wales has also been analyzed and mapped, but the Welsh approach, called LANDMAP, uses a different methodology from that used in England and Scotland. The LANDMAP methodology separates landscape into five aspects: geology (geology, geomorphology and hydrology); landscape habitats (vegetation); visual; sensory; historic landscape and cultural landscape. |

3.9 Planting and Water Bodies Near Airfields

Relevant Bodies/ Authorities	**Civil Aviation Authority; Airports Operators Association; General Aviation Awareness Council**
Relevant Guidelines	• Safeguarding Aerodromes Advice Note No. 3 – 'Potential Bird Hazards from Amenity Landscaping and Building Design' 2003. • Civil Aviation Publication 772 – 'Birdstrike Risk Management for Aerodromes Bird Control' 2007.
Consultation	• Aerodromes can lodge 'safeguarding maps' with Planning Authorities that indicate a zone of a 13 km radius from the centre of the aerodrome. • Consultation is required with the aerodrome where hazards to aviation are proposed within that 13 km radius.
Bird Strike Hazards	• Landscaping will attract birds by providing and feeding, nesting and roosting habitats. • Water features including the enhancement of existing wet areas or watercourses or creating new lakes or drainage channels, balancing ponds, SUDS (Sustainable Urban Drainage systems), etc. create a wide range of exploitable habitats for birds. • Hazardous birds include those that form large roosts or flocks (starlings, thrushes, wood pigeons, pigeons finches or rooks) or are attracted to open water (ducks, gulls, waders, herons, coots, moorhen and cormorants) or are large species that could move onto the airfield from nearby water or landscape and cause bird strikes (swans, herons, geese).
Significant Hazards created by Landscape Schemes	• Create dense vegetation that may become a roost for starlings, rooks, woodpigeons and other aviation hazard bird species. • Provide abundant winter food supply in the form of fruits and berries for large flocks of starlings, fieldfares and redwings which may also move onto an adjacent aerodrome to feed on soil invertebrates. • Create standing water or watercourses that attract gulls and other waterfowl which are large and cause increased bird movements between existing waters and the new site over and around the aerodrome.

Safeguarding Strategy	Where a proposed development within 13 km of an aerodrome has the potential to attract hazardous bird species the developer will be required to have undertaken a bird hazard assessment, and modify the proposals to mitigate the risk. This may include a Bird Hazard Management Plan. CAP772 does acknowledge that landscaping schemes attract smaller concentrations of birds from a smaller area and have less potential for increasing bird strike risk than developments such as landfills, sewage treatment plants and wetlands. Therefore bird attraction and potential bird strike risk of most landscape developments, except for wetlands and starling roosts is limited to within 6.5km of an aerodrome or less.
Fruits, Berries and Roosts	Species of plants that are attractive to birds because of their food supply or their roosting/nesting potential.

Species of plants that are attractive to birds because of their food supply or their roosting/nesting potential.

- Berberis spp. (Barberry)
- Cotoneaster spp.
- Crataegus monogyna (Hawthorn)
- Aucuba
- Buddleia
- Callicarpa (Beauty Berry)
- Chaenomeles
- Clerodendrum
- Danae (Butchers Broom)
- Daphne
- Euonymus (Spindle)
- Fagus sylvatica (Beech)
- Fraxinus excelsior (Ash)
- Hypericum (St Johns Wort)
- Lonicera (Honeysuckle)
- Conifers – especially young unthinned plantations.
- Ilex aquifolium (Holly)
- Sorbus aucuparia (Rowan)
- Mahonia
- Malus (Crab Apple)
- Viburnum
- Pernettya (Prickly Heath)
- Prunus avium (Wild Cherry)
- Pyracantha (Firethorn)
- Quercus spp (Oak)
- Rhus (Sumach)
- Ribes (Currant)
- Rosa canina (Dog Rose)
- Sambucus nigra (Elder)
- Skimmia
- Stransvaesia
- Symphoricarpus (Snowberry)
- Taxus (Yew)

Reducing the Attractiveness of Landscape	• Eliminating the most attractive species. • Reducing their numbers and proportions. • Dispersing them among other species so they do not form blocks. • Using varieties that do not produce berries or using male plants only. • Keep Hawthorn hedges trimmed to limit berry production. • Restrict woodland tree planting to 4 m centres. • Trees that grow above 20 m should not be planted within 3 km of an aerodrome. Allow for thinning as part of a management plan. • Have a grass management policy.
Reducing the Hazards of Water	• Water should be deeper than 4 m to minimize bottom growing vegetation with steeply shelving banks preferably near vertical to prevent birds walking in and out of the water. • Simplify the shape to circular or square to restrict bays, promontories and islands that are to attractive birds. • On larger areas of water introduce netting or visible wires to prevent birds taking off or landing on water. • Do not stock with fish or permit angling. • Perimeters – paving or long grass regime including wildflower meadows areas up to 200 mm high but not wetland grass or dense vegetation.

Source/Copyright Permission: Civil Aviation Authority for CAP 772 Bird Strike Risk Management for Aerodromes and Safeguarding Aerodromes Advice Note 3 – Potential Hazards from Amenity Landscaping and Building Design.

3.10 Guidelines for Construction Around Trees

Available Guidelines	BS 5837: 2005: 'Trees in Relation to Construction – Recommendations' *Refer to Guidelines for full details.*
Tree Survey	A tree survey should be carried out by an arboriculturalist and recorded in a tree survey schedule listing: • Species; • Condition category A–C and Remove; • Tag reference No. (shown on a plan); • Height in metres; • Stem diameter at 1.5 m above GL; • Crown spread at 4 cardinal points accurately plotted on the plan; • Height above GL; • Age class; • Estimated remaining years; • Management recommendations.
Arboricultural Assessment	An arboriculturalist should review the impact of the development proposals on the trees and provide an impact assessment to enable the development layout to be finalized.
Tree Protection Plan and Root Protection Area	A Tree Protection Plan should follow relating the tree survey to the proposed development and clearly indicating trees to be retained and trees to be removed for development or due to condition. The Root Protection Area of each tree requires to be calculated (refer to BS 5837) to enable the construction exclusion zone to be determined and tree protection measures shown on the Tree Protection Plan.
Construction Exclusion Zone	All trees being retained should be protected by barriers and or ground protection to exclude damaging construction activities and storage.
Barriers	• Scaffold framework 2.3 m high comprising vertical and horizontal framework clamped together, braced and with weldmesh panels wired to framework on inside of barrier. Vertical uprights should be at 3.0 m centres minimum and driven into the ground by 60 mm. • Site compound/buildings may form part of the barrier system. • Or as agreed with LPA.

Ground Protection	Where construction access, adjacent demolition or scaffolding is required within the Root Protection Area and has been agreed with the LPA that ground protection will be required. • Pedestrian access – scaffold boards on top of a compressible layer on a geotextile membrane. • Vehicular access – designed by an engineer to withstand loading (Reinforced slabs or a proprietary system). • The barrier should still be retained.
Additional Protection	Avoid the following: • Material that will contaminate the soil should not be discharged within 10 m of the tree stem (e.g. oil, concrete waste), • No fires where flames can extend within 5 m of foliage/branches or tree trunk. • Fixing of notice boards or cables to protected trees. Preventative pruning may also be undertaken by an arboriculturalist.
Avoiding Root Damage	Precautions to protect the condition and health of the root system should be carried out by: • Preventing physical damage to the root structure. • Maintaining the soil structure by avoiding compaction. • Making provision for water and oxygen to reach the root system. This can be achieved by: • Herbicide treating existing ground cover prior to installing protective surface. Obtain specialist advice on the appropriate herbicide to be used to prevent leaching and damaging roots. • Loose organic matter/turf can be removed carefully using hand tools and the new surface established over a granular fill which does not inhibit vertical gaseous diffusion such as no fines gravel, washed aggregate or cobbles. Depending on the CBR (California Bearing Ratio) of the soil it may require a load suspension layer such as cellular confinement system. • Restrict new impermeable surfacing within the RPA to a maximum of 3.0 m width and situated tangentially to one side of the tree and confined to an area of no greater than 20% of the root system.

	• All excavations should be carried out by hand and avoiding damage to protective bark covering of larger roots. Exposed roots should be wrapped in dry clean Hessian to prevent desiccation. Roots less than 25 mm/diameter can be pruned back to a side branch using proprietary cutting tools. Roots larger than 25 mm can only be removed after consultation with an arboriculturalist. • Ensure any surfacing in the RPA is sloped away from the tree to prevent waterlogging.			
Foundations in the RPA	This is justifiable if it allows the retention of a Class A or B tree, but foundations must be designed to avoid root damage. Strip foundations should be avoided and uses of piles, radial foundations or suspended slabs are preferable. Engineering/arboricultural advice will be required.			
Avoiding Damage to New Structures by New Trees	Minimum distances (metre) between young trees or new tree planting and structure to avoid damage to structure from future tree growth.			

Structure	Diametre of stem at 1.5 m above GL at maturity		
	<30 cm	30–60 cm	>60 cm
Buildings and heavy loaded structures	–	0.5	1.2
Lightly loaded structures (garages/porches)	–	0.7	1.5
Underground services/drains <1.0 m deep >1.0 m deep	0.5 –	1.5 1.0	3.0 2.0
Masonry boundary walls	–	1.0	2.0
In situ concrete paths/drives	0.5	1.0	2.5
Paths/drives with flexible surfaces or paving slabs	0.7	1.5	3.0

Source/Copyright: Extracts derived or taken directly from BS5837: 2005 is granted by BSI. British Standards can be obtained from BSI Customer Services, 389 Chiswick High Road, London W4 4AL. Tel: +44(0)20 8996 9001. E-mail: cservices@bsi-global.com

3.11 Glossary of Contracts

ICE (Institute of Civil Engineering) Contracts	This is a family of standard conditions of contract for civil engineering works produced by the Conditions of Contract Standing Joint Committee (CCSJC). The ICE Conditions of Contract, which have been in use for over 50 years, were designed to standardise the duties of contractors, employers and engineers and to distribute the risks inherent in civil engineering to those best able to manage them. • Measurement Version 7th Edition – 1999 • Design and Construct 2nd Edition – 2001 • Term Version 1st Edition – 2002 • Minor Works 3rd Edition – 2001 • Partnering Addendum – 2003 • Tendering for Civil Engineering Contracts – 2000 • Archaeological Investigation 1st Edition – 2004 • Target Cost 1st Edition – 2006 • Ground Investigation 2nd Edition – 2003.
New Engineering and Construction Contract (NEC) 3rd Edition 2005	Produced by the ICE, the NEC represents a non-adversarial approach to contracts. It is a family of standard contracts that embraces the concept of partnership and encourages employers, designers, contractors and project managers to work together through both a powerful management tool and a legal framework of project management procedures to facilitate the creation of engineering and construction projects of all sizes. It includes a series of different documents based on a project management system to suit different procurement arrangements selected by the employer: • Option A – Priced Contract with Activity Schedule • Option B – Priced Contract with BQ • Option C – Target Contract with Activity Schedule • Option D – Target Contract with BQ • Option E – Cost Reimbursement Contract • Option F – Management Contract. The contract strategy is further refined by selecting from 15 secondary options depending on the main option selected.
Engineering and Construction Short Contract (ECSS)	The ECSS has been specially produced for use with contracts that do not require sophisticated management techniques, comprise only straightforward works and impose only low risk on both the employer and the contractor.

Joint Contracts Tribunal (JCT) Building Contracts 2005	Issued by the JCT which publishes a whole family of building contracts catering for different sizes of development and approaches to procurement. Most of the contracts were reissued in 2005. • **SBC 05** – Standard Building Contract for traditional procurement. • **DB 05** – Design and Build Contract for design and build procurement. • **IC 05** – Intermediate Building Contract with Contractors Design for works of smaller value and less complexity. • **ICD 05** – Intermediate Building Contract for works of smaller value and less complexity and where the contractor assumes responsibility for the design of discrete parts. • **MW 05** – Minor Works Building Contract for works of a minor nature that are relatively straightforward. • **MP 05** – Major Project Construction Contract for major works where the Employer regularly procures large-scale construction work. • **CM 05** – Construction Management Agreement for construction management procurement. • **MC 05** – Management Building Contract for management contracting procurement. • **MTC 05** – Measured Term Contract for use where the employer requires maintenance works to be executed on a regular basis. • **FA 05** – Framework Agreement for the procurement of construction/engineering-related works over a period of time. There are three variants of SBC 05 for use in different circumstances: • **With Quantities** – Works are defined in BQ and the design is provided by the Employer through his agent – the architect.

Joint Contracts Tribunal (JCT) Building Contracts 2005 (Continued)	• **Without Quantities** – As above, but the works are not defined in the BQ but more typically through as schedule of rates. • **With Approximate Quantities** – Used where the works have been substantially designed but not completely detailed so the quantities are approximate and subject to re-measurement.
Joint Contracts for Landscape Industries (JCLI) Agreement for Landscape Works 2008	Produced by the JCLI. Used for new landscape construction contracts up to a value of £250 000.00. Similar to JCT Minor Works with additional clauses for nominated sub-contractors, vandalism, certification, fluctuations and nominated suppliers. Does not provide for maintenance of plants.
JCLI Agreement for Maintenance Works 2002	Designed for maintenance work and not new landscape works. It must be used with JCLI contract to allow for maintenance of the works.
JCLI Form of Agreement with Contractors Design 2008	Produced by JCLI for works that include contractor's design elements for contract values upto £250 000.00.

Government Construction (GC) Works Range of Contracts	The GC Works family of contracts are standard Government forms of contract intended for use in connection with government construction works.
	
	• **GC/Works/1** (1998 and 1999)
	   A standard form of contract for major UK building and civil engineering works, available with Model Forms and Commentary, in the following versions:
	   – With Quantities (1998)
	   – Without Quantities (1998)
	   – Single Stage Design and Build (1998)
	   – Two Stage Design and Build Version (1999)
	   – With Quantities Construction Management Trade Contract (1999).
	• **GC/Works/2** (1998) Contract for Building and Civil Engineering Minor Works.
	• **GC/Works/3** (1998) for mechanical and electrical engineering.
	• **GC/Works/4** (1998) for small building, civil, mechanical and electrical work.
	• **GC/Works/5** (1998) procurement of professional services. Designed for use with the 1998 and 1999 editions of GC/Works contracts for the appointment of the relevant consultancy services associated with the construction works.

	• **GC/Works/5** General Conditions for the Appointment of Consultants: Framework Agreement (1999). Designed for use with the (1998) and (1999) editions of GC/Works contracts for the appointment of consultancy services (associated with the construction works) on a "call-off" basis over a 3–5 year period. • **GC/Works/6** General Conditions of Contract for a Daywork Term Contract (1999). Applicable to work of a jobbing type nature. Based on a 3–5 year contract period. Payment is relatively straightforward: labour at schedule of rates; materials at cost plus a percentage addition. • **GC/Works/7** General Conditions of Contract for Measured Term Contracts (1999). Based on a schedule of rates, with orders being placed with the contractor as necessary/required over a 3–5 year contract period. • **GC/Works/10** General Conditions of Contract for Facilities Management (2000). This standard form of contract is intended for procuring Facilities Management services. The introduction in the contract advises that the Facilities Management Contractor can either be appointed as a one-stop-shop or as a managing agent.
Built Environment Collaborative Contract (BCC) 2003	Issued by Collaborating for the Built Environment formed in 2002. The aim is a standard form of contract that is shorter, simpler and easier to administer than current JCT Forms. The BCC seeks to encourage collaboration within the contract rather than having a separate partnering agreement. 'The Overriding Principal' is *to work together with each other in a co-operative and collaborative manner and in good faith and in the spirit of mutual trust and respect.* It comprises two basic elements: • A Purchase Order, which is signed by both parties and includes the project details and the services to be provided. • The Collaborative Construction Terms, i.e. The Contract Conditions. There are two payment options: target cost (with or without GMP) or fixed price. There is no provision for retention.

Project Partnering Contract (PPC) 2000	Published by the Association of Consultant Architects, the PPC is the first standard form of project partnering contract and is a radical change. It is a single multi-party contract where the employer, the contractor and all consultants work together under the same terms and conditions. Each partnering team member owes responsibilities to all other team Members. PPC 2000 provides for KPI with milestones.

3.12 Construction (Design and Management) Regulations 2007

Relevant Legislation	**Construction (Design and Management) Regulations (CDM) 2007** Came into force on 6 April 2007 Replaced the Construction (Design and Management) Regulations 1994 and the Construction (Health, Safety and Welfare) Regulations 1996
Contents	The Regulations are divided into five parts: • Part 1: Interpretation and Application of the Regulations. • Part 2: General Management Duties – which apply to ALL construction projects. • Part 3: Additional Management Duties – which apply to *notifiable* projects. • Part 4: Based on the former Construction (Health, Safety and Welfare) Regulations 1996 and applies to ALL construction work. • Part 5: Civil Liability Issues.
Application of the Regulations	CDM 2007 applies to **ALL** construction works including those which are non-notifiable from small extensions to large scale projects like Heathrow's Terminal 5.
Notification to the Health and Safety Executive (HSE)	**Is the Project Notifiable? Yes:** • if the works are expected to last more than 30 working days, **or** • it is anticipated that the works will involve more than 500 person days. The HSE does not have to be notified if the project is for a domestic client although the Regulations will still apply.
Duty Holders	The Regulations name the key duty holders under Part 1: • The Client • The Designer • The Principal Contractor • The Contractor • The CDM Co-ordinator – replaces the former Planning Supervisor under the 1994 Regulations.

Clients Duties	**All Construction Projects**
	Be satisfied as to the competency of:
	• CDM-C Co-ordinator
	• Designers
	• Principal Contractor.
	Provide all relevant pre-construction information promptly to the appointed designer and contractor and identify that there are suitable management arrangements in place to ensure that:
	• All construction work can be carried out safely.
	• Welfare arrangements are suitable and in place.
	• All structures are designed to meet the Workplace Regulations 1992.
	Allow sufficient time and resources for all stages of the project including sufficient mobilisation period for the Principal Contractor prior to going on-site.
Additional Client Duties	**Notifiable Projects**
	• Appoint a CDM Co-ordinator as is practicable after initial design is underway (RIBA Stage B/C).
	• Appoint a Principal Contractor.
	• Ensure the construction phase does not start unless there are suitable welfare arrangements in place and a suitable and sufficient Construction Stage Plan is in place.
	• Provide all necessary information relating to the Health and Safety File to the CDM-C.
	• Retain and provide access to the Health and Safety File.
	Note
	• On the failure or late appointment of a CDM-C, the client is deemed by default to be the CDM-C as well as client.
	• All appointments must be in writing.
	• The client signs the F10 (notification Form to HSE) – previously it was the Planning Supervisor and the Principal Contractor.
	• The client can no longer appoint a Client's Agent.

Designers Duties	**All Construction Projects** • Do not commence work until the client is aware of his duties. • Be satisfied that he is competent to carry out his duties. • Avoid foreseeable risks and eliminate hazards through their design to ensure the health and safety to any person constructing, maintaining or using the designed structure. • Take account of the Workplace Regulations 1992 in the design or use of materials. • Provide information about the design, its construction or maintenance to assist clients, other designers and contractors.
Additional Designers Duties	**Notifiable Projects** • Do not progress beyond initial design work (RIBA Work Stage B/C) until a CDM-C has been appointed. • Take all reasonable steps to provide sufficient information to assist the CDM-C.
Principal Contractors	**All Construction Projects** • Ensure that the client is aware of his duties and has appointed CDM-C. • Plan, manage and monitor the construction phase in liaison with other contractors. • Prepare, develop and implement a written plan and site rules. • Give contractors relevant parts of the plan. • Ensure suitable welfare facilities are provided from the start and maintained. • Check competence of all appointees. • Ensure provision of information, instruction and training to all. • Consult with the workforce. • Liaise with the CDM-C regarding ongoing design. • Secure the site at all times.

Duties of CDM-C	• Give suitable and sufficient advice and assistance to the client.
	• Ensure that suitable arrangements are made and implemented for the co-ordination of health and safety measure during planning and preparation for the construction phase.
	• Liaise with the principal contractor regarding the contents of the Health and Safety Plan, any information required to prepare the Construction Phase Plan, and any design development which may affect planning and management of the construction work.
	• Collect pre-construction information and provide promptly in a convenient form to the designers, principal contractor and appointed contractors.
	• Ensure co-operation between designers and principal contractor during the construction phase in relation to any design changes.
	• Prepare the Health and Safety File at the end of the construction phase and pass to the client.
	• Ensure the HSE are notified of the project using Form F10. This notice must be signed by the client.
The Contractors Duties	**All Construction Projects**
	• Shall not carry out construction work unless the client is aware of his duties.
	• Shall plan, manage and monitor construction work carried out by him or under his control in a way which ensures it is carried out without risks to health and safety.
	• Ensure that any contractor whom he appoints is informed of the minimum amount of time which will be allowed to him for planning and preparation before he begins construction work.
	• Shall provide every construction worker with information and training, including a site induction.
	• Shall prepare site rules.
	• Shall not begin construction work unless the site is secure.

The Contractors Duties	**Notifiable Projects**
	• A contractor shall not carry out construction work in relation to the project unless:
	  – the CDM-C and principal contractor have been named;
	  – the CDM-C has been given access to such part of the construction phase plan as is relevant to the work to be performed by him;
	  – notice of the project has been given to the HS Executive.
	• Shall provide the principal contractor with any information which might affect the health or safety of any person carrying out the construction work or of any person who may be affected by it; or might justify a review of the construction phase plan; or has been identified for inclusion in the Health and Safety file.
	• Identify to the principal contractor any contractor whom he appoints for the project.
	• Comply with any directions of the principal contractor and any site rules.
	• Provide the principal contractor with the information in relation to any death, injury, condition or dangerous occurrence which the contractor is required to notify or report under the Reporting of Injuries, Diseases and Dangerous Occurrences Regulations 1995.
	• Ensure that the construction work is carried out in accordance with the construction phase plan.
	• Take appropriate action to ensure health and safety where it is not possible to comply with the construction phase plan in any particular case.
	• Notify the principal contractor of any significant finding which requires the construction phase plan to be altered or added to.

All Duty Holders	• Check their own competence.
	• Co-operate with each other to ensure health and safety of:
	  Those carrying out construction works
	  Others who may be affected by the works
	  The end user.
	• Report obvious risks.
	• Take account of and apply the principals of prevention when carrying out duties.

Prosecutions	Failure to comply with Health and Safety Legislation is a criminal offence. Under CDM Regulations 2007 the maximum penalties that can be imposed by the courts are:
	• An unlimited fine • Two years imprisonment.

Source: The Construction (Design and Management) Regulations 2007.
Refer to the Regulations for more detailed information.

4 Design Guidelines

4.1 Dimensional Data

People

Average walking speed is 80 m/min, 400 m in five minutes or 800 m in ten minutes
Average shoulder height – 1310–1425 mm
Average height – 1610–1740 mm
Average eye level – 1505–1630 mm
Average seated eye level – 1180–1230 mm
Average seated head height – 1290–1350 mm
Average sitting space – 550 mm
Upward reach – 1905–2060 mm

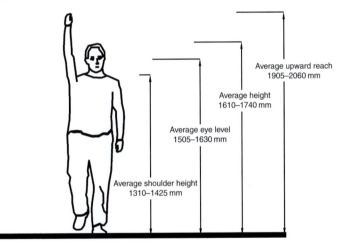

Average upward reach
1905–2060 mm

Average height
1610–1740 mm

Average eye level
1505–1630 mm

Average shoulder height
1310–1425 mm

Seating

Perch seating – 650–800 mm with a median of 700 mm above ground level.

Conventional seat height varies between 420 and 580 mm, with an average seat height of 450 mm and with widths recommended to be a minimum of 500 mm.

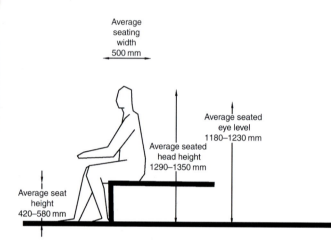

Wheelchairs

Minimum passage width for a typical wheelchair	900 mm
Eye level of typical wheelchair user	960–1250 mm
Eye level of typical scooter user	1080–1315 mm
Seated height of typical wheelchair user	1300–1400 mm
Seated height of typical scooter user	1200–1450 mm
Knee height of typical wheelchair user	500–690 mm
Seat height of typical wheel chair	460–490 mm
Ankle height of typical wheelchair user (manual)	175–300 mm
Ankle height of typical wheelchair user (electric)	380–520 mm
Typical height of bottom of foot support	60–150 mm
The typical space required for a self-propelled wheelchair to manoeuvre through 90°	1345 mm × 1450 mm
The typical space required for a self-propelled wheelchair to manoeuvre through 180°	1500 mm × 1950 mm

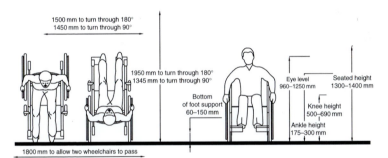

1500 mm to turn through 180°
1450 mm to turn through 90°

1950 mm to turn through 180°
1345 mm to turn through 90°

Bottom
of foot support
60–150 mm

Eye level
960–1250 mm

Seated height
1300–1400 mm

Knee height
500–690 mm

Ankle height
175–300 mm

1800 mm to allow two wheelchairs to pass

Footpaths

Minimum preferred obstacle-free width for busy footways	1800 mm
Preferred minimum obstacle-free footway width for less busy routes	1500 mm
Preferred minimum obstacle-free footway width for rarely used routes	1200 mm
Preferred minimum width for paths providing access to a single dwelling	900 mm
Preferred width at bus stops	3000 mm
Preferred width at shops	3500–4500 mm
Absolute minimum width at obstacles (max length 6 m)	1000 mm
Minimum path width for a stick user	750 mm
Minimum path width for a double crutch user/walking frame user	900 mm
Minimum path width for a long cane user/adult plus assistance dog	1100 mm
Minimum path width for an adult and child	1100 mm
Minimum path width for an adult plus helper	1200 mm
Width to allow two wheelchair users to pass each other	1800 mm
Preferred unobstructed height above footways	2300 mm
Preferred cross-fall of a path/level access route	1:50

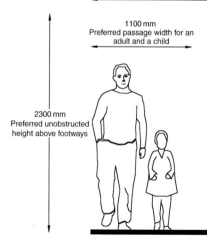

1800 mm
Preferred obstacle
free footway

1100 mm
Preferred passage width for an
adult and a child

2300 mm
Preferred unobstructed
height above footways

Cycling

- Average cycling speed is 12 kph or 200 m/min.
- Average length of a bike 1.9 m, width 560 m, height 1070 mm.
- Average width of a cyclist mounted on a bicycle is 750 mm.
- Minimum headroom required for a cyclist – 2.4 m, preferably 2.7 m.

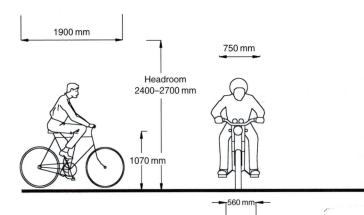

1900 mm

Headroom
2400–2700 mm

750 mm

1070 mm

560 mm

Cycle parking

The preferred spacing of cycle racks is at 1000 mm centres to allow two bicycles to be stored per metre run. An absolute minimum of 800 mm may be used where space is limited. The outermost stands should be a minimum of 550 mm from a wall with a minimum of 550 mm between the ends of stands and a parallel wall.

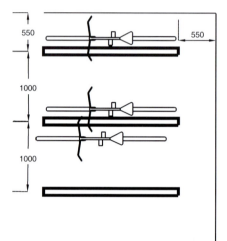

Horse riding

- Acceptable width of bridle path depends on gradient, ground conditions and surface finish. However, the recommended minimum width is 2.3 m with 0.5 m deemed as the absolute minimum width of a ride-able path.
- Approximate height of mounted rider is 2.55 m above ground level.
- Minimum headroom required for a mounted rider is 3 m, preferably 3.7 m.

Motorcycles

Average length 2250 mm, width 600 mm, height 800 mm.

The recommended space for parking motorcycles is 2000 mm × 800 mm per motorcycle. Where a rail is required for security, it should be set at 600 mm above ground level.

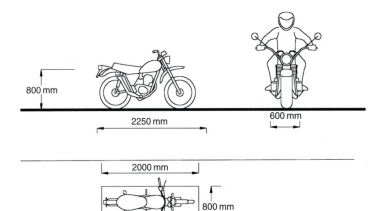

Vehicles

Vehicle movement

Width of carriageway, which can accommodate two cars to pass comfortably on a straight section of carriageway with clear visibility:

*   −5.5 m

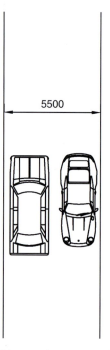

5500

Manoeuvring space requirements needed to access parking spaces can typically be, for a 2.4 m wide bay:

*   90 degrees parking – 6.0 m width
*   60 degrees parking – 4.2 m width
*   45 degrees parking – 3.6 m width

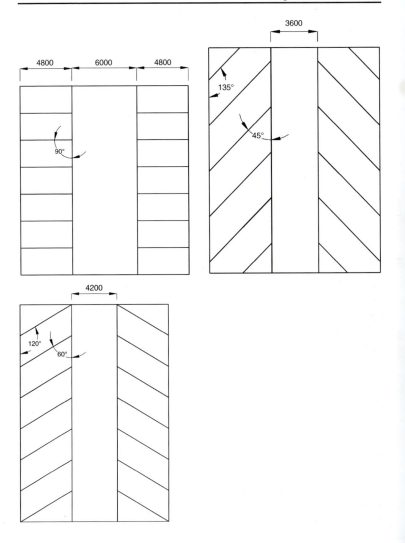

Parking bays

Minimum/standard parking bay	4800 mm × 2400 mm
Off-street parking for disabled motorists:	
Bays parallel to access aisle and access available from the side	As above with an additional 1800 mm in length
Bays perpendicular to access aisle	As above with an additional 1200 mm along each side plus 1200 mm safety zone at vehicle access end
On-street parking for disabled motorists:	
Bays parallel to the kerb	Minimum of 6600 mm × 2700 mm (preferably 3600 mm wide)
Bays at an angle to the kerb	Minimum of 4200 mm × 3600 mm

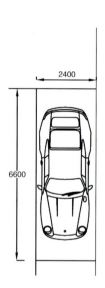

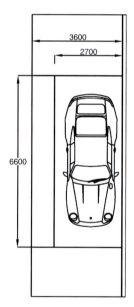

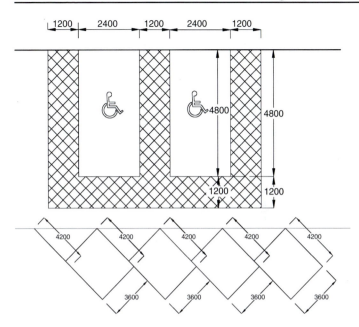

Car parking provision

Car parking for disabled motorists should be provided within 50 m of the facilities served by the car park with level or ramped access.

Minimum recommended number of disabled parking bays in off-street parking	
Car parks for existing employment premises	2% of total parking capacity with a minimum of one space
Car parks for new employment premises	5% of total parking capacity to include both employees and visitors
Shopping, recreation and leisure facilities	Minimum of one space for each employee who is disabled plus 6% of the total capacity for visiting disabled motorists
At railway stations	<20 spaces: a minimum of 1 reserved space 20–60 spaces: a minimum of 2 reserved spaces

The above figures are guidelines only and will vary in relation to site specific requirements.

Minimum recommended number of disabled parking bays in off-street parking	
At railway stations *(continued)*	61–200 spaces: 6% of capacity plus a minimum of 3 reserved spaces
	Over 200 spaces: 4% of capacity plus 4 reserved spaces

Sources/Copyright: Additional information available from DFT Traffic Advisory Leaflet Department of Transport – Inclusive mobility. A guide to Best Practice on Access to Pedestrian and Transport Infrastructure.

The above figures are guidelines only and will vary in relation to site specific requirements.

4.2 Senses, Communication and Space

People generally walk at just under 5 km/h (3 mph). The human senses are adapted to this condition.

Sense	Distance	Distance	Distance	Distance	Distance
Sight	0–100 m	20–25 m	30 m	70–100 m	500–1000 m
	This is the social field of vision. It is possible to see other individuals.	It is possible to perceive another, person's facial features and facial expressions.	Facial features can be seen.	Possible to determine, age, sex and activity and recognize someone you know.	The presence of other people can be determined, depending on lighting and their level of activity.
Sound	Up to 7 m	Up to 35 m	More than 35 m	More than 1000 m	
	It is possible to hold a conversation, with relatively little detail.	It is possible to communicate but it is difficult to hold a conversation.	It is possible to hear people who shout but difficult to understand.	It is only possible to hear very loud noises such as an aeroplane, explosion and so on.	
Smell	Up to 1 m	2–3 m	More than 3 m		
	It is possible to experience weak odours.	It is possible to experience stronger odours	Only stronger smells are perceived.		

Note: Further information can be found in *Life Between Buildings: Using Public Spaces* by Jan Gehl, 1987, English Translation, First published, Livet Mellum Husene, Arkitektens Forlag, 1980, Springer Science and Business Media.

4.3 Walkable Neighbourhoods

Walking

The following guidelines set out parameters for the design of ease of walking, which may help to discourage the use of the car and promote a walkable neighbourhood. The distances assume that there are no major obstructions such as busy roads or railway lines.

Facility	Distance (m)	Journey time on foot (min)
Post box or telephone	250	2–3
Newsagent	400	5
Local shops, bus stop, health centre	800	10
Local parks	250–400	3–5

A widely used benchmark is for mixed development neighbourhoods to cover a 400 m radius, equating to about 5 min walk. This translates into about 50 hectares.

Public transport

The table below outlines the ideal catchment area per stop for viability of different types of public transport, based on a density of a minimum of 80 persons per hectare, a catchment of 2000 people per bus stop.

A ratio of 100 people per hectare provides a catchment of around 2500 people per bus stop. Densities below 80 people per hectare may not be attractive to transport providers.

Mode of transport	Minibus	Bus	Guided bus	Light rail	Rail
Stop interval (m)	200	200	300	600	1,000+
Corridor width (m)	800	800	800	1,000	2,000+
Catchment per stop (number of people)	320–640	480–1,760	1,680–3,120	4,800–9,000	24,000

Pedestrian crossings and traffic flow

- Streets with up to 500 vehicles per hour (two way) offer pedestrians easy opportunities to cross the road.
- Street with between 500 and 1000 vehicles per hour (two way) will require specific crossing opportunities to be incorporated to allow for pedestrians to cross.
- Flows of over 1000 vehicles per hour mean that pedestrians will have to wait to cross the road at designated controlled crossings.

Source/Copyright: Urban Design Compendium, English Partnerships/The Housing Corporation.

4.4 Creation of Positive Outdoor Space

Animation, life and interest are added to a street by an active frontage. The following table provides a scale to judge the performance of designs according to the amount of active frontage. Grade A is the ideal and most active frontage. Active frontages mean frequent doors and windows with few blank walls, narrow frontage buildings giving vertical rhythm to the street scene, articulation of facades with projections, such as bays and porches incorporated, providing a welcoming feeling and on occasion lively internal uses visible from the street or spilling onto the street.

Active frontage guidelines	
Grade A frontage	
• More than 15 premises every 100 m • More than 25 doors and windows every 100 m • A large range of frontages	• No blind facades and few passive ones • Much depth and relief in the building surfaces • High-quality materials and refined details
Grade B frontage	
• 10 to 15 premises every 100 m • More than 15 doors and windows every 100 m • A moderate range of frontages	• A few blind facades and few passive ones • Some depth and modelling in the building surfaces • Standard materials and refined details
Grade C frontages	
• 6 to 10 premises every 100 m • Some range of frontages	• Less than half blind or passive facades • Very little depth and modelling in the building surfaces • Standard materials and few details
Grade D frontages	
• 3 to 5 premises every 100 m • Little or no range of functions	• Predominantly blind or passive facades • Flat building surfaces • Few or no details
Grade E frontages	
• 1 or 2 premises every 100 m • No range of functions	• Predominantly blind or passive facades • Flat building surfaces • No details and nothing to look at

Note: This design performance can be used to assess existing situations or determine requirements for new streets.
Source/Copyright: Urban Design Compendium, English Partnerships/The Housing Corporation.

4.5 Steps and Ramps

Sam's sense of humour suddenly disappeared without trace.

Note on the Disability Discrimination Act

There are no dimensional regulations associated with the Disability Discrimination Act. There are, however, numerous best practice guidelines. Part 3 of the DDA requires that '*reasonable*' measures are taken to avoid physical barriers to access to buildings or services. Compliance with DDA is subject to change as the test of '*reasonableness*' is established by Case Law.

Steps

Minimum number of steps in a flight	3
Maximum number of steps in a flight	12
Preferred riser height	150 mm
Minimum riser height	100 mm
Maximum riser height	170 mm
Preferred tread depth (going)	300 mm
Minimum tread depth (going)	250 mm
Minimum unobstructed width of steps (between handrails, if applicable)	1000 mm
Maximum cross-fall	1:50
Landing at top and bottom	At least the width of the steps and a minimum of 1200 mm long and with tonal contrast to the surfacing of the steps.

Notes: The preferred range: twice the riser + the going = 550 – 700 mm.
The ideal range for external steps: twice the riser + the going = 630 mm.
The appropriate width of a flight of steps and associated landings will depend on how intensely the access will be used and how many people are likely to use it.

Ramps

Slopes steeper than 1:20 (5%) are ramps. Where a ramp has a gradient of 1:20 or steeper, it should comply with the recommendations for ramps.

Minimum surface width of ramp	1200 mm
Minimum unobstructed width (between handrails)	1000 mm
Preferred gradient	There is general agreement among guidelines from various bodies and countries that 1:12, 8%, is the maximum that should be used with 1:20, 5%, the preferred.
General rule of thumb in relation to gradient and length of ramp	1:12 over a maximum of 2 m 1:13 over a maximum of 3 m 1:14 over a maximum of 4 m 1:15 over a maximum of 5 m 1:16 over a maximum of 6 m 1:17 over a maximum of 7 m 1:18 over a maximum of 8 m 1:19 over a maximum of 9 m 1:20 over a maximum of 10 m
Landing at top and bottom	At least the width of the ramp and a minimum of 1200 mm long and with tonal contrast to the ramp surfacing.
Intermediate landing	1500 mm long
Maximum cross-fall	1:50
Construction	Non-slip surface with 100 mm kerb up stand on either side and with handrails.

Note: The appropriate width of a ramp and associated landings will depend on how intensely the access will be used and how many people are likely to be using it.

Source/Copyright: Department of Transport – Inclusive mobility. A guide to Best Practice on Access to Pedestrian and Transport Infrastructure.

Additional sources of information: BS 8300, Design of buildings and their approaches to meet the needs of disabled people – Code of Practice.

Where ramps are required, and are not associated with access to buildings or services and the terrain dictates steeper grades, the following grades and lengths are suggested.

Gradient	Application/maximum lengths
1:20	Maximum slope for access to buildings or services
1:12	Ideal maximum gradient for bridle paths (with short sections of 1:7)
1:20–1:16	For up to 240 m
1:14	For up to120 m
1:12	For up to 90 m
1:11	For up to 60 m
1:10	For up to 30 m
1:9	For up to 15 m

Points to note:

- Ramps should be no longer than 15 m before a rest is provided.
- The maximum cross slope for any path should be no steeper than 1:40 (2.5%).
- On paths with wheelchair access, a camber profile of 1:25–1:50 should be used in preference to a cross-fall.
- Where sections of a path have a gradient between 1:60 and 1:20, level landings for each 500 mm rise would assist with accessibility.
- Landings to be provided for every 750 mm of vertical climb on slopes with a gradient steeper than 1:20.

4.6 Guarding and Handrails

Handrails to ramps and stairs

Ideally handrails should be provided on either side of a ramp or stepped access. The minimum unobstructed width between handrails should be 1000 mm but not more than 1800 mm. A public ramp or set of steps wider than 1800 mm should be divided into two with a handrail in the centre.

The height of the top of the handrail should be between 900 and 1100 mm, from the pitch line of the flights of steps or the surface of the ramp and placed not more than 100 mm from the outer edge of the ramp or flight of steps.

Handrails

Circular section diameter	40–50 mm
Non-circular section	50 mm × 38 mm
Clearance from wall	60 mm
Maximum distance from the edge of the ramp or step	100 mm
Extension beyond the start or end of the steps or ramp	300 mm and terminated in a manner to avoid clothing, etc., from being caught
Height above step nose or ramp surface	900–1100 mm

Source: Department of Transport – Inclusive mobility. A guide to Best Practice on Access to Pedestrian and Transport Infrastructure.

Guarding should be provided to prevent falls where there is a danger of people falling and/or where the drop or a rise is greater than 600 mm. Guarding should be constructed such that a 100 mm sphere cannot pass through any openings.

Recommended heights of guarding

Location	Guarding height from ground level (mm)
External balconies and edges of roofs	1100
Stairs and ramps	900–1100
Handrails on bridges used by horses	1800 – 1500 (depending on height of drop below)
Handrails on bridges used by cyclists	1400
Guardrails and barriers at the side or across footways	1100 or 1200
Tapping rail for visually impaired cane users and wheelchair users	150 mm upstand

Additional sources of information: BS 8300, Design of buildings and their approaches to meet the needs of disabled people – Code of Practice.

4.7 Tactile Surfaces and Warning Paving

There are seven recognized types of tactile surfaces recommended for use in the United Kingdom. A number of guidance documents, standards and codes of practice exist to provide a level of consistency, and BS 7997 sets out construction standards for the materials of tactile surfaces. The seven recognized tactile surfaces are:

- Blister surface
- Corduroy hazard warning surface
- (Off street) Platform edge warning
- (On street) Platform edge warning
- Segregated shared cycle track/footway surface with central delineator strip
- Guidance path surface
- Information surface.

The following provides a summary of the guidance and applications for the two most commonly used tactile surfaces; blister and corduroy paving.

Tactile surface	Purpose	Profile of surface	Layout/depth of surface
Blister paving	Provides a warning in the absence of a kerb upstand or of a kerb less than 25 mm to differentiate between the footway and the road carriageway at pedestrian crossing points.	Rows of flat-topped blisters 25 mm diameter, 5 mm high with chamfered edges set out at 64, 66.8 or 67 mm centres. Laid across the full width of the crossing with the back edge of the tactile surface at right angles to the direction of travel.	At a controlled crossing, where the dropped kerb is in the direct line of travel, the tactile surface should be laid to a depth of 1200 mm, otherwise laid at a depth of 800 mm. A stem of the surfacing, 1200 mm wide, should extend back from the crossing point at the side next to the push button control box and be laid in line with the direction of travel.

Tactile surface	Purpose	Profile of surface	Layout/depth of surface
Blister paving (*Continued*)			At an uncontrolled crossing close to a junction the tactile surface should be laid at a depth of 400 mm where the crossing is inset.
			Where the crossing is in the direct line of pedestrian travel, the depth should be 1200 mm.
			At an uncontrolled crossing away from a junction the tactile paving should be laid at a depth of 800 mm.

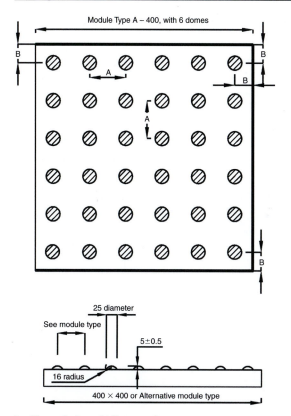

Profile and plan of blister surface.

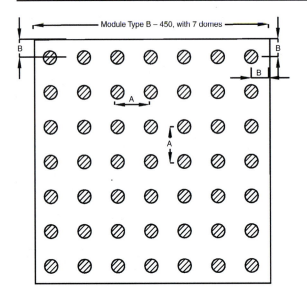

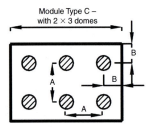

Module Type	Size	Pitch dimensions	
		A	**B**
A	450 × 450	64	33
B	400 × 400	66.8	33
C	200 × 133	67	33

Tactile surface	Purpose	Profile of surface	Layout/depth of surface
Corduroy hazarad warning	Provides a warning of a specific hazard: steps, level crossings, the approach to on-street light rapid transit platforms or where a footway joins a shared surface.	Rounded bars laid to run transversely across the direction of pedestrian travel. Bars are 6 mm high, 20 mm wide and at 50 mm centres.	Laid at top and bottom of stairs. Installed across the full width of stairs and extending 400 mm beyond the width on each side. Installed to a depth of 800 mm at 400 mm from the nosing. Where a pedestrian would have to make a conscious turn to encounter the steps, a depth of 400 mm is sufficient.
			Ramps – 800 mm depth across the full width at the foot only.
			Level crossings where there is a barrier – 400 mm, otherwise 800 mm where there is no barrier across the full width.
			Entrance to an unprotected railway station platform – 800 mm depth across the full width of the entry.

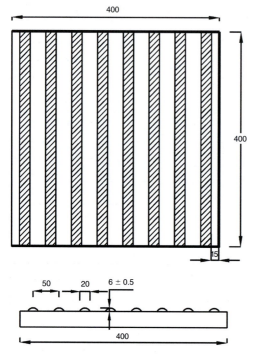

Profile and plan of corduroy surface.

It is recommended that the tactile surface be in a contrasting colour to adjacent surfaces. BS7997: 2003 specifies that red tactile 'blister' surfacing is used at controlled pedestrian crossings and this colour is restricted to use for this purpose.

Source/Copyright: Guidance on the use of tactile paving surfaces, Department of the Environment, Transport and the Regions, Department for Transport, Inclusive Mobility.

4.8 Design of Cycleways

CHECKLIST FOR DESIGN AND CONSTRUCTION OF OFF-ROAD CYCLEWAYS

Width	2–3 m, 2.5 optimum.
Gradient	Generally no greater than 1:35 to 1:20.
	Short Ramps (no more than 1.5 m) can be 1:12.
Angles and Corners	Rounded with minimum 6 m radius of curvature on lengths.
Camber/cross slope	1:35 maximum.
Path surface	Hard and firm with few loose stones.
Edging	Depends on situation, location and construction.
Construction	100–150 mm base course (depending on ground conditions).
	Surface – 50–60 mm bitmac, whin, bound gravel or similar.
Head room	2.4 m above ground level.
Surface gaps	That is, grills, boards, gratings – maximum 12 cm gap at right angles to direction of travel.
Lighting	Only where necessary for safety reasons, i.e. commuter paths in towns.
Signage	Use smallest appropriate sign. Avoid clutter. Signs to be placed off the path. Posts to contrast in colour with surroundings.
Access barriers	Ensure access controls to prevent unauthorized access. Avoid access barriers which make cyclists dismount. Chicanes 1.2 m high, offset gap 1.2 m minimum.
Isolate restrictions	Ensure 1.2 m min width.
Kerbs and crossing points	Maximum gradient 1:12. Flush area 1.2 m.
Pedestrian segregation	If flows more than 100 bicycles/h.

Source/Copyright: SUSTRANS
Refer to Sustrans publications 'Making Traffic Free paths more accessible' and 'Making Ways for the bicycle' for further detailed information.

4.9 Playgrounds and Playground Equipment

Relevant BS EN 1176

Part 1: General safety requirements and test methods
Part 2: Additional specific safety requirements and test methods for swings
Part 3: Additional specific safety requirements and test methods for slides
Part 4: Additional specific safety requirements for runways
Part 5: Additional specific safety requirements for carousels
Part 6: Additional specific safety requirements for rocking equipment
Part 7: Guidance for installation, inspection, maintenance and operation.

BS EN 1177 Impact absorbing playground surfacing
- Safety requirements and test methods.

BS 7188 Impact absorbing playground surfaces
- Performance requirements.

BS 5696 Minimum use zone
- Space occupied by equipment
- Free space
- Falling space.

LOCATION OF PLAY GROUNDS

Away from hazards such as:
- Overhead power lines
- Major roads
- Hidden/secluded areas
- Railway lines
- Waterways.

SELECTING EQUIPMENT

- Equipment should meet British Standard
  Proof/copies of certificates should be provided by the manufacturer or supplier before an order is placed.
  All equipment should carry the appropriate identification label.

SURFACING

Types of surfacing are:
- Rubber tiles
- Wet pour
- Loose fills
- Bark mulch or woodchip.

Suppliers should provide surfacing that has been tested to BS EN 1177 and BS 7188. It should have the required critical fall height properties for the height of fall required by the equipment or recommended by the supplier. Test certificates should be supplied.

All playground equipment suppliers should supply information on dimensions and depth of safety surfacing.

LAYOUT
Free spaces and falling spaces
- Falling spaces have impact areas that are based on the maximum free fall height of the equipment and these may overlap.
- Free spaces, i.e., where the equipment has forced movement, e.g. a slide, fire pole or swing, the free spaces must not overlap with each other or with adjacent falling space. (Refer to BS 1176 or RoSPA guidelines for calculation of falling and free space.)

PROTECTION AGAINST INJURIES IN FREE SPACE
- No obstacles allowed in free space
- Traffic flow should not go through free space
- Free height of fall should not exceed 3 m
- No obstacles in falling space
- Platforms with fall heights of 1 m between them require impact absorbency
- Impact absorbency should be sufficient for free fall heights.

All playground manufacturers should supply information on free space and fall space in relation to the equipment.

CIRCULATION WITHIN THE PLAY AREA
Circulation space should be considered in addition to free space and falling space.

This can be spilt into two areas:

1. Children who are generally running around from one piece of equipment to the next. Space required depends on anticipated user numbers.
2. As a general rule it is suggested that a minimum of 2.50 m should be allowed between two items of static equipment with free fall height of no more than 600 mm and a minimum of 2.50 m between a swing seat and static item.

POST INSTALLATION
Required:

- Post-installation inspection and report provided by RoSPA should be provided for the clients information and use.

PLAYGROUND FURNITURE

Fences: Entrapment requirements – no less than 89 mm between vertical palings, no horizontal access and 'hoop' tops should pass neck and head probe.

Gates: Self closing to prevent unwanted access by dogs.

Seats: Locate at least 300 mm from fence to prevent potential entrapment.

Litter bins: Locate at least 500 mm from seats.

Cycle racks: Locate at playground entrance.

Source/Copyright: RoSPA
Association of Play Industries
Refer to RoSPAs guidelines on European Playground Equipment and Surfacing Standards and Association of Playgrounds guidelines for playground layout and design.

4.10 Designing for Schools: Rules of Thumb

The new school furniture brought out a nasty superiority complex in little Nicola.

Introduction	Each Local Authority Education Department will have specific requirements for the design, layout and content of play areas for nursery/infant, primary/junior and secondary schools. These will be based on national guidelines. The following are rules of thumb that are based on national guidelines.
Relevant Guidance	Learning Through Landscapes Guidelines Secured by Design Guidelines Department for Children Schools & Families (Dfes) – Building Bulletins
Fencing Heights	Nursery/Primary Play Areas: 1.5 or 1.2 m with separating planting Boundary: Dependent on Insurance requirements – normally 2.4 m

Hard Play Surface Area	Nursery/Infant: 70% of external play space or 7 m² per pupil Primary/Junior: 400 + (1.5 × total pupil no.) = Area required in m² or approximately 5 m² per pupil Secondary: 400 + (1.5 × total pupil no.) = Area required in m²
Soft Play Surface Area	Nursery/Infant: 30% of external play space or 3 m² per pupil Primary/Junior: 800 + (1.5 × total pupil no.) = Area required in m² Secondary: 800 + (1.5 × total pupil no.) = Area required in m²
Seat Heights	Nursery/Infant: 280 mm Primary/Junior: 350 mm Secondary: 450 mm
Seat Totals	10% of pupil numbers
Play or other features that are considered desirable	**Nursery/Infant** • Variety of hard surfaces (decking, slabs, rubber safety surface, etc.) • Variety of play features and furniture (covered sandpit, stepping stones, moveable play elements that can be stored, picnic benches and planting tubs) • Variety of planting and soft landscape features (shade trees and educational or sensory planting) **Primary/Junior** • Variety of hard surfaces that allow for marking out of informal playground games or sports games. Age groups 4–5 and 6–7 should be separated from the overall playground • Quiet informal seating areas • Dining areas with picnic tables • Fenced play area with a variety of equipment and safety surface • Outdoor teaching area • Variety of soft landscape of small trees, shade trees, shrubs, grass, meadows, bulb planting and an enclosed area for school cultivation. The emphasis should be on native planting where practical and appropriate for environmental education.

	Secondary • Variety of hard surfaces for formal and informal play activities. Hard surfaces should be located adjacent to school entrances • Informal seating areas for socialising • Outdoor dining areas with picnic tables • Variety of soft landscape of trees, shrubs, grass, meadows and bulb planting. The emphasis should be on native planting where practical
Habitat Areas	Fenced and suitable for environmental education. Could include bird tables, compost bins, bird boxes, habitat planting types, sensory planting types, planting boxes, bog garden, meadow areas, willow arches, seating and work benches. Refer to Section 2.4 for plants for encouraging wildlife.
Other Furniture	Litter bins Cycle storage Chat room shelters
Sports Facilities	The requirement for sports facilities will vary per school **Primary/Junior**: Most will look for a minimum of a grass or synthetic 7-a-side sports pitch or a Multi-Use Games Area (MUGA) **Secondary**: Likely to include, football, hockey, rugby pitches either grass or synthetic and hard surfaced netball/tennis courts Refer to Section 4.11 for further information on sports pitch dimensions.

4.11 Standard Sports Markings

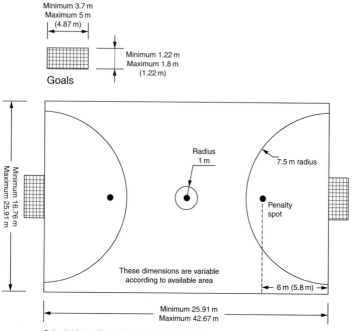

Minimum 3.7 m
Maximum 5 m
(4.87 m)

Goals

Minimum 1.22 m
Maximum 1.8 m
(1.22 m)

Minimum 16.76 m
Maximum 25.91 m

Radius
1 m

7.5 m radius

Penalty
spot

These dimensions are variable
according to available area

6 m (5.8 m)

Minimum 25.91 m
Maximum 42.67 m

School children dimensions are shown in brackets

Small side football (up to 7 a side)

See www.minisoccer.co.uk.

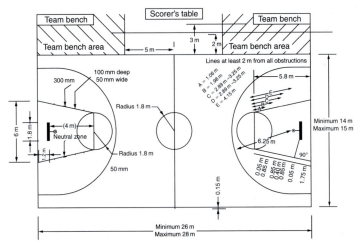

Mini rules, dimensions are shown in brackets
Outer boundary is a minimum of 2 m

Basketball

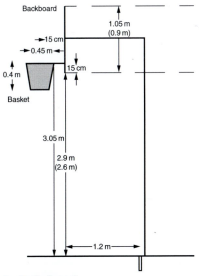

Basketball goals

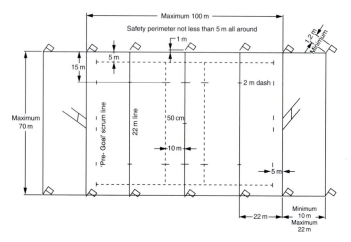

Rugby Union

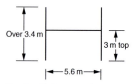

Rugby Union goals

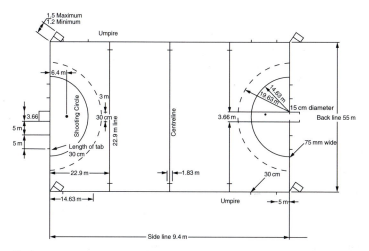

Hockey

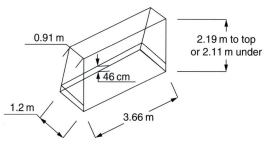

Hockey goals

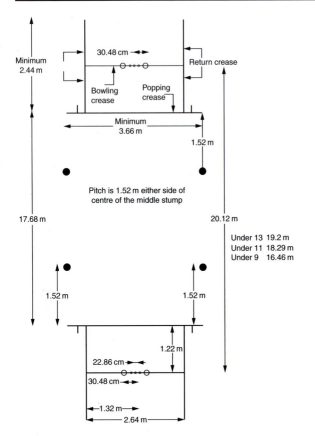

Cricket

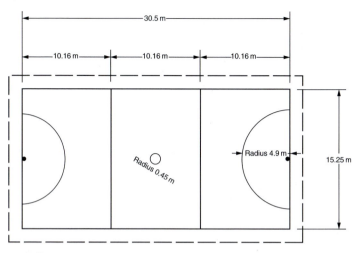

Netball

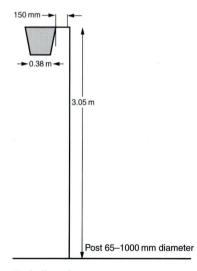

Netball goals

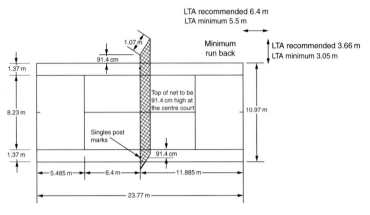

Lawn tennis

Source/Copyright: Groundsman's Field Handbook (909) Sportsmark Group Ltd. www.sportsmark.net. Tel.: 0208 560 2010.

4.12 Construction of Free Standing Walls

Rules of thumb

The rules of thumb for the maximum height of a wall and minimum width of the foundation for the four wind exposure zones are shown on the next page. The recommendations given here for height and foundation width should be taken as limits above which a design check by a qualified engineer is recommended to ensure stability.

Notes on rules of thumb

Wind exposure zones are based on wind speed distribution across the United Kingdom.

Local exposure conditions allow for differences in exposure within the zones. Sheltered locations are typical urban situations or areas where the wind flow is considerably interrupted. Exposed locations are typical rural or open areas where there is no local shelter from trees or buildings.

For the given exposure zone, the rules of thumb for wall height (measured from the lowest ground level to the top of the capping or coping) and the foundation width can be read off, from the table, against the common wall thicknesses. In the absence of other information, intermediate thicknesses can be built to the rules of thumb for the next smallest thickness given. The figures given are for an average slope of up to 1 in 20 within a 1 km radius of the site. For slopes of between 1 in 10 and 1 in 20 the wall heights given should be reduced by 15%.

Rules of thumb may not apply if the wall is:
- Adjacent to a vehicle access area where a robust crash barrier, or other protection, is not provided.
- Adjacent to a public area where there may be crowd pressure against the wall or children playing around the wall*.
- Where there may be excessive vibration.
- Close to a medium or high-rise building (more than four storeys), i.e. nearer than a distance equal to the height of the building.
- On the crest of a hill or in the vicinity of an extensive hill or mountain range.
- Where the soil substrate is soft or unstable.
- Where the average slope of the ground is greater than 1:10.
- Where the wall may be required to support a large gate or door.
- Where the difference in ground level between each side of the wall exceeds twice the thickness of the wall.

---

*The use of reinforced design should be used in these circumstances.

Structural advice should be sought where any of the above conditions apply.

UK wind exposure zones

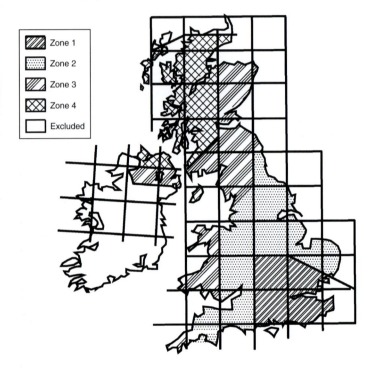

Maximum above-ground height and minimum foundation width

Zone/wall thickness	Sheltered		Exposed	
	Wall height limit (mm)	Foundation width (mm)	Wall height limit (mm)	Foundation width (mm)
ZONE 1				
Brickwork				
Half brick	725	350	525	375
One brick	1925	525	1450	600
One and a half brick	2500	525	2400	725
Blockwork				
100 mm	625	300	450	325
200 m	1400	375	1050	450
300 mm	2500	450	2000	600
ZONE 2				
Brickwork				
Half brick	650	350	450	375
One brick	1750	550	1300	625
One and a half brick	2500	575	2175	775
Blockwork				
100 mm	550	300	400	350
200 m	1275	400	925	450
300 mm	2425	525	1825	625
ZONE 3				
Brickwork				
Half brick	575	375	400	400
One brick	1600	575	1175	650
One and a half brick	2500	650	2000	800
Blockwork				
100 mm	550	325	350	350
200 mm	1150	425	850	475
300 mm	2200	550	1650	650

Zone/wall thickness	Sheltered		Exposed	
	Wall height limit (mm)	Foundation width (mm)	Wall height limit (mm)	Foundation width (mm)
Zone 4				
Brickwork				
Half brick	525	375	375	400
One brick	1450	575	1075	650
One and a half brick	2450	725	1825	850
Blockwork				
100 mm	450	325	325	350
200 mm	1050	425	775	500
300 mm	2025	575	1525	700

NB: An upper height limit of 2500 mm has been applied.

Movement joints

Movement joints should be continuous for the full height of the wall and spaced as below. For lateral stability, slip ties (stainless steel) should be incorporated at movement joints and where a freestanding wall abuts a building.

Brick/block type	Joints	Location of first joint from an end of a wall
Clay	16 mm wide movement joints every 12 m	No more than 6 m
Calcium silicate	Butt movement joint with separator every 9 m	No more than 4.5 m
Dense concrete block	Butt movement joint with separator every 6 m	No more than 3 m

Source/Copyright: BRE Good Building Guide 14, Building simple plan brick or blockwork free standing walls, IHS BRE Press, 1994.

Advice on free standing walls is extracted from the above publication. Copyright BRE. Reproduced with permission.

4.13 Water Features and Ponds

"That'll do nicely Frank – though I was hoping for a bit of decking…"

Water bodies could be considered to fall into three main types:
1. Natural-based lakes
2. Constructed lakes and ponds of natural appearance
3. Formal water bodies

1. **Natural-based lakes** Located in a natural valley setting where the sub-strata can retain water naturally or a dam is built to create a reservoir. This would usually be designed by an engineer and in fact, it is a legal requirement that an engineer designs and certifies any large water feature. The landscape architecture would probably be involved in the water margins and treatment of banking including aesthetics and planting proposals.
2. **Constructed lakes and ponds** Constructed using liners, some of which are listed below. In this case an overflow or drain will be required.
3. **Formal water bodies** These are designed according to functional requirements. Use of any appropriate material for the liner, usually concrete, which can then be faced to provide a desirable aesthetic effect.

Liners

There are two methods of lining ponds and water features:
• Clay puddling
• Impermeable liners

1. **Clay puddling** is the traditional method but is very labour intensive. The clay is laid by hand in thin layers of a minimum of 150 mm. Clay is liable to cracking if allowed dry out.

2. **Impermeable liners**
   - **Concrete** – this material is very strong but affected by extremes in temperature. For most water features the concrete will need to be reinforced.
   - **Butyl** (a form of synthetic rubber) or laminated liner can be moulded into any shape. It is unaffected by temperature fluctuation. Used for small water features, lakes and ponds due to its flexibility. It is also unaffected by ultra violet rays. Its life cycle is up to 100 years. The best butyl lining is 0.8 mm, black which exaggerates the clear reflective properties of a deep pool.
   - **Blue laminated PVC** will provide a shallow visual effect and is useful for small ponds.
   - **Pre-formed pool** – resin-bonded fibre or semi-rigid plastic.
   - **Polyethylene** – this comes in a wide range of densities and is relatively cheap. High-density polyethylene (HDPE) is used for landfill and capping as well as large water features. Low-density polyethylene (LDPE) is used for lining of lakes where greater flexibility is required.
   - **PVC** – Polyvinylchloride is used in smaller domestic situations. It has a slightly shorter lifespan than other materials apart from polythene and is only available in small units. Highly elastic, good resistance to acids, alkalis and alcohols. It can become brittle at low temperatures and decays on exposure to ultra violet light.

Control of water level

1. **Disposal and replenishment**
   - Disposal – In small pools a cistern could be used. In larger water features a water control devise such as a penstock and overflow would be considered.
   - Replenishment – Could be any of the following depending on the situation:
     - storm water
     - mains supply
     - surface run off
     - natural sources.

2. **Cleansing and emptying**
   The means of emptying the pool/lake/water feature will dictate the position of the overflow pipe. It would be in the deepest part of the pool or there is a requirement to leave an area for fish.

3. **Water circulation**
   A natural balance occurs when a balanced ecosystem has been achieved. Often this is not the case and mechanical aid is required to provide oxygen and prevent stagnation.
   Aeration. Examples below:
   - Natural streams or waterfalls.
   - Pumps or fountains – mixing oxygen in the water by mechanical means. Pump specification will depend on the style and size of the water feature and can be submerged or dry.

- Electrical aerators – self-contained unit connected to a single power control. Rule of thumb – 2 horsepower of pump capacity per surface acre.
  5 m deep and over – deep bottom diffusers
  Shallow water – floating aerator.
- Fountain aerators added value – fountains: aesthetic, water droplets on surface of water dissolve oxygen, create waves.

It is recommended that a water feature specialist and civil engineer be involved in the design and construction of water features.

PLANTS

Plants are useful for the biological balance of a pond, they oxygenate the water, shade the water and aid in the control of the water temperature and provide breeding places for wildlife.

Submerged or floating leaved

Curled pondweed	Potamogeton crispus
Water starworts	Callitriche sp.
Rigid hornwort	Ceratophyllum demersum
Water crowfoot	Ranunculus sp.
Spiked water-milfoil	Myriophyllum spicatum
Marestail	Hippuris vulgaris
*Broad-leaved pondweed	Potamogeton natans
*Yellow water lily	Nuphar lutea
*White water lily	Nymphaea alba

*Tolerant of range of conditions.

Plants for shallow water

Yellow iris	Iris pseudacorus
Great pond-sedge	Carex riparia
Marsh Woundwort	Stachys palustris
Reed canary grass	Phalaris arundinacea
Gipsywort	Lycopus europaeus
Reed sweet grass	Glyceria maxima
*Purple loosestrife	Lythrum salicaria
*Branched bur-reed	Sparganium erectum
*Rush species	Juncus sp.
*Bulrush	Typha latifolia
*Great water dock	Rumex hydrolapathum

*Not suitable for small ponds as very vigorous.

Base rich soil herbs and grasses for pond margins

Amphibious bistort	Persicaria amphibia
Water forget-me-not	Myosotis scorpioides
Floating sweet-grass	Glyceria sp.
Water mint	Mentha aquatica
Creeping bent	Agrostis stolonifera
Common water-plantain	Alisma plantago-aquatica
Watercress	Nastursium officinale
Marsh foxtail	Alopecurus geniculatus
Marsh marigold	Caltha palustris
Fool's water-cress	Apium nodiflorum
Common spike-rush	Eleocharis palustris
Marsh pennywort	Hydrocotyle vulgaris

Marginal plants for acid soils

Star sedge	Carex echinata
Common sedge	Carex nigra
Soft rush	Juncus effusus
Bottle sedge	Carex rostrata
Hard rush	Juncus inflexus
Ragged robin	Lychnis flos-cuculi
Marsh thistle	Cirsium palustre
Creeping forget-me-not	Myosotis secunda
Tufted hair grass	Deschampsia caespitosa
Bog myrtle	Myrica gale
Common spike-rush	Eleocharis palustris
Lesser spearwort	Ranunculus flammula
Marsh willowherb	Epilobium palustre
Yellow iris	Iris pseudacorus
Floating sweet-grass	Glyceria fluitans
Marsh violet	Viola palustris
Articulated rush	Juncus articulus
Sharp-flowered rush	Juncus acutiflorus
Marsh speedwell	Veronica scutellata
Bulbous rush	Juncus bulbosus
Bog stitchwort	Stellaria uliginosa

4.14 Signage

A considerable amount of research has been undertaken on the design of signage and printed material. The general principles are summarized in the following sections and refer principally to signage associated with the Department of Transport. Signage may be used in conjunction with other means of communication such as tactile information or audible information.

Letter size

Various research studies have produced a range of preferred size of letters in relation to the distance and degree of visual impairment. As a general rule it is suggested that the letter height should be at least 1% of the distance at which the message will usually be read subject to a minimum height of 22 mm. If space permits the letter height should be greater than 1%. The general principles are summarized below.

The Sign Design Guide recommends the following:

Distance (m)	Character size (mm)
Long-distance reading such as at building entrances/external locations	Minimum 150
Medium-range reading such as direction signs	50–100
Close-up reading such as wall-mounted information signs	15–25

Symbol sizes

Research by TransVision for Transport Canada produced the following table relating to reading distance and symbol size. The size is actual for square symbols and nominal for circular and triangular.

Distance (m)	Symbol size (mm)
3–6	40
6–9	60
9–12	80
12–15	100
15–18	120
18–24	160
24–30	200
30–36	240
36–48	320
48–60	400
60–72	480
72–90	600

Typefaces

General recommendations indicate that the following attributes of typeface are more distinguishable:

- Lower case lettering
- Sans Serif
- Arabic numbers
- Width to height ratio of between 3:5 and 1:1
- Stroke width to height ratio of between 1:5 and 1:10, preferably 1:6 to 1:8
- Horizontal character spacing 25–50% of character widths and 75–100% between words
- Vertical spacing between lines should be at least 50% of character height.

Colour contrast

Characters on signs should contrast with the background; dark text on a light background, light text on a dark background.

Signs should have a matt finish and should be well and evenly lit with a uniform lux of between 100 and 300. The signboard should contrast with its background to assist with visibility. The table below shows appropriate colour relationships.

Schedule of colour contrast for signs		
Background	**Signboard**	**Legend**
Red brick or dark stone	White	Black, dark green or dark blue
Light brick or light stone	Black/dark	White or yellow
Whitewashed walls	Black/dark	White or yellow
Green vegetation	White	Black, dark green or dark blue
Back-lit sign	Black	White or yellow

Reproduced from the Merseyside Code of Practice.

Positioning of signage

Optimum viewing for signs mounted on vertical plane are:

- +/− 30° from eye level in the vertical plane
- Up to 20° either side of 90 line to the sign on the horizontal.

Wall-mounted signs which contain detailed information, e.g. timetables, maps or diagrams – the sign should be centred, 1400 mm from the ground level, with the bottom edge not less than 900 mm above the ground level and the top edge at 1800 mm above the ground level. The recommended height for a wheelchair user is 1000–1100 mm and for someone standing 1400–1700 mm.

Source/Copyright: Department of Transport – Inclusive mobility. A Guide to Best Practice on Access to Pedestrian and Transport Infrastructure.

5 General Information

5.1 Landscape Architectural Work Stages

'The Landscape Consultant's Appointment' published by The Landscape Institute sets out clearly the services required by the client and the terms and conditions relating to the provision of them. Preliminary and Standard Services covering design, construction and management are set out under a series of work stages A–L and covers Inception to Completion of the project. Refer to The Landscape Consultants Appointment for further detail.

Work Stage A	**Preliminary Services: Inception** • Brief • Information provided by the client • Site appraisal • Advice on appointment of other consultants/specialists • Programme
Work Stage B	**Preliminary Services: Feasibility** • Feasibility studies • Agree extent of services required
Work Stage C	**Standard Services: Outline Proposals** • Outline proposals • CDM designers duties
Work Stage D	**Standard Services: Sketch Scheme Proposals** • Sketch scheme proposals • Changes in scheme proposals • Outline planning application • Other approvals
Work Stage E	**Standard Services: Detailed Proposals** • Detailed proposals • Cost checks and changes to proposals • Detailed statutory approvals
Work Stages F and G	**Standard Services: Production Information & Bills of Quantities** • Production Information • Bills of Quantities

Work Stages H and J	**Standard Services: Tender Action and Contract Preparation** • Letting of advanced contracts • Tender lists • Tender action or negotiation • Contract document preparation
Work Stage K	**Standard Services: Operations on Site During Construction and 12 Months Maintenance** • Contract administration • Inspections • Accounts and certificates • Financial appraisal and programme
Work Stage L	**Standard Services: Completion** • Administering the terms of the contract regarding completion

5.2 Setting a Sundial

Sundials measure time as it is based on the idea that a day is the time between two successive noons. It is not equivalent to 'clock time' which assumes that each day is exactly 24 hours long. The length of a day varies slightly throughout the year, i.e. the length of time between the noons when the sun reaches its highest point (when it crosses the meridian). Sundials measure the days as they are, varying in length from 23 hours and 59 minutes and 29 seconds on 25 December to 24 hours and 19 seconds on 1 September.

Robert displayed his usual enthusiasm at the sun-dial demonstration

To set a sundial accurately, it must be installed at solar noon using solar time at the place it is to be installed, and not standard time which is based on a prime meridian somewhere else. Solar noon is the most practical time to install a sundial. To find the time of local solar noon:

- **Find out the longitude of the place where the sundial is to be installed.**
- **Find out the longitude of your standard meridian.**

The world is divided into time zones 15° apart, measured from longitude 0 in Greenwich, England. Thus, the standard meridian for the United Kingdom, Ireland and Portugal is the prime meridian of 0°, while the rest of continental Europe keeps European Time, for which the standard meridian is 15° east of Greenwich (which passes through Prague, the capital of the Czech Republic). For example, the time zones of North America are:

Zone	Prime meridian degree W	City near that longitude	Hours earlier than Greenwich
Atlantic	60°	Glace Bay, NS	4
Eastern	75°	Philadelphia, PA	5
Central	90°	Memphis, TN	6
Mountain	105°	Santa Fe, NM	7
Pacific	120°	Fresno, CA	8

- **Calculate the difference between your longitude and the prime meridian.**

  For example, consider 4° 10′ for West Plymouth. Subtract the longitude of the prime meridian of your time zone (e.g. 0° for Greenwich). Since the sun takes 1 hour to traverse 15°, the sun crosses the longitude of Plymouth later than it is at Greenwich. It will be 4 minutes later for each degree of longitude, and 4 seconds later for each minute of longitude. Therefore 4° 10′ means that solar noon in Plymouth will be 16 minutes and 40 seconds later than it is at Greenwich.

Place	Plymouth, England	Santiago de Compostela, Spain	New Harbor, Maine	Boise, Idaho
Longitude of place	4° 10′ W	8° 33′ W	69° 30′ W	116° 12.8′ W
Longitude of prime meridian	0°	15° E	75° W	105° W
Difference	+4° 10′	−12° 51.5′	−5° 30′	+11° 37.2′
Time equivalent	+16 min 40 seconds	+90 min 26 seconds	−22 min 0 seconds	+46 min 29 seconds

- **Look up the time of solar noon at your prime meridian in the table below.**
  Time of solar noon at the prime meridian

	1st	Correction/day	11th	Correction/day	21st	Correction/day
	hh:mm:ss	sec	hh:mm:ss	sec	hh:mm:ss	sec
January	12:03:09	+20.5	12:07:38	+21	12:11:05	+12
February	12:13:33	+4.5	12:14:19	+3	12:13:49	−9.5
March	12:12:34	−13.5	12:10:18	−17	12:07:28	−20
April	12:04:08	−20	12:01:16	−13.5	11:59:00	−11
May	11:57:09	−5	11:56:20	+6	11:56:26	+7
June	11:57:42	+9.5	11:59:21	+12.5	12:01:28	+12.5
July	12:03:33	+10.5	12:05:16	+6	12:06:15	0
August	12:06:16	−6	12:05:14	−12	12:03:16	−17
September	12:00:12	−20	11:56:52	−21	11:53:20	−21
October	11:49:55	−17.5	11:46:58	−13	11:44:45	−6
November	11:43:40	+2	11:44:00	+12.5	11:45:44	+18
December	11:48:46	+25	11:52:58	+29	11:57:44	+30

- **Calculate the time of solar noon at your location** (if it is sunny that day at the time of solar noon). For example, on 11 March, solar noon is at 12:10:18 at the prime meridian, so solar noon at Plymouth is 12:10:18 plus 16:40 which gives 12:26:58 by your watch. The calculation is tabulated below.

Place	Plymouth, England	Barcelona, Spain	New Harbor, Maine	Boise, Idaho
Time of solar noon at prime meridian	12:10:18	12:10:18	12:10:18	12:10:18
Time equivalent of longitude (see above)	+16 min 40 seconds	−51 min 26 seconds	−22 min 0 seconds	+46 min 29 seconds
Time by your watch of solar noon at this location	12:26:58	11:18:52	11:48:18	12:56:45
See note on daylight saving time below				
Sundial apparently fast or slow by your watch	26 min 58 s slow	41 min 8 s fast	11 min 42 seconds fast	56 min 45 seconds slow

If your country operates Daylight Saving Time or Summer Time when all clocks are altered to read an hour ahead of the standard time, add 1 h to your calculated time of solar noon. For example, on 11 August, solar noon occurs at 12:05:14 at the prime meridian, so solar noon at Plymouth is 12:05:14 plus 16:40 plus 1 h which gives 13:19:53 on your watch.

- **Set your watch accurately by a radio time signal.**
- **Set up your sundial**. At the exact time of solar noon which you have calculated, rotate the sundial on the base plate until the ray of sunlight falling between the slot in the gnomon is exactly over the dotted noon line.

Source/Copyright: The spot-on sundial, www.spot-on-sundials.co.uk

5.3 Conversions and Calculations

To convert to imperial, multiply by the factor To convert from imperial, divide by the factor			To convert from metric, multiply by the factor To convert to metric, divide by the factor
		LENGTH	
0.6214	miles	kilometres	1.6093
1.093	yards	metres	0.9144
3.280	feet	metres	0.3048
3.93	inches	millimetres	25.4
0.393	inches	centimetres	2.54
		AREA	
0.386	square miles	square kilometres	2.59
0.0039	square miles	hectares	258.999
1.196	square yards	square metres	0.8361
0.00155	square inches	square millimetres	645.16
0.155	square inches	square centimetres	6.4516
		MASS	
0.001	tonnes	kilograms	1016.05
0.984	tonnes	tonnes	1.016
0.020	hundred weights	kilograms	50.8023
0.0787	quarters	kilograms	12.7006
0.157	stones	kilograms	6.3503
2.205	pounds	kilograms	0.4536
		VOLUME	
1.308	cubic yards	cubic metres	0.7646
35.315	cubic feet	cubic metres	0.0283
0.0353	cubic feet	cubic decimetres	28.3168
0.061	cubic inches	cubic centimetres	16.3871
		CAPACITY	
0.220	gallons	litres	4.546
1.760	pints	litres	0.568

Approximate metric/imperial Equivalents

Area	Length
1 hectare (ha) = 10,000 m^2	25 mm = 1″
1 hectare = 2 ½ acres	100 mm = 4″
0.4 hectare = 1 acre	3000 mm = 10′0″
1 acre (a) = 100 m^2	1 micron (μm) = 1.0 × 10^{-6} m

Capacity	Weight
1 litre = 1¾ pints	1 kg = 2¼ pounds
	28 grams = 1 ounce
Units	100 grams = 3½ ounces
π = 3.1416	454 grams = 1 pound

Calculations
Volume

Cone = 1/3 $\pi r^2 h$
Sphere = 4/3 $\pi r^3 h$
Cylinder = $\pi r^2 h$

Circumference

Circle = π × diameter
Cone = π × main axis + ½ minor axis

Surface area

Circle = π × r^2
Cylinder = circumference × length + area of both ends
Sphere = πr × $diameter^2$
Triangle = ½ base × perpendicular height

5.4 Gradients

Slope	Percentage	Degrees	Height of rise in 1 m length (mm)
1:1	100	45	1000
1:2	50	26.56	500
1:3	33.3	18:43	333
1:4	25	14	250
1:5	20	11.3	200
1:6	16.6	9.46	166
1:7	14.3	8.13	143
1:8	12.5	7.12	125
1:9	11.1	6.34	111
1:10	10	5.71	100
1:11	9	5.19	
1:12	8.3	4.76	83
1:13	7.7	4.39	
1:14	7.1	4.08	
1:15	6.6	3.81	67
1:16	6.25	3.57	
1:20	5	2.86	50
1:25	4	2.29	
1:30	3.3	1.9	33
1:40	2.5	1.43	25
1:50	2	1.14	20
1:60	1.6	0.95	16.6

See the next page for how to work out a gradient.

To work out a gradient as 1:G

$$G = \frac{\text{length of ramp (Y)}}{\text{Height rise (Z)}}$$

To work out the gradient as a percentage (P)

$$P\% = \frac{\text{Height rise (Z)} \times 100}{\text{Length of ramp (Y)}}$$

To convert 1:G to a percentage (P)

$$P\% = \frac{100}{G}$$

To convert a percentage (P) to 1:G

$$G = \frac{100}{P\%}$$

5.5 Weights of Materials

Material	Tonnes per cubic metre	Cubic metres per tonne	Litres per tonne
Ashes	0.96	1.04	–
Ballast, all in, containing sand	1.60	0.62	–
Bitumen	1.37	0.73	–
Bituminous emulsion	–	–	1000
Brickwork, solid – pressed bricks	2.12	0.47	
Brickwork, solid – ordinary	1.92	0.53	
Cement – aluminous	1.40	0.71	
Cement – Portland	1.44	0.70	
Cement – rapid hardening	1.28	0.79	
Chalk	2.24	0.45	
Clay	1.92	0.53	
Clinker	0.80	1.24	
Coke	0.57	1.70	
Concrete – gravel or ballast	2.24	0.45	
Concrete – breeze	1.44	0.69	
Earth top soil	1.60	0.62	
Earth vegetable	1.23	0.82	
Flint	2.59	0.38	
Gravel, coarse with sand	1.76	0.57	
Lime, ground – quicklime	0.96	1.04	
Lime, slaked	0.48	2.08	
Loam	1.60	0.62	
Marl	1.76	0.57	
Media-filter	0.88	1.13	
Pitch	1.16	0.87	
Sand, fine, clean pit	1.44	0.70	
Sand, medium pit	1.53	0.65	
Sand, Thames or washed river	1.69	0.59	
Shale	2.60	0.38	
Slag	1.51	0.67	
Slate	2.89	0.34	

Material	Tonnes per cubic metre	Cubic metres per tonne	Litres per tonne
Snow – freshly fallen	0.12	8.33	
Snow – old lying and compacted	0.52	1.92	
Stone – solid, ballast	2.77	0.36	
Stone – solid, bath	2.00	0.50	
Stone – solid, granite	2.67	0.38	
Stone – solid, Kentish rag	2.64	0.38	
Stone – solid, limestone	2.41	0.41	
Stone – solid, Portland	2.44	0.41	
Stone – solid, Purbeck	2.60	0.39	
Stone – solid, sandstone	2.33	0.44	
Stone – solid, traprock	2.73	0.37	
Stone – solid, whinstone	2.77	0.36	
Tar	–	–	873

Approximate weight of wet mortar		
Type of mortar	Tonnes per cubic metre	Cubic metres per tonne
Cement lime mortar	1.96	0.51
Lime mortar	1.73	0.59
Portland cement mortar	2.00	0.50

Average weight of building stone	
Type of stone	Cubic metres per tonne
Bath	0.44
Portland	0.41
Sandstone	0.41
York	0.40
Limestone	0.40
Purbeck	0.39
Granite	0.38
Marble	0.37

Weight of kerb per metre		
Size of kerb per metre	Type of kerb and weight in tonnes per metre	
	Concrete	Granite
125 × 50	0.011	0.013
175 × 50	0.022	0.025
250 × 100	0.066	0.077
250 × 125	0.077	0.088
250 × 150	0.088	0.099
250 × 200	0.110	0.132
300 × 150	0.099	0.121
300 × 200	0.132	0.165

Weight of artificial stone paving	
Thickness of stone (mm)	Tonnes per square metre
50	0.12
63	0.15

Weight of precast concrete manhole rings	
Diameter of ring (mm)	Weight per metre (kg)
675	281
900	467
1050	624
1200	760
1350	869
1500	1036
1800	1449

Weight of agricultural drainage pipes	
Diameter of piper (mm)	Kilograms per 1000
50	900
62	1250
75	1750
100	2300
1500	5000

Weight of road foundation materials			
Nature of material	Weight in the solid Kilograms per cubic metre	Weight of crushed material	
		Tonnes per cubic metre	Cubic metres per tonne
Basalt	2809	1.53	0.65
Brick	2123	1.16	0.86
Clinker	–	0.80	1.24
Concrete	2286	1.24	0.81
Granite	2711	1.48	0.67
Kentish rag	2694	1.47	0.68
Limestone	2449	1.33	0.69
Sandstone	2367	1.29	0.75
Shingle	–	1.51	0.66
Slag, cold blast	2580	1.40	0.72
Slag, hot blast	2531	1.37	0.73
Whinstone	2809	1.53	0.65
Note: The data shown are based on 45% voids.			

Weight of road surfacing materials			
Nature of material	Weight in the solid Kilogrammes per cubic metre	Weight in the loose as delivered on the site	
		Tonnes per cubic metre	Cubic metres per tonne
Ashes	–	0.96	1.04
Clinker	–	0.80	1.24
Gravel	–	1.52	0.66
Hardcore, brick	2123	1.16	0.86
Hardcore, chalk	2286	1.24	0.81
Hardcore, concrete	2286	1.24	0.81
Pitching, granite	2711	1.48	0.68
Pitching, limestone	2367	1.29	0.78
Pitching, sandstone	2449	1.33	0.75
Pitching, whinstone	2804	1.53	0.65

Weight of road surfacing materials			
Nature of material	Weight in the loose as delivered on the site		
	Weight in the solid Kilograms per cubic metre	Tonnes per cubic metre	Cubic metres per tonne
Asphalt, bottom course	–	2.12	0.51
Asphalt, top course	–	2.24	0.45
Asphalt, mastic	2711	2.33	0.43
Tarred granite	–	1.53	0.62
Tarred gravel	2449	1.53	0.65
Tarred limestone	2531	1.57	0.64
Tarred slag	2804	1.40	0.70
Tarred whinstone	–	1.56	0.61

Approximate weight of brickwork			
Type of brick	Approximate weight of one brick (kg)	Approximate weight of 1000 bricks (tonnes)	Approximate number of bricks per tonne
Flettons	2.54	2.50	400
Facing bricks	2.72	2.68	373
Stocks	3.06	3.00	332
Firebricks	3.17	3.12	320
Wirecuts	3.26	3.21	311
Pressed bricks	3.62	3.57	280
Blue staffs	3.97	3.90	256
Engineering bricks	4.20	4.13	242

5.6 Volumes in Relation to Depth and Area

Area (m²)	Volume (m³)				
	Depth 300 mm	Depth 200 mm	Depth 150 mm	Depth 100 mm	Depth 50 mm
0.50	0.15	0.10	0.08	0.05	0.30
1.00	0.30	0.20	0.15	0.10	0.05
2.00	0.60	0.40	0.30	0.20	0.10
3.00	0.90	0.60	0.45	0.30	0.15
4.00	1.20	0.80	0.60	0.40	0.20
5.00	1.50	1.00	0.75	0.50	0.25
6.00	1.80	1.20	0.90	0.60	0.30
7.00	2.10	1.40	1.05	0.70	0.35
8.00	2.40	1.60	1.20	0.80	0.40
9.00	2.70	1.80	1.35	0.90	0.45
10.00	3.00	2.00	1.50	1.00	0.50
11.00	3.30	2.20	1.65	1.10	0.55
12.00	3.60	2.40	1.80	1.20	0.60
13.00	3.90	2.60	1.95	1.30	0.65
14.00	4.20	2.80	2.10	1.40	0.70
15.00	4.50	3.00	2.25	1.50	0.75
16.00	4.80	3.20	2.40	1.60	0.80
17.00	5.10	3.40	2.55	1.70	0.85
18.00	5.40	3.60	2.70	1.80	0.90
19.00	5.70	3.80	2.85	1.90	0.95
20.00	6.00	4.00	3.00	2.00	1.00
21.00	6.30	4.20	3.15	2.10	1.05
22.00	6.60	4.40	3.30	2.20	1.10
23.00	6.90	4.60	3.45	2.30	1.15
24.00	7.20	4.80	3.60	2.40	1.20
25.00	7.50	5.00	3.75	2.50	1.25
26.00	7.80	5.20	3.90	2.60	1.30
27.00	8.10	5.40	4.05	2.70	1.35
28.00	8.40	5.60	4.20	2.80	1.40
29.00	8.70	5.80	4.35	2.90	1.45
30.00	9.00	6.00	4.50	3.00	1.50
31.00	9.30	6.20	4.65	3.10	1.55

Area (m²)	Volume (m³)				
	Depth 300 mm	**Depth 200 mm**	**Depth 150 mm**	**Depth 100 mm**	**Depth 50 mm**
32.00	9.60	6.40	4.80	3.20	1.60
33.00	9.90	6.60	4.95	3.30	1.65
34.00	10.20	6.80	5.10	3.40	1.70
35.00	10.50	7.00	5.25	3.50	1.75
36.00	10.80	7.20	5.40	3.60	1.80
37.00	11.10	7.40	5.55	3.70	1.85
38.00	11.40	7.60	5.70	3.80	1.90
39.00	11.70	7.80	5.85	3.90	1.95
40.00	12.00	8.00	6.00	4.00	2.00
41.00	12.30	8.20	6.15	4.10	2.05
42.00	12.60	8.40	6.30	4.20	2.10
43.00	12.90	8.60	6.45	4.30	2.15
44.00	13.20	8.80	6.60	4.40	2.20
45.00	13.50	9.00	6.75	4.50	2.25
46.00	13.80	9.20	6.90	4.60	2.30
47.00	14.10	9.40	7.05	4.70	2.35
48.00	14.40	9.60	7.20	4.80	2.40
49.00	14.70	9.80	7.35	4.90	2.45
50.00	15.00	10.00	7.50	5.00	2.50
51.00	15.30	10.20	7.65	5.10	2.55
52.00	15.60	10.40	7.80	5.20	2.60
53.00	15.90	10.60	7.95	5.30	2.65
54.00	16.20	10.80	8.10	5.40	2.70
55.00	16.50	11.00	8.25	5.50	2.75
56.00	16.80	11.20	8.40	5.60	2.80
57.00	17.10	11.40	8.55	5.70	2.85
58.00	17.40	11.60	8.70	5.80	2.90
59.00	17.70	11.80	8.85	5.90	2.95
60.00	18.00	12.00	9.00	6.00	3.00
61.00	18.30	12.20	9.15	6.10	3.05
62.00	18.60	12.40	9.30	6.20	3.10
63.00	18.90	12.60	9.45	6.30	3.15
64.00	19.20	12.80	9.60	6.40	3.20
65.00	19.50	13.00	9.75	6.50	3.25

Area (m²)	Volume (m³)				
	Depth 300 mm	Depth 200 mm	Depth 150 mm	Depth 100 mm	Depth 50 mm
66.00	19.80	13.20	9.90	6.60	3.30
67.00	20.10	13.40	10.05	6.70	3.35
68.00	20.40	13.60	10.20	6.80	3.40
69.00	20.70	13.80	10.35	6.90	3.45
70.00	21.00	14.00	10.50	7.00	3.50
71.00	21.30	14.20	10.65	7.10	3.55
72.00	21.60	14.40	10.80	7.20	3.60
73.00	21.90	14.60	10.95	7.30	3.65
74.00	22.20	14.80	11.10	7.40	3.70
75.00	22.50	15.00	11.25	7.50	3.75
76.00	22.80	15.20	11.40	7.60	3.80
77.00	23.10	15.40	11.55	7.70	3.85
78.00	23.40	15.60	11.70	7.80	3.90
79.00	23.70	15.80	11.85	7.90	3.95
80.00	24.00	16.00	12.00	8.00	4.00
81.00	24.30	16.20	12.15	8.10	4.05
82.00	24.60	16.40	12.30	8.20	4.10
83.00	24.90	16.60	12.45	8.30	4.15
84.00	25.20	16.80	12.60	8.40	4.20
85.00	25.50	17.00	12.75	8.50	4.25
86.00	25.80	17.20	12.90	8.60	4.30
87.00	26.10	17.40	13.05	8.70	4.35
88.00	26.40	17.60	13.20	8.80	4.40
89.00	26.70	17.80	13.35	8.90	4.45
90.00	27.00	18.00	13.50	9.00	4.50
91.00	27.30	18.20	13.65	9.10	4.55
92.00	27.60	18.40	13.80	9.20	4.60
93.00	27.90	18.60	13.95	9.30	4.65
94.00	28.20	18.80	14.10	9.40	4.70
95.00	28.50	19.00	14.25	9.50	4.75
96.00	28.80	19.20	14.40	9.60	4.80
97.00	29.10	19.40	14.55	9.70	4.85
98.00	29.40	19.60	14.70	9.80	4.90
99.00	29.70	19.80	14.85	9.90	4.95
100.00	30.00	20.00	15.00	10.00	5.00

5.7 Rules of Thumb for Planting Plans

Planting densities

Centres/per m²	Plants/per m²
150 mm	45
200 mm	25
300 mm	11
400 mm	6.3
500 mm	4
600 mm	2.8
750 mm	1.98
800 mm	1.6
900 mm	1.2
1000 mm	1.0
1500 m	0.44
2000 m	0.3

Planting on a 1:3 slope

1:1 slope – multiply plan area by 1.41 (40%)

1:2 slope – multiply plan area by 1.12 (12%)

1:3 slope – multiply plan area by 1.05 (5%)

5.8 Quantities and Rates of Sowing Grass Seed for Sports Use

Total quantities of grass seed are required at the following sowing rates:

Application	Area	Sowing rate (g/m²)		
		20 g/m²	35 g/m²	50 g/m²
Bowling Green	40 × 40 m (1600 m²)	32	56	80
Cricket Square	22.8 m × 22.8 m (520 m²)	10.4	18	26
Lawn Tennis	23.8 m × 11 m (262 m²)	5.2	9	13
Rugby Football	100 m × 69 m (6900 m²)	138	241	234
Association Football	9 m × 46 m (4140 m²)	82.8	145	207
18 Golf Greens	500 m² (9000 m²)	180	315	450

6 Graphics

Mrs. Ponsonby was very proud of Giles' early promise as a graphic designer.

6.1 Paper Sizes

The A series	The A series of paper sizes is an international scale used for all drawings and written material
Calculation of sizes	The A range is based on a rectangle AO, 1.1, and of area 1 m² with sides x and y where x:y = 1:√2 (i.e. x = 841 mm and y = 1189 mm) The other sizes in the series are derived downwards by progressively halving the size above across its larger dimension. The proportion of the sizes remain constant 1:2

A sizes	A Size	Dimensions in mm
	A0	841 × 1189
	A1	594 × 841
	A2	420 × 594
	A3	297 × 420
	A4	210 × 297
	A5	148 × 210
	A6	105 × 148
	A7	74 × 105
	A8	52 × 74
	A9	37 × 52
	A10	26 × 37

6.2 Common Digital File Extensions

Adobe family		
	.pdf	Portable document format
	.ai	Illustrator
	.ait	Illustrator template
	.psd	Photoshop document
	.indd	InDesign
Autodesk family		
	.dwg	AutoCAD drawing file
	.dwf	Drawing web format
	.dwt	Drawing template
	.dxf	Drawing exchange format
	.shx	Shape file
	.bak	Backup file
	.sv$	Auto-save file
Windows/system files		
	.exe	Program file
	.bmp	bitmap image file
	.wmf	Windows metafile
	.jpg	Photo file
	.tif	Integrated image file
	.doc	Word document
	.xls	Excel spread sheet
	.dot	Word document template
	.ppt	Powerpoint template
	.pps	Powerpoint slide show
	.htm	Web page
	.html	Web page
	.msg	Outlook message
	.txt	Text file
	.rtf	Rich text format
	.xlt	Excel template
	.mpg	Movie file
	.avi	Audio visual file
Other software for consideration	Quark Microstation Sketch-up Zip programs	

6.3 AutoCAD Printing Scales

Zoom Scales	Model space in metres		Model space in millimetres	
	1:1	100xp	1:1	1xp
	1:2	500xp	1:2	0.5xp
	1:5	200xp	1:5	0.2xp
	1:10	100xp	1:10	0.1xp
	1:20	50xp	1:20	0.05xp
	1:25	40xp	1:25	0.04xp
	1:50	20xp	1:50	0.02xp
	1:100	10xp	1:100	0.01xp
	1:200	5xp	1:200	0.005xp
	1:250	4xp	1:250	0.004xp
	1:500	2xp	1:500	0.002xp
	1:1000	1xp	1:1000	0.001xp
	1:1250	0.8xp	1:1250	0.0008xp
	1:2000	0.5xp	1:2000	0.0005xp
	1:2500	0.4xp	1:2500	0.0004xp
	1:5000	0.2xp	1:5000	0.0002xp
	1:10,000	0.1xp	1:10,000	0.0001xp

6.4 Typical Survey Annotations

Annotations					
AP	Anchor Point	**FS**	Flagstaff	**PZ**	Piezometre
AV	Air Valve	**G**	Gully	**RE**	Rodding Eye
BH	Borehole	**GV**	Gas Valve	**RP**	Reflector Post
BL	Bollard	**IC**	Inspection Cover	**RS**	Road Sign
BS	Bus Stop	**IL**	Invert Level	**SA**	Soakaway
BT	Telecom IC	**IN**	Inclinometre	**SC**	Stop Cock
CL	Cover Level	**JB**	Junction Box	**SF**	Soffit Level
C.MK	Cable Marker	**KO**	Kerb Outlet	**SI**	Trial Pit
CTV	Cable TV IC	**LP**	Lamp Post	**SS**	Survey Station
DP	Down Pipe	**MH**	Manhole	**ST**	Stump
DR	Drain	**MK**	Marker	**SV**	Stop Valve
EIC	Electricity IC	**NB**	Notice Board	**TBM**	Site Bench Mark
EP	Electricity Pole	**OS**	O.S. Trig. Station	**TL**	Threshold Level
ER	Earthing Rod	**OSBM**	O.S. Bench Mark	**TL**	Telegraph Pole
FH	Fire Hydrant	**P**	Post	**TP**	Traffic Light
FL	Floor level	**PE**	Pipe	**VP**	Vent Pipe
		PGM	Perm. Ground Marker	**WM**	Water Meter

Fence types		Wall types	
CBF	Close-Boarded Fence	**BW**	Brick Wall
CPF	Chestnut Paling Fence	**CW**	Concrete Wall
IRF	Iron Railing Fence	**DSW**	Dry Stone Wall
OBF	Open-Boarded Fence	**RTW**	Retaining Wall
PBW	Post and Barbed Wire	**SW**	Stone Wall
PCLF	Post and Chain Link		
PSW	Post and Sheep Wire		
PW	Post and Wire		
PWM	Post and Wire Mesh		

Symbols

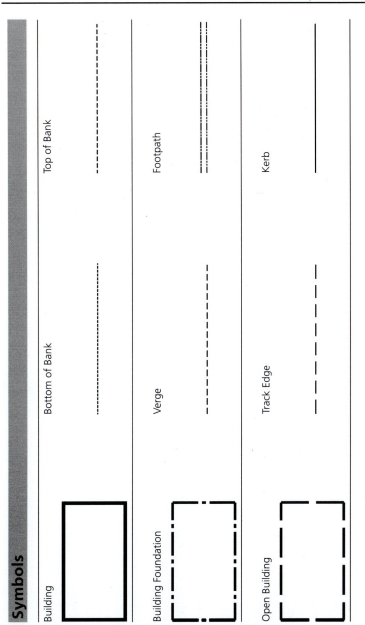

Building	Bottom of Bank	Top of Bank
Building Foundation	Verge	Footpath
Open Building	Track Edge	Kerb

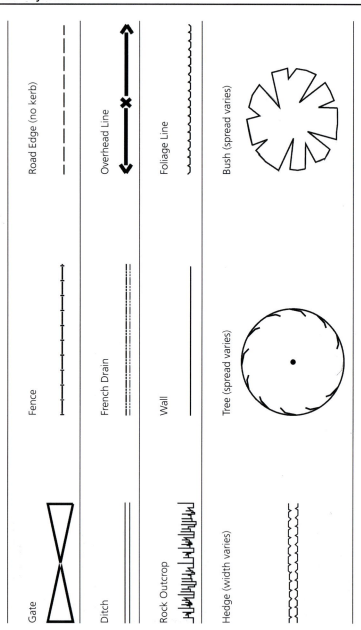

Gate

Fence

Road Edge (no kerb)

Ditch

French Drain

Overhead Line

Rock Outcrop

Wall

Foliage Line

Hedge (width varies)

Tree (spread varies)

Bush (spread varies)

6.5 Common Graphic Symbols

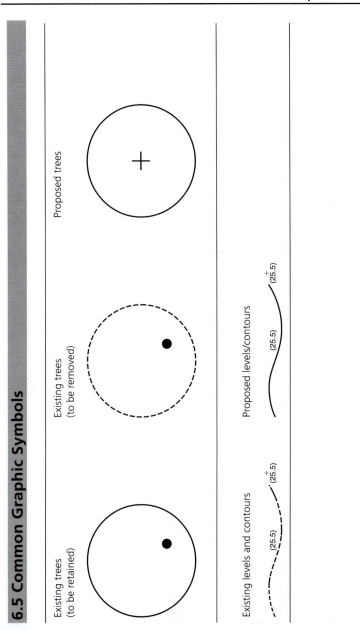

Existing trees
(to be retained)

Existing trees
(to be removed)

Proposed trees

Existing levels and contours

(25.5)   +(25.5)

Proposed levels/contours

(25.5)   +(25.5)

Glossary

air entrained and plasticized   Admixtures to a mortar. Mortar plasticizers which entrain air impart good working qualities. The air serves to increase the volume of the binder paste filling the voids in the sand and improving working qualities.

alloy   A metallic material which is a homogeneous mixture or solid solution of two or more metals or metallic with non-metallic elements added or something added that lowers value or purity.

anneal   To bring to a desired consistency, texture or hardness by a process of gradually heating and cooling.

anodizing   To coat a metallic surface electrolytically with a protective or decorative oxide.

austenitic steel   Austenitic stainless steels have high ductility, low yield stress and relatively high ultimate tensile strength, when compared to carbon steel. Austenitic grades are not magnetic. The austenitic stainless steels, because of their high chromium and nickel content, are the most corrosion resistant of the stainless group providing unusually fine mechanical properties.

brazing   To solder two metal surfaces together by fusing a layer of high melting point solder or brass between them.

bull nose   This refers to a rounded corner on a brick, kerb or cope. Bricks with two rounded corners are double bull nose.

capping units   Units at the top of a parapet free-standing or retaining wall which are flush with the wall that they are protecting and do not incorporate a throating or similar feature, designed to shed water. Flush cappings do not protect bricks below from saturation.

cardinal points/cardinal directions   The directions are *north, east, south* and *west*.

case hardening   When stone is first taken from the ground, it is relatively soft. As it dries out, and salts are drawn to the surface, a patina or harder outer skin known as the case hardening, is formed.

cementitous lime staining   There can be confusion between lime staining and efflorescence. In its most common form, lime staining emanates from the bottom of the cross joints. The lime deposited on the surface of the brickwork then carbonates as a water-insoluble blemish.

contour scaling   This is the term used to describe the process where salt crystallization detaches the case hardening.

conviction on indictment   Indictable offences are more serious offences and can be tried by jury.

copping   A unit at the top of a parapet free-standing or retaining wall and is a unit which sheds water clear of all exposed faces of the wall it is protecting.

corrosion   The breaking down or destruction of a material through chemical reactions. Rusting is a form of corrosion which occurs when iron combines with oxygen and water.

curtilage   It is a legal term describing the enclosed area of land around a dwelling.

delamination   The detachment or loss of a layer of stone that follows the alignment of bedding planes.

designated mix or designed mix   A concrete mix selected from a restricted range, where the producer must hold a current accredited product conformity certification.

ductile   Easily drawn into wire or hammered thin.

duplex stainless steel   Duplex stainless steel strip, a mixed microstructure with about equal proportions of ferrite and austenite. Duplex is also roughly double the strength of standard austenitic stainless steels. Duplex is a stainless steel designed to combine improved resistance to stress corrosion cracking, pitting, crevice corrosion and high strength when compared with other stainless alloys.

edge bedding   Means of laying stone where the layers of the stone are vertical and run at 90° to the plane of construction.

efflorescence   This typically appears as a white powdery deposit on brick faces which have dried out after brickwork has been saturated. This can be distinguished from other stains as it will tend to disappear when rubbed with a wet thumb.

face bedding   Means of laying stone where the layers of the stone are vertical and parallel to the plane of the construction. Usually leads to extensive powdering and scaling of the stone.

ferrous   Derived from or containing iron.

fibre optics   *Glass* or *plastic* fibre designed to guide *light* along its length. Optical fibres are widely used in *fibre-optic communication*, which permits transmission over longer distances and at higher data rates than other forms of communications. Fibres are used instead of metal wires because signals travel along them with less *loss*, and they are immune to *electromagnetic interference*.

flat sawn timber   Timber cut tangentially to the annual growth rings, often called through and through.

forging   To form, metal, by heating and beating or hammering into shape.

frogged brick   This brick has a depression formed in one or more bed faces of the unit in order to save weight. The total volume of all such depressions should not exceed a certain limit of the overall volume of the unit.

gnomon   A stationary object that projects a shadow, used as an indicator, on a sundial.

IP ratings   (Ingress Protection) EN 60529 outlines an international classification system for the sealing effectiveness of enclosures of electrical equipment against the intrusion into the equipment of foreign bodies (i.e. tools, dust, fingers) and moisture.

Joule (J) It is the international sytem of units (SI) of *energy* – measuring *heat, electricity* and *mechanical work*. One joule is the work done, or energy expended, by a *force* of one *newton* moving one *metre* along the direction of the force. Or one joule is the work done to produce power of one *watt* continuously for one *second*.

Kelvin (K) A unit of *thermodynamic temperature*, taken as one of the base units of the *International System of Units* (SI). The Kelvin is defined by setting the thermodynamic temperature of the triple point of water at 273.16 K. In measuring temperature intervals, the degree Celsius is equal to the Kelvin. The Celsius temperature scale is defined by setting 0°C equal to 273.16 K.

lath A thin, narrow strip of wood, that can be oak, chestnut or softwood often found in traditional buildings. They are nailed to the rafters, studs, or floor beams of a building, for the purpose of supporting the tiles, plastering, etc. A corrugated metallic strip or plate is sometimes used.

lumen (lm) It is the *SI* unit of *luminous flux*, a measure of the perceived power of *light*. Luminous flux differs from *radiant flux*, the measure of the total power of light emitted, in that luminous flux is adjusted to reflect the varying sensitivity of the human *eye* to different *wavelengths* of light.

luminaires It is a complete lighting unit that consist of a lamp or lamps. Luminaires also refer to the parts that help position, protect and connect the lamps.

mass concrete Any volume or placement of normal concrete with dimensions large enough to require that measures be taken to cope with the generation of heat due to hydration of the cement and attendant volume change to minimize cracking.

micrometre This (symbol μm) is one millionth of a metre, or equivalently one thousandth of a millimetre. It is also commonly known as a micron. It can be written in scientific notation as 1×10^{-6} m, meaning 1/1,000,000 m.

mill finish Mill finish is the finish obtained by standard extrusion practices and produced without the aid of any subsequent operations as metal.

m/m Mass

organic solvent Solvents are substance that acts as a dissolving agent for solids, liquids or gases. Organic solvents are carbon-containing chemicals. The most widely used solvent is water. Other compounds valuable as solvents are acetone, alcohol, benzene (or benzol), carbon disulphide, carbon tetrachloride, chloroform, ether, ethyl acetate, furfural, gasoline, toluene, turpentine and xylene (or xylol).

oxidization The addition of oxygen to a compound.

Peacocking This is a type of discolouration which often occurs on blue or similarly fired bricks or pavers. Usually, the effect is a darkening around the edges or a more widespread petrol-stain effect. Peacocking to a degree is, and always has been, a normal feature of blue clay brickwork. However, protective measures will minimize the visual impact and limit the extent of the effect.

Portland cement A hydraulic cement made by heating a limestone and clay mixture in a kiln and pulverizing the resulting material.

Portland cement mortar   It (often referred to as cement mortar) is created by mixing Portland cement with sand and water. The Portland cement mortar is the basis for concrete, a mixture usually composed of this particular mortar with the addition of gravel or suitable aggregate.

quarry sap   This is the moisture found in most newly quarried stone which quickly dries out forming the case hardening.

quarter sawn timber   Cut radially from the log to give an edge vertical or straight grained appearance.

satin finish   Also known as brushed or matte finish, where a series of very fine parallel lines are scratched on the surface of metal to create a texture. The finish is achieved by sandblasting or brushing with a stiff wire brush, or chemically altering a high shine surface. This semi-glossy finish has reduced reflectivity.

slaked lime   Calcium oxide. Limestone is heated until it breaks down to form calcium oxide and carbon dioxide. Calcium oxide is also called quicklime. Calcium oxide reacts with water to form calcium hydroxide, also called slaked lime.

soldering   A fusible alloy such as tin or lead for joining two metal surfaces. The surfaces are soldered by melting the alloy so that it forms a thin layer between the two parts.

spalling   A general term applied to stonework on which the outer face is peeling off. A spall is a small piece of stone.

summary conviction   Summary conviction offences encompass the most minor offences.

tempered   Reduce the brittleness of a hardened metal or glass to improve its elasticity. Made appropriately hard or flexible by tempering. Having the requisite degree of hardness or elasticity. Used on glass or a metal.

vitreous enamel   It is the fusing of powdered glass on to a substrate to form a durable protective finish usually fired between 750°C and 850°C. The powder melts and flows and hardens to a smooth, durable vitreous coating on metal, glass or ceramic.

weld   To join metals or plastic by softening by applying heat, sometimes with pressure by hammering and sometimes with a filler metal having a high melting point.

Associations, Institutes and Further Sources of Information

Acorn Planting Products Ltd Little Money Road, Loddon, Norwich, N14 6JD www.acord-p-p.co.uk	tel:	01508 528763
Aluminium Federation National Metalforming Centre, 47 Birmingham Road, West Bromwich, West Midlands B70 6PY email: alfed@alfed.org.uk www.alfed.org.uk	tel: fax:	0121 601 6363 0870 138 9714
API (Association of Playground Industries) Rederatiion House, Stoneleigh Park Warwickshire, CV8 2RF www.api-play.org	tel:	01476 414999 ext 208
Barbour Ludgate House, 245 Blackfriars Road, London, SE1 9UY email: barbour-cmc@cmpi.biz www.barbour.info	tel: fax:	01344 884121 01344 884845
Brick Development Association (BDA) Woodside House, Winkfield, Windsor, Berkshire, SL4 2DX email: brick@brick.org.uk www.brick.org.uk	tel: fax:	01344 885 651 01344 890 129
British Board of Agrément, Bucknalls Lane, Garston, Watford WD25 9BA email: contact@bba.star.co.uk www.bbacerts.co.uk	tel: fax:	01923 665300 01923 665301
British Cement Association Riverside House, 4 Meadows Business Park, Station Approach, Blackwater, Camberley Surrey, GU17 9AB email: info@bca.org.uk www.cementindustry.co.uk	tel: fax:	01276 608700 01276 608701

British Research Establishment (BRE) BRE, Bucknalls Lane, Watford WD25 9XX email: enquiries@bre.co.uk www.bre.co.uk	tel:	01923 664000
British Seed Houses Ltd. Camp Road, Witham St. Hughes Lincoln, LN6 9QJ www.britishseedhouses.com	tel:	01522 868714
British Stainless Steel Association Broomgrove, 59 Clarkehouse Road, Sheffield S10 2LE, United Kingdom email: enquiry@bssa.org.uk www.bssa.org.uk	tel: fax:	0114 267 1260 0114 266 1252
British Standards Institute BSI British Standards, 389 Chiswick High Road, London, W4 4AL email: cservices@bsigroup.com www.bsi-uk.com	tel: fax:	020 8996 9001 020 8996 7001
BTCV Sedium House, Mallard Way Doncaster, DN4 8DB www2.btcv.org.uk	tel:	01302 388883
Building Centre The Building Centre, Store Street London, WC1E 7BT www.buildingcentre.co.uk	tel:	0207 692 4000
Centre for Accessible Environments and the Access Lab 70 South Lambeth Road, London SW8 1RL email: info@cae.org.uk www.cae.org.uk		020 7840 0125 020 7840 5811
Concrete Centre The Concrete Centre, Riverside House, 4 Meadows Business Park Station Approach, Blackwater, Camberley, GU17 9AB email: enquiries@concretecentre.com www.concretecentre.com	tel:	01276 606 800

Concrete Society The Concrete Centre, Riverside House, 4 Meadows Business Park Station Approach, Blackwater, Camberley, GU17 9AB www.concrete.org.uk	tel:	1276 607140
Central Point of Expertise on Timber **Procurement** email: cpet@proforest.net www.proforest.net	tel:	01865 243766
Commission for Architecture and the Built (CABE), Environment, 1 Kemble Street, London, WC2B 4AN www.cabe.org.uk	tel: fax:	02070706700 02070706777
Copper Development Association 5 Grovelands Business Centre, Boundary Way Hemel Hempstead HP2 7TE www.cda.org.uk	fax:	01442 275716
Corus 30 Millbank, London SW1P 4WY email: feedback@ corusgroup.com www.corusgroup.com	tel: fax:	020 7717 4444 020 7717 4455
Department of Transport Department for Transport Great Minster House, 76 Marsham Street, London, SW1P 4DR email: FAX9643@dft.gsi.gov.uk www.dft.gov.uk	tel: fax:	020 7944 8300 020 7944 9643
English Heritage 1 Waterhouse Square, 138 – 142 Holborn, London, EC1N 2ST email: customers@english-heritage.org.uk www.english-heritage.org.uk	tel: fax:	020 7973 3000 020 7973 3001
English Partnerships Corporate Headquarters, 110 Buckingham Palace Road, London, SW1W 9SA email: mail@englishpartnerships.co.uk www.englishpartnerships.co.uk	tel: fax:	020 7881 1600 020 7730 9162

Environment Agency National Customer Contact Centre, PO Box 544, Rotherham, S60 1BY email: enquiries@environment-agency.gov.uk www.environment-agency.gov.uk	tel:	08708 506506
Forestry Commission Forestry Commission GB and Scotland.Silvan House, 231 Corstorphine Road Edinburgh, Scotland, EH12 7AT email: enquiries@forestry.gsi.gov.uk www.forestry.gov.uk	tel: fax:	0131 334 0303 0131 334 3047
Forests Forever and the Timber Trade Federation The Building Centre, 26 Store Street, London, WC1E 7BT email: ttf@ttf.co.uk www.forestsforever.org.uk	tel: fax:	020 3205 0067 020 7291 5379
Forest Stewardship Council FSC UK,11-13 Great Oak Street, Llanidloes, Powys, SY18 6BU email: info@fsc-uk.org www.fsc-uk.org	tel: fax:	01686 413916 01686 412176
Galvanizers Association Wren's Court, 56 Victoria Road Sutton Coldfield, West Midlands B72 1SY email: ga@hdg.org.uk www.galvanizing.org.uk	tel: fax:	0121 355 8838 0121 355 8727
Green-Tech Sweethills Park, Nun Monkton York, YO26 8ET www.green-tech.co.uk	tel:	01423 332100
Heicom 4 Frog Lane, Tunbridge WellsKent, TN1 1YT www.treesand.co.uk	tel:	01892 522360
Helios Wensley, Keyworth Road, Wysall, Nottinghamshire NG12 5QQ UK email: info@gohelios.co.uk www.gohelios.co.uk	tel:	01509 609 121

Highways Agency 123 Buckingham Palace Road, London SW1W 9HA email: ha_info@highways.gsi.gov.uk www.highways.gov.uk	tel:	0121 335 8300
Historic Scotland Head Office, Historic Scotland, Longmore, House, Salisbury Place Edinburgh, EH91SH email: hs.inspectorate@scotland.gsi.gov.uk www.historic-scotland.gov.uk	tel:	0131 668 8600
Horticultural Trades Association 19, High Street, Theale, Reading, RG7 5AH www.the-hta.co.uk	tel:	0118 930 8940
Ibstock Building Products Ltd Leicester Road, Ibstock, Leicestershire, LE67 6HS email: leicester.sales@ibstock.co.uk www.ibstock.com	tel: fax:	01530 261999 01530 257457
Institution of Highways and **Transportation** 6 Endsleigh Street, London WC1H 0DZ email: info@iht.org www.iht.org	tel: fax:	020 7387 2525 020 7387 2808
Landscape Institute Landscape Institute, 33 Great Portland Street, London, W1W 8QG email: mail@landscapeinstitute.org www.landscapeinstitute.org	tel: fax:	020 7299 4500 020 7299 4501
Lathams Ltd, Unit 3, Swallow Park, Finway Road, Hemel Hempstead, Hertfordshire, HP2 7QU email: marketing@lathams.co.uk www.lathams.co.uk	tel: fax:	01442 849100 01442 267241
Limetechnology Unit 126, Milton Park, Abingdon Oxfordshire, OX14 4SA email: info@limetechnology.co.uk www.limetechnology.co.uk	tel: fax:	0845 603 1143 0845 634 1560

Maccaferri 7600 The Quarum, Oxford business Park, North Easington Road, Oxford, OX4 2JZ www.maccaferri.co.uk	tel:	01865 770555
Melcourt Industries Ltd. Bolbridge Brake, Long Newnton Tetbury, Glos., GL8 8RT www.melcourt.co.uk	tel:	01666 502711
National Building Specification The Old Post Office, St Nicholas Street, Newcastle upon Tyne, NE1 1RH email: info@theNBS.com www.thenbs.com	tel:	0845 456 9594
National Joint Utilities Group 28 Broadway, Westminster, London, SW1H 9JX email: info@njug.org.uk www.njug.org.uk	tel:	020 7340 1423
Natural England Northminster House, Peterborough PE1 1UA www.naturalengland.org.uk	tel: fax:	0845 600 3078 01733 455103
Plaswood Products Ltd. Threxton House, Threxton Road, Industrial Estate, Watton, Thetford, Norfolk, IP25 6NG www.plaswood.co.uk	tel:	01953 884774
ProForest South Suite, Frewin Chambers Frewin Court, Oxford, OX1 3HZ email: info@proforest.net www.proforest.net	tel:	01865 243439
Rigby Taylor Ltd. The Riverside Estate, Portsmouth Road, Peasmarsh, Guildford, Surrey, GU3 1LZ www.rigbytaylor.com	tel:	0800 424919 01482 446900
ROSPA ROSPA House, Edgbaston Park, 353 Bristol Road, Edgbaston Birmingham, B5 7ST www.rospa.com	tel:	0121 248 2000

Salix River & Wetland Services Ltd. Blackhills Nurseries, Blackhills Lane Fairwood, Swansea, SA2 7JN www.salixrw.com	tel:	0870 350 1851
Scottish Natural Heritage Great Glen House, Leachkin Road, Inverness, IV3 8NW email: enquiries@snh.gov.uk www.snh.org.uk	tel: fax:	01463 725000 01463 725067
Sportsmark Ltd. Sportsmark House, 4 Clere water Place, Lower Way, Thatcham, Berkshire RG19 3RF www.sportsmark.net	tel: fax:	01635 867 537 01635 864 588
Spot-on sundial Spot-On Sundials PO Box 292, Epsom, KT174YP, England email: info@spot-on-sundials.co.uk www. spot-on-sundials.co.uk	tel:	01372 747767
Stone Federation Great Britain Channel Business CentreIngles Manor, Castle Hill Avenue, Folkestone, Kent, CT20 2RD email: enquiries@stone-federationgb.org.uk www.stone-federationgb.org.uk	tel: fax:	01303 856123 01303 856117
Sureset UK Ltd. 32 Dexerill Road, Trading Estate Sutton Veny, Warminster, BA12 7BZ www.sureset.co.uk	tel:	01985 841180
Sustrans 2 Cathedral Square, College Green, Bristol, BS1 5DD www.sustrans.org.uk	tel:	0117 926 8893
Tarmac Ltd. Muirfields Road, Ettingshall Wolverhampton, West Midlands, WV4 6JP www.tarmac.co.uk	tel: Info:	01902 353 522 0800 1 218218

Tensar International Cunningham Court, Shadsworth Business Park, Blackburn, BB1 2QX www.tensar.co.uk	tel:	01254 262431
Terraaqua Land & Water Group Ltd. Westen Yard, She Sheet Alburn, Surrey, GU5 9AT www.land-water.co.uk	tel:	01483 202733
Terram Ltd. Mamhilad, Pontypool, Gwent www.terram.com	tel: tech.	01495 757722 01495 767444
TRADA Technology Ltd. Stocking Lane, Hughenden Valley High Wycombe, HP14 4N D email: information@trada.co.uk www.trada.co.uk	tel: fax:	01494 569600 01494 565487
Tubex Ltd. Units 12-14, Aberman Park Aberdare, South Wales, CF44 6DA www.tubex.com	tel:	01685 883833
Woodland Trust (England) Finburn Park, Dysart Road Grantham, NG31 6IL www.woodland-trust.org	tel:	01476 581111
Wood Protection Association 1 Gleneagles House, Vernongate Derby DE1 1UPemail: info@wood-protection.org www.wood-protection.org		
Wrap (Waste Resources Action Programme) The Old Academy, 21 House FairBanbury, Oxon, OX16 0AH www.wrap.org.uk	tel:	0808 100 2040
Zinc Information Centre Wrens Court, 56 Victoria Road, Sutton Coldfield, West Midlands, B72 1SY email: zincinfocentre@hdg.org.uk www.zincinfocentre.org	tel: fax:	0121 362 1201 0121 355 8727

Bibliography

Architects Guide to Stainless Steel, 1997, The Steel Construction Institute, Nancy Baddoo, Rana Burgan, Raymond Ogden, SCI publication 179.

BDA Design Note 7, Brickwork Durability, 2006, Brickwork Development Association.

BRE Digest 380, Damp-Proof Courses, 1993, Building Research Establishment, IHS BRE Press.

BRE Good Building Guide 14, 1994, Building Simple Plan Brick or Blockwork Ffree Standing Walls, IHS BRE Press.

BS 1282 Guide to the Choice, Use and Application of Wood Preservatives, British Standards Institute, 1999.

BS 3882:2007 Specification for Topsoil and Requirements for Use, British Standards Institute.

BS 5837:2005 Trees in Relation to Construction.

BS EN 351-1 Durability of Wood and Wood-Based Products, Preservative-treated solid wood. Classification of preservative penetration and retention, British Standards Institute.

BS EN 771-1 European Standard Specification for Clay Masonry compared to BS 3921 British Standard Specification for Clay Bricks, 2003, Ibstock.

BS EN 771-1 Technical Information Sheet 9, 2007, Ibstock.

Civil Aviation Publication 772, 'Birdstrike Risk Management for Aerodromes Bird Control', 2007.

Compost Specifications for the Landscape Industry, WRAP, in conjunction with the LI, BALI & NBS.

Construction (Design and Management) Regulations, 2007.

DfEs Building Bulletins.

The Green Guide to Housing Specification, BRE Press.

Groundsman's Field Handbook (909), Sportsmark Group Ltd.

Guidance on the Use of Tactile Paving Surfaces, 1998, Department of the Environment, Transport and the Regions, and The Scottish Office, Department for Transport.

Guide to Playground Layout and Design, API.

Guidelines for European Playground Equipment and Surfacing Standards ROSPA.

Guidelines for Landscape and Visual Impact Assessment, 2002.

Inclusive Mobility: A Guide to Best Practice on Access to Pedestrian and Transport Infrastructure, 2002, Department for Transport.

Industrial Wood Preservation – Specification and Practice, 2007, The Wood Protection Association, British Wood Preserving and Damp Proof Association.

Landscape Character Assessment: Guidance for England and Scotland, 2002.

'The Landscape Consultants Appointment', The Landscape Institute.

Learning Through Landscapes Guidelines.

LI/WRAP Compost Specifications for the Landscape Industry.

Life between buildings, Using Public Spaces, 1987, Jan Gehl, English Translation, First published, Livet Mellum Husene, Arkitektens Forlag, 1980, Springer Science and Business Media.

Lorenz Van Ehren Nursery Manual.

Maccaferri, Soil Engineering Design Guide.

Making Traffic Free Paths More Accessible, 2004 SUSTRANS.

Making Ways for the Bicycle, 1994 SUSTRANS.

Materials, 1986, Alan Everett, Longman Scientific and Technical.

Mortars for Masonry, 2005, The Concrete Society Good Concrete Guide 4, The Concrete Society.

Planting Native Trees and Shrubs, 1979, Kenneth and Gillian Beckett.

Preserving Confidence in Timber, 2003, The Wood Protection Association, British Wood Preserving and Damp Proof Association.

Professional Practice for Landscape Architects, 2006, 2nd Edition, Elsevier.

ROSPA, 2002, A Guide to European Playground Equipment and Surfacing Standards, 4th Edition.

Safeguarding Aerodromes Advice Note 3, Potential Bird Hazards from Amenity Landscaping and Building Design, 2005.

Secured by Design Guidelines.

Sustrans 'Making traffic free paths more accessible' 'Making ways for the bicycle'.

Technical Information Sheet 21, 2007, Ibstock.

Terram 'Ground Stabilisation'.

The Town and Country Planning (Environmental Impact Assessment), 1999, England and Wales.

Urban Design Compendium, 2000, English Partnerships/The Housing Corporation.

WRAP 'Guide to recycled content of mainstream construction products'.

Index

Acid-washed finish, 6
Adobe family, 267
Adoptable lighting, 70
Aggregates, 84
Agri-environment schemes, 157
Agricultural drainage pipes, weight of, 257
Alder, 97
Alder buckthorn, 99
Aluminium, 9
Amenity grass, 138
'Amsterdam Tree Soil', 131
Ancient monuments and archaeological areas, 156
Anodizing, 13
Antisocial Behaviour Act 2003 Part 8, 164
Apatite, 3
Aquatic plants, 117
Areas of Great Landscape Value (AGLV), 158
Areas of Outstanding Natural Beauty (AONB), 158
Artificial stone paving, weight of, 257
Ash, 97
Ashes, weight of, 255, 258
Aspen, 97
Asphalt, 83, 86
   weight, 259
Association football, 264
Austenitic stainless steel, 14
AutoCAD printing scales, 268
Autodesk family, 267

Badgers and Setts, 158
Balancing and attenuation ponds, 81
Ballast, weight of, 255
Bare root plants, 120
Bark mulches, 131
Barriers, for construction around trees, 177
Basalt, weight of, 258
Basins, 80
   and ponds, 81
Basketball court, 227
   goals, 227
Bath, weight of, 256

Bats and bat roosts, 158
Bee-loving plants, 102–4
Beech, 97
Berries, 175
   and fruit, for birds, 103–4
Bilberry, 99
Birch (Downey), 97
Birch (Silver), 97
Bird strike hazards:
   in planting and water bodies near airfields, 174
Bitumen, 61, 64, 85, 255
Bituminous emulsion, weight of, 255
Blackthorn, 99
Blast furnace slag, 84
Blister paving, guidance and applications for, 213–14
Blister surface, profile and plan of, 215
Blue staffs, weight of, 259
Bog myrtle, 99
Bowling green, 264
Bramble, 99
Bricks and brickwork construction, 37–50
   bond, types of:
      English bond, 39
      English garden wall bond, 40
      Flemish bond, 39
      Flemish garden wall bond, 40
      garden wall bonds, 40
      header bond, 38
      stretcher bond, 38
   brickwork dimensions, 42–3
   clay bricks, 43–5
   definitions, 37
   engineering bricks, 45–6
   joint profiles, 41–2
   selection of bricks and mortars for durability, 46–50
   weight, 255, 258, 259
British native trees and shrubs, 97–101
British Research Establishment:
   Environmental Assessment Method (BREEAM) ratings, 82
British Standard Code of Practices, 51
Broom, 100
Brushed finish, 7

BS 5628, 55
BS 5696, 220
BS 7188, 220
BS 8500-1:2006 Concrete, 51
BS 8500-2:2006 Concrete, 51
BS EN 206-1:2000 Concrete, 51
BS EN 459-1, 55, 57
BS EN 998-2, 55
BS EN 1176, 220
BS EN 1177, 220
BS5489-1:2003, 72
BS7997: 2003, 218
BSEN 60598: Luminaires, 72
Building stone, weight of, 256
Built Environment Collaborative Contract
        (BCC) 2003, 183–4
Bulbs, 137
Bush hammer finish, 6
Butchers broom, 100
Butterfly loving plants, 103
Butyl liner, 238

Cadmium, 130
Calcite, 3
Calcium silicate bricks, 37
Cappings, 47
Carriageways, gulley spacing for, 74
Case Law, 166
Cast iron, 11
Cement, weight of, 255
Cement lime mortar, weight of, 256
Cement lime sand mortar, 57
Cement mortar, *see* Portland Cement
        mortar
Central Point of Expertise on Timber
        Procurement (CPET), 24
Chain of Custody (COC), 25
Chalk, weight of, 255
'The Character of England' (1995), 172
Charry (bird), 97
Cherry (wild), 97
China clay, 85
Chromium, 130
CIBSE (SLL) Lighting Guide, 6, 72
Circle:
    circumference of, 252
    surface area of, 252
Circulation space, within play area, 221
Circumference
    of circle, 252
    of cone, 252

Clay, 114
    bricks, 43–5
    loam, 114
    puddling, 237
    weight, 255
Cleaning methods, of stainless steel, 22
Climbers, 138
Clinker, weight of, 255, 258
Coatings, metal, 12
Coke, weight of, 255
Colchicum, 117
Colour contrast, design guidelines for,
        244
Colour effects, in lighting, 71
Colour rendering, of lamps, 69
Composts, 127
Concrete:
    making, 51
    retaining walls, 48
    selection, 51–2
    site mixed concrete, 53
    weight, 255, 258
Cone:
    circumference of, 252
    volume of, 252
Conifers and evergreens, 117
Conservation areas, 155
Construction (Design and Management)
        Regulations (CDM) 2007:
    additional client duties, 186
    additional designers duties, 187
    all duty holders, 189
    application, 185
    CDM-C, duties of, 188
    clients duties, 186
    contents, 185
    contractors duties, 188–9
    designers duties, 187
    duty holders, 185
    Health and Safety Executive (HSE),
        notification to, 185
    principal contractors, 187
    prosecutions, 190
    relevant legislation, 185
Construction around trees, guidelines for,
        177–9
Container grown plants, 117
Contracts, glossary of, 180–4
Convention on International Trade in
        Endangered Species of Wild Fauna
        and Flora (CITES), 23

Conversions and calculations, 251–2
'Co-ordinating size (CO)', of brick, 42
Copings, 47
Copper, 8, 130
Cor–Ten steel, 11
Corduroy hazarad warning, 217
Corduroy surface, profile and plan of, 218
Corns, 117
Corundum, 3
Country Parks, 158
Crab apple, 97
Cricket pitch, 230
Cricket square, 264
Cycle parking, design guidelines for, 196
Cycleways, design of, 219
Cycling, design guidelines for, 195
Cylinder:
    surface area of, 252
    volume of, 252

Damp-proof courses (DPCs), 50, 59
    high level DPCs, 59
    low level DPCs, 59
    material selection, 60–4
    purpose, 59
Damp-proof membranes, 65
Dark red meranti, 28
DC, definition of, 53
Deciduous trees and shrubs, 117
Deer fencing, 125–6
Department for Environment, Food and
    Rural Affairs (DEFRA), 23, 24
Design guidelines:
    cycleways, design of, 219
    dimensional data, 191–202
    free standing walls, construction of,
        233–6
    guarding and handrails, 211–12
    playgrounds and playground
        equipment, 220–2
    positive outdoor space, creation of,
        206
    schools, designing for, 223–5
    senses, communication and space, 203
    signage, 242–4
    standard sports markings, 226–32
    steps and ramps, 207–10
    tactile surfaces and warning paving,
        213–18
    walkable neighbourhoods, 204–5
    water features and ponds, 237–41

Development, definition of, 151
Diamond, 3
Digital file extensions, 267
Disability Discrimination Act (DDA),
    208–10
Dogwood, 100
Douglas fir, 30
Drainage, 73–81
Dried bulbs, 117
Ductile iron, 11
Duplex stainless steel, 14
Durability, 46

Earth top soil, weight of, 255
Earth-retaining walls, 48
Earth vegetable, weight of, 255
18 golf greens, 264
Electroplating, 12
Elm (Wych), 98
Energy use and maintenance, of lighting,
    71
Engineering and Construction Short
    Contract (ECSS), 180
Engineering bricks, 37, 45–6
    weight, 259
England:
    landscape character assessment, 172
English bond, 39
English garden wall bond, 40
The Environment Act 1995 (Part V), 163
Environmental impact assessment (EIA),
    167–9
Environmental Protection Act 1990, 166
Environmental Statement (ES), of
    Environmental Impact Assessment
    (EIA), 167
Environmentally Sensitive Areas (ESA),
    157
Equivalent common mortar mixes, 56
Escherica coli, 130
EU Forest Law Enforcement, Governance
    and Trade (FLEGT) Action
    Plan, 24
'Exposure Classes', 53

Facing bricks, 37
    weight, 259
Falling spaces, 221
Feldspar, 3
Fence coding, 125
Fencing heights, in school, 223

Ferrous metals:
  cast iron, 11
  Cor–Ten steel, 11
  mild steel, 10
  stainless steel, 10
  wrought/ductile iron, 11
Filter drains and permeable surfaces, in
    SUDS, 78
Filter strips and swales, in SUDS, 77
Firebricks, weight of, 259
Flamed finish, 6
Flemish bond, 39
Flemish garden wall bond, 40
Fletton:
  brick, 37
  weight, 259
Flint, weight of, 255
Flood storage reservoirs, 81
Flourescent light, 66
Fluorspar, 3
Fly ash, 84
FND, definition of, 53
Fodder Plant Seed Regulations 1985, 108
Football court, 226
Footpaths, 86
  design guidelines for, 194
  edging, 88–90
Forest Law Enforcement, Governance and
    Trade (FLEGT), 24
Forest Stewardship Council (FSC), 24
Formal water bodies, 237
Free spaces, 221
Free standing wall, construction of, 48
  maximum above-ground height and
    minimum foundation width,
    235–6
  movement joints, 236
  rules of thumb, 233
  UK wind exposure zones, 234
Fruits, 175

Galvanized coating, 12
Garden wall bonds, 40
Garden waste, 85
GEN, definition of, 53
General Permitted Development Order
    (GPDO) 1995, 151
Geotextiles, 148–9
  civil engineering uses, 148
  landscape uses, 148
  laying, 148

  materials used in, 148
  'non-woven' textiles:
    design and selection of, 149
    for ground stabilization, 149
Glass, 84
Golf course mixes, 108
Gorse, 100
Government Construction (GC) Works
    Range of Contracts, 182–3
Gradient limits:
  for paved areas, 73
  for surfaces, 73
Gradients, 253–4
Granite, 2, 4
  weight, 256, 258
Graphics, 265
  AutoCAD printing scales, 268
  common digital file extensions, 267
  paper sizes, 266
  survey annotations, 269–70
  symbols, 271–3
Grass seed mixes, 108–9
  common grasses, 108
  cutting heights, 109
  drought, tolerance to, 109
  dry shade, 109
  golf course mixes, 108
  lawns, 109
  low maintenance/hard wearing, 109
  reclamation mixes, 109
  road verges, 109
  sowing methods, 109
  sports mixes, 108
  SUDs areas and wet areas, 109
Grass seed sowing, for sport use, 264
Gravel, weight of, 255, 258
Green belt, 157
Green bulbs, 117
Green roofs, 142–7
  design considerations, 144
  extensive, 143
    plant selection for, 147
    substrate, 145
  intensive, 143
    plant selection for, 147
    substrate, 146
  make up of, 145
  roof drainage, 146
  semi-intensive, 144
    plant selection for, 147
    substrate, 146

substrate, 145
types, 143
Guarding and handrails, design guidelines for, 211–12
Guelder rose, 100
Guidelines for construction around trees, 177–9
'Guidelines for Landscape and Visual Impact Assessment' 2002, 170
Gulley spacing:
  for carriageways, 74
  for paved areas, 74
Gypsum, 3

Habitat Areas, in schools, 225
Habitats and species, 160
Halogen light, 66
Handmade bricks, 37
Handrails and guarding, design guidelines for, 211–12
Hard landscape:
  bricks and brickwork construction, 37–50
  concrete, 51–3
  damp-proof courses, 59–64
  damp-proof membranes, 65
  drainage, 73–5
  footpath edging, 88–90
  footpaths, 86–7
  lighting, 66–72
  metals, 8–13
  mortar, 54–8
  natural stone, 1–7
  recycled materials and products, 84–5
  stainless steel, 14–22
  sustainability, of materials and life span, 82–3
  sustainable urban drainage systems (SUDS), 76–81
  timber, 23–32
    exterior finishes, 33–6
Hard play surface area, in schools, 224
Hardcore, weight of, 258
Hardwood, 25
Hawthorn, 100
Hazardous birds, 174
Hazards
  bird strike hazards, 174
  created by landscape schemes, 174
Hazards of water, reducing, 176
Hazel, 100

Header bond, 38
Health and Safety Executive (HSE), notification to, 185
Heath, 100
Heather (bell), 100
Heather (cross leaved), 100
Hedgerow legislation, 163–4
The Hedgerow Regulations 1997, 163
Hedgerows, 158
Hedges, 137
Herbaceous plants, 117
High calcium lime (HCL) mortar, 57
High-density polyethylene (HDPE), 238
High tensile wire, 125
Hinged joint fencing, 124
Historic gardens and designed landscapes, 157
Hockey court, 229
  goals, 229
Holly, 100
Honed finish, 6
Horizontal brick dimensions, 42
Hornbeam, 98
Horse riding, 196
Horticultural Trades Association, 91
Hydraulic lime (HL) mortar, 57
  mix proportions, 58
Hydraulic mortar, 55

ICE (Institute of Civil Engineering) Contracts, 180
Idigbo, 29
Igneous rock, 1, 2
ILE Guidance Notes on the Reduction of Light Pollution 2000, 72
Impermeable liners, 238
Incandescent light, 66
Infiltration technique, 79
Inground fitting (water ingress), 70
Intensive green roof systems, 143
International Union for the Conservation of Nature and Natural Resources (IUCN) Red List, 23
IP ratings (EN 60529), 69
Iroko, 29
Ivy, 101

Jarrah, 29
Joint Contracts for Landscape Industries (JCLI) Agreement, 182, 183

Joint Contracts Tribunal (JCT) Building
       Contracts 2005, 181–2
Juniper, 101

Kentish rag, weight of, 258
Kerb per metre, weight of, 257
Knotted joint fencing, 124

Lagoons, 81
Lakes and ponds, constructed, 237
LANDMAP methodology, 173
Landscape character assessment,
       172–3
'The Landscape Consultant's
       Appointment', 245
Larch, 29
Large trees, planting method of, 120–1
Lawn tennis, 232, 264
Lead, 130
Legislation, 151
Letter size, 242
Life cycle costing, 71
Light Emitting Diodes (LEDs), 68
Lighting:
   adoptable lighting, 70
   colour rendering, 69
   design, 71
   energy and maintenance, 71
   inground fittings, 70
   light fittings:
      degree of protection IP rating, 69
      shock resistance IK ratings, 70
      touch surface temperature, 70
   light pollution, 71
   light types, 66–8
   relevant legislation and Codes of
       Practice, 72
Lime (small leaved), 98
Lime, weight of, 255
Lime mortar, 54, 57–8
   weight, 256
Limestone, 2, 5
   pavements, 158
   weight, 256, 258
Load classes, for manhole covers, 75
Loam, weight of, 255
Local Planning Authorities (LPAs), 154,
       161, 162, 168
Long grass, with bulbs, 139
Low-density polyethylene (LDPE), 238

Mahogany, Brazilian, 30
Manhole covers, load classes for, 75
Manufactured topsoil, 113, 132
Maple (field), 98
Marble, 2, 5, 6
   weight of, 256
Marginal plants, for acid soils, 241
Marine NR, 159
Marl, weight of, 255
Materials:
   recycled materials, 84–5
   sustainability of, 82–3
   weights of, 255–9
Media-filter, weight of, 255
Medium loam, 114
Meranti (Red), 28, 30
Mercury, 130
Metal Halide light, 67
Metals, 8
   finishes for:
      chemical treatments, 13
      coatings, 12
      mechanical treatments, 13
   typical properties of:
      ferrous metals, 10–11
      non ferrous metals, 8–9
Metamorphic rock, 1, 2
Metric/imperial equivalents, 252
Midland hawthorn, 101
Mild steel, 10
Moh's Scale of Relative Hardness, 3
Mortar, 54
   common types, 54
   components, 54
   equivalent common mortar mixes, 56
   lime mortar, 57–8
   making of, 54
   selection of, 54
   standards and guidance, 55
   terminology, 55
Motorcycles, 197
Mound and ridge planting, 120
Mulches, 129, 131
   bark mulches, 131
   uses, 131

National NR, 159
National Plant Specification, 91, 94
National Scenic Areas (NSA), 158
Natural-based lakes, 237

Natural durability, of timber, 25–6
Natural hydraulic lime (NHL) mortar, 57
Natural stone, 1–7
   igneous rock, 1, 2
   metamorphic rock, 1, 2
   sedimentary rock, 1, 2
Nature reserves (NR), 159
Netball court, 225, 231
New Engineering and Construction
     Contract (NEC), 180
Nickel, 130
Non ferrous metals:
   aluminium, 9
   copper, 8
   zinc, 9
Non-hydraulic mortar, 55, 57
Non-woven geotextiles:
   design and selection of, 149
   for ground stabilization, 149
Notch planting, 120
Notice of Intention to Develop (NID), 153
Notifiable weeds, 165–6
Nursery and Contractors Certification
     Schemes, 91

Oak, 30, 98
Off-road cycleways, checklist for design
     and construction of, 219

Padauk, 31
Painting and coating, 12
Paper, 85
   sizes, 266
PAV, definition of, 53
Paved areas:
   gradient limits for, 73
   gulley spacing for, 74
Pear (wild), 98
Pedestrian crossings and traffic flow,
     design guidelines for, 205
People, design guidelines for, 191
Perch seating, 192
Permitted development, 152
Phytotoxicity, 130
Pig netting, see Stock netting
Pine (Scots), 98
Pit planting, 120
Pitching, weight of, 255, 258
Planning (Northern Ireland) Order 1991
     and Amendment 2003, 151

Planning and Compensation Act 1991,
   151
Planning and Compulsory Purchase Act
   2004, 151
Planning and development control, 151–4
Planning and legislation:
   Construction (Design and
     Management) Regulations 2007,
     185–90
   construction around trees, guidelines
     for, 177–9
   contracts, glossary of, 180–4
   Environmental Impact Assessment
     (EIA), 167–9
   Hedgerow legislation, 163–4
   landscape character assessment, 172–3
   listed and protected areas:
     for heritage, amenity, landscape
      quality, cultural and natural
      habitat, 155–60
   notifiable weeds, 165–6
   planning and development control,
     151–4
   planting and water bodies near
     airfields, 174–6
   Tree Preservation Orders (TPO), 161–2
   visual assessment and landscape,
     170–1
The Planning etc (Scotland) 2006, 151
Planning permission, 151
   application, 153
   duration, 154
   procedure, 154
   types, 153
Plant protection, 123
   deer fencing, 125–6
   fence coding, 125
   high tensile wire, 125
   rabbit fencing, 126
   stock netting, 124
   tree guards, 124
   tree shelters, 124
   wire netting, 125
Planting:
   on 1:3 slope, 263
   densities, 263
   times of year for, 117
   and water bodies near airfields,
     174–6
Planting boxes, 47

Planting method:
    of large trees, 120–1
    of small trees, 120
Plants:
    base rich soil herbs and grasses, for
        pond margins, 240
    for encouraging wild life, 102–4
    marginal plants for acid soils, 241
    for shallow water, 240
    submerged/floating leaved plants, 239
Plastic coating, 12
Plastics, 84
Playgrounds and playground equipment,
        220–2
Poisonous plants:
    to animals, 106
    to humans, 105
Polished surface finish, 6
Polishing, 13
Polyester powder coating, 12
Polyethylene, 238
Polystyrene, 85
Polythene, 84
Polyvinylchloride (PVC), 238
Ponds, 81
Ponds and water features, *see* Water
        features and ponds
Portland Cement mortar, 54
    weight of, 256
Portland, weight of, 256
Positive outdoor space, creation of, 206
Precast concrete manhole rings, weight
        of, 257
Pre-planting care, 119
Pressed bricks, weight of, 259
Privet, 101
Programme for the Endorsement of Forest
        Certification (PEFC), 24
Project Partnering Contract (PPC) 2000,
        184
Protected areas, 155–60
Public transport, design guidelines for,
        204
Purbeck, weight of, 256
Purging buckthorn, 101
PVC, *see* Polyvinylchloride

Quartz, 3

Rabbit fencing, 126
Ramps and steps, design guidelines for,
        207–10

Ramsar Sites, 160
RC, definition of, 53
Recycled products, 84
Red meranti, 28
Refusal, dealing with, 154
Retention ponds, 81
Ringlock fencing, 124
Riparian woodland, 134–5
Road foundation materials, weight of,
        258
Road surfacing materials, weight of,
        258–9
Roosts, 175
Root balled plants, 119
Root damage, avoidance of, 178
Root Protection Area (RPA):
    foundations in, 179
    and Tree Protection Plan, 177
Rowan, 98
Rubber, 85
Rugby football, 264
Rugby union court, 228
    goals, 228
Rules of thumb, for planting plans, 263
'Rylock', *see* Stock netting

Safeguarding strategy, 175
Salmonella spp., 130
Sand, 114
    weight of, 255
Sand blasted finish, 6
Sand blasting, 13
Sandstone, 2, 4
    weight of, 256, 258
Sandy loam, 114
Sapele, 30
Saw cut refined finish, 6
Sawn finish, 6
Schools, designing for, 223–5
Scotland and Wales:
    landscape character assessment, 173
Sea buckthorn, 101
Seat Heights, in schools, 224
Seat Totals, in schools, 224
Seating, 192
Sedimentary rock, 1, 2
Seeds, 110
    sowing rates, 110
    sowing times, 110
Seeds Regulations 1982, 108
Semi-intensive green roof systems, 144
Shale, weight of, 255

Sheep netting, *see* Stock netting
Sheet membranes, 65
Sheradizing, 12
Shingle, weight of, 258
Shrub, 102–3, 135–6
  British native shrubs, 99–101
Shrub sizes:
  definition and specification of,
    94–6
Sight sense, 203
Signage, 242–4
  colour contrast, 244
  letter size, 242
  positioning, 244
  symbol sizes, 243
  typefaces, 243
Sills, 47
Silty loam, 114
Site mixed concrete, 53
Site of Special Scientific Interest, 159
Slag, weight of, 255, 258
Slate, 2, 5
  weight of, 255
Small trees, planting method of, 120
Smell sense, 203
Snow, weight of, 256
Sodium lamps, 67
Soft landscape, 91
  British native trees and shrubs,
    97–101
  composts, 127
  geotextiles, 148–9
  grass seed mixes, 108–9
  green roofs, 142–7
  maintenance, 133–9
  maintenance programme, 140–1
  mulches, 131
  plant protection, 123
    deer fencing, 125–6
    fence coding, 125
    high tensile wire, 125
    rabbit fencing, 126
    stock netting, 124
    tree guards, 124
    tree shelters, 124
    wire netting, 125
  planting, times of year for, 117
  plants, for encouraging wile life,
    102–4
  poisonous plants:
    to animals, 106
    to humans, 105

product specification, 128–30
shrub sizes, 94–6
topsoil, 112–16
tree:
  sizes, 91
  specification requirements for,
    92–3
tree planting, 118
  large trees, planting method of,
    120–1
  preferences, 119
  pre-planting care, 119
  root ball sizes and weights, of tree,
    122
  season, 119
  small trees, planting method of,
    120
  storage, 119
  supporting tree, methods for, 121
  urban tree soil, 131–2
  wild flower mixes, 110–11
Soft Play Surface Area, in schools, 224
Softwood, 25
Soil herbs and grasses, for pond margins,
    240
Soil improvement, for general landscape
    works, 128
Solar noon time, at prime meridian,
    249
Sound sense, 203
Southern yellow pine, 30
Special architectural/historic interest,
    buildings of, 156
Special Protection Areas (SPA), 160
Sphere:
  surface area of, 252
  volume of, 252
Split faced finish, 7
Sports facilities, in schools, 225
Sports markings, *see* Standard sports
    markings
Stainless steel, 10
  grades:
    for atmospheric applications, 15
    and attributes, 14
  maintenance, cleaning and remedial
    repairs, 22
  performance improvement and
    corrosion prevention in, 16
  product range, 20–1
  surface finishes of, 17–19
Standard brick, 37

Standard sports markings:
  basketball, 227
  cricket, 230
  football, 226
  hockey, 229
  lawn tennis, 232
  netball, 231
  rugby union, 228
Steps and ramps, design guidelines for,
  207–10
Stock bricks, 37
Stock netting, 124
Stocks, weight of, 259
Stones:
  characteristics, 4–5
    and properties, 2
  finishes for, 6–7
  natural stones, 1–7
  weight of, 256
Stove enamel coating, 12
Stretcher bond, 38
Sundial, setting, 247–50
Sunrise light, 66
Surface area:
  of circle, 252
  of cylinder, 252
Surfaces, gradient limits for, 73
Surfacing, types of, 220–1
Survey annotations, 269–70
Sustainability, of materials and life span,
  82–3
Sustainable Urban Drainage Systems
  (SUDS), 76
  basins and ponds, 80–1
  benefits, 76
  filter drains and permeable surfaces, 78
  filter strips and swales, 77
  infiltration devices, 79
  techniques, 77
Symbol sizes, design guidelines for, 243
Symbols, 271–2
  in graphics, 273

Tactile surfaces and warning paving,
  213–18
Talc, 3
Tar, weight of, 256
Tarred granite, weight of, 259
Tarred gravel, weight of, 259
Tarred limestone, weight of, 259

Tarred slag, weight of, 259
Tarred whinstone, weight of, 259
Tennis court, 232
Thuja plicata, 29
Timber, 23–32
  exterior finishes of, 33–6
  properties, 29–32
    finishes for, 34–6
  selection, 25–35
    in-service environment, 26
    life service, 26
    natural durability, 25–6
    sustainable sources, 23–5
Timber Procurement Policy, 24
Top dress and grass maintenance, 128
Topaz, 3
Topsoil, 112–16, 129
  characteristics, 113–14
  definition, 113
  manufactured topsoil, 113, 132
  phytotoxic elements, 114
  stones, 114
  textural classification, 116
  zoo toxic elements, 115
Town and Country Planning Act 1990,
  151
Travellers joy, 101
Tree, 102, 134
  British native trees, 97–9
  sizes, 91
  specification requirements for, 92–3
Tree guards, 124
  uses, 124
Tree planting, 118
  large trees, planting method of,
    120–1
  preferences, 119
  pre-planting care, 119
  root ball sizes and weights, of tree, 122
  season, 119
  small trees, planting method of, 120
  storage, 119
  supporting tree, methods for, 121
Tree preservation orders (TPO), 155,
  161–2
Tree Protection Plan and Root Protection
  Area, 177
Tree shelters, 124
  grow cones, 124
  shelter guard, 124

spiral shelter, 124
uses, 124
Triangle, surface area of, 252
Tubers, 117
Tumbled finish, 7
Tutsan, 101
Typefaces, design guidelines for, 243
UK Species and habitats, 159
Urban centres and public amenity areas,
    lighting in, 72
Urban tree soil, 131–2
Utile, 30
Vehicles:
    car parking provision, 201–2
    movement, 198–9
    parking bays, 200–1
Visual assessment and landscape, 170–1
Vitreous enamel coating, 12
Volume, 252
    of cone, 252
    of cylinder, 252
    related to depth and area, 260–2
Walkable neighbourhoods, 204–5
    pedestrian crossings and traffic flow,
      205
    public transport, 204
    walking, 204
Walking, 204
Wall-mounted signs, 244
Water hazards, reducing, 176
Water features and ponds:
    clay puddling, 237
    constructed lakes and ponds, 237
    formal water bodies, 237
    impermeable liners, 238
    natural-based lakes, 237
    plants:
      base rich soil herbs and grasses, for
        pond margins, 240
      marginal plants for acid soils, 241
      for shallow water, 240
      submerged/floating leaved plants,
        239

water level, control of:
    cleansing and emptying, 238
    disposal, 238
    replenishment, 238
    water circulation, 238–9
Waterstruck brick, 37
Wayfaring tree, 101
Weathering steel, 10, 11
Weed seeds, 130
The Weeds Act 1959, 165
Wet mortar, weight of, 256
Wetlands, 81
Wheelchairs, 193
Whinstone, weight of, 258
White oak, 30
White Son light, 68
Whitebeam, 98
Wild flower mixes, 110–11
    maintenance, 110
    plugs, 110
    pots, 110
    seeds, 110
Wild life, plants for encouraging, 102–4
Wildflower areas, 139
Wildflower plugs, 117
Wildlife and Countryside Act 1981
    Schedule 9 Section 14, 165
Willow, 99
Windows/system files, 267
Wire-cut/Extruded brick, 37
Wire netting, 125
Wirecuts, weight of, 259
Wood, 84
Work stages, of landscape architecture,
    245–6
World Heritage Sites, 160
Wrought/ductile iron, 11

Yew, 99
York, weight of, 256

Zinc, 9, 130
Zintec coating, 12